T0238037

Lecture Notes in Artificial Intelligence   2872

Edited by J. G. Carbonell and J. Siekmann

Subseries of Lecture Notes in Computer Science

Gianluca Moro
Claudio Sartori
Munindar P. Singh (Eds.)

Agents and Peer-to-Peer Computing

Second International Workshop, AP2PC 2003
Melbourne, Australia, July 14, 2003
Revised and Invited Papers

 Springer

Series Editors

Jaime G. Carbonell, Carnegie Mellon University, Pittsburgh, PA, USA
Jörg Siekmann, University of Saarland, Saarbrücken, Germany

Volume Editors

Gianluca Moro
Università di Bologna
Dipartimento di Informatica, Elettronica e Sistemistica (DEIS)
Via Venezia 52, 47023 Cesena, Italy
E-mail: gmoro@deis.unibo.it

Claudio Sartori
Università di Bologna
CSITE - CNR
Viale Risorgimento, 2, 40136 Bologna, Italy
E-mail: claudio.sartori@unibo.it

Munindar P. Singh
North Carolina State University
Department of Computer Science
Raleigh, NC 27695-7535, USA
E-mail: singh@ncsu.edu

Library of Congress Control Number: 2004116524

CR Subject Classification (1998): I.2.11, I.2, C.2.4, C.2

ISSN 0302-9743
ISBN 3-540-24053-5 Springer Berlin Heidelberg New York

Springer is a part of Springer Science+Business Media

springeronline.com

© Springer-Verlag Berlin Heidelberg 2004
Printed in Germany

Typesetting: Camera-ready by author, data conversion by PTP-Berlin, Protago-TeX-Production GmbH
Printed on acid-free paper   SPIN: 11365105   06/3142   5 4 3 2 1 0

Preface

Peer-to-peer (P2P) computing is attracting enormous media attention. Typical applications are file sharing, as in Gnutella, and exploiting distributed computing power, as in the SETI (Search for Extra Terrestrial Intelligence) project.

The most popular applications at present are limited in their scope, but they are highlighting some of the key challenges of P2P computing and exposing the limitations of traditional approaches to addressing such challenges. First, the peers are autonomous entities: they can cooperatively participate or not according to their own choice. Second, the peers are heterogeneous, meaning that in general we would not be justified in making strong assumptions about how they are designed or how their information structures are conceptually modeled.

The applications of P2P computing go beyond file sharing or load balancing of computing resources. Understood more generally, P2P computing is a natural approach to the development of large systems from autonomous, heterogeneous components. The obvious idea would be for entities to function as peers that provide services or expose resources for sharing. Services or resources can then be composed dynamically to yield novel functionalities. Rigorous composition techniques are a major research direction.

First, let's consider heterogeneity. One aspect of the above-mentioned techniques for developing P2P systems is dealing with the information structures of the various peers. Another aspect is dealing with the underlying processes. How do we ensure that peers are able to share knowledge and able to act in unison? Addressing both aspects involves modeling the peers appropriately and reconciling their conceptual differences.

Next, let's consider autonomy. Since the participants are autonomous and not governed by any central agency, certain new challenges must be addressed. One, we need mechanisms for trust and reputation, and, related to these, for governance and regulation. Two, we need to develop economic environments or incentive mechanisms that foster knowledge sharing and collaboration, i.e., lead the peers to prefer cooperative over non-cooperative behaviors in sharing resources. Systems such as Gnutella already suffer from the problem of *free riding*, where some participants take advantage of the system but never contribute to it. What business models would properly support those who contribute or give an incentive to the peers to cooperate? What techniques would sustain such business models?

Interestingly and significantly, research on multiagent systems and on large-scale information systems has at least partially addressed many of the challenges of P2P systems. The work on information systems has studied the consequences of heterogeneity of knowledge and process. The work on multiagent systems has studied the consequences of autonomy. In particular, the basic doctrine of multiagent systems—that the member agents are autonomous—agrees with what P2P systems require. Research on topics such as task decomposition, protocols, economic models involving game theory and decision theory, and coordination and teamwork all feed naturally into P2P systems.

For the above reasons, this workshop series aims at addressing the following nonexhaustive list of topics:

- Intelligent agent techniques for P2P computing
- P2P computing techniques for multi-agent systems
- The Semantic Web and semantic coordination mechanisms for P2P systems
- Scalability, coordination, robustness and adaptability in P2P systems
- Self-organization and emergent behavior in P2P systems
- E-commerce and P2P computing
- Participation and contract incentive mechanisms in P2P systems
- Computational models of trust and reputation
- Community of interest building and regulation, and behavioral norms
- Intellectual property rights in P2P systems
- P2P architectures
- Scalable data structures for P2P systems
- Services in P2P systems, including service definition, discovery, filtering, composition, and so on
- Knowledge discovery and P2P data mining
- P2P-oriented information systems
- Information ecosystems and P2P systems
- Security considerations in P2P networks
- Ad hoc networks and pervasive computing based on P2P architectures and wireless communication devices.

The workshop series emphasizes discussions about methodologies, models, algorithms and technologies, strengthening the connection between agents and P2P computing. These objectives are accomplished by bringing together researchers and contributions from these two disciplines but also from more traditional areas such as distributed systems, networks, and databases.

This volume is the postproceedings of AP2PC 2003, the 2nd International Workshop on Agents and P2P Computing,[1] which took place in Melbourne on July 14, 2003 in the context of the 2nd International Joint Conference on Autonomous Agents and Multi-agent Systems (AAMAS 2003).

This volume is organized according to the sessions held at the workshop. Besides the invited papers related to the invited talk and to the panel, these were framed into the following topics:

- Paradigm integration and challenges
- Trust
- Self-organization
- Incentives
- Search and systems
- Adaptive applications

---

[1] http://p2p.ingce.unibo.it/

– Mobile agents

This proceedings brings together papers presented at the workshop, fully revised to incorporate reviewers' comments and discussions at the workshop, plus three invited papers related to the panel. After the call for papers we received 22 submissions. All submissions were reviewed for scope and quality; finally, 11 were accepted as full papers and 6 as short papers. AP2PC 2003 drew over 40 attendees. Given the dual threats of SARS and war this year and logistical challenges of getting to Melbourne, it is not surprising that this was one of the better attended workshops at AAMAS.

We express our deepest appreciation to the participants for their lively discussions. We would like to acknowledge the contributions of the invited speaker, the authors for their excellent submissions, and the program committee members for their diligence in reviewing submissions on a tight schedule. We would also like to thank the panel chair, Aris M. Ouksel, and the invited panelists, Sonia Bergamaschi (University of Modena and Reggio-Emilia), Rajkumar Buyya (University of Melbourne), and Onn Shehory (IBM Haifa). We would like to acknowledge the steering committee for its guidance and encouragement.

This workshop followed the successful first edition, which was held in conjunction with AAMAS in Bologna in 2002. In recognition of the interdisciplinary nature of P2P computing, a sister event called the International Workshop on Databases, Information Systems, and P2P Computing was held in Berlin in September 2003 in conjunction with the International Conference on Very Large Data Bases (VLDB).

Gianluca Moro
Claudio Sartori
Munindar P. Singh

Executive Committee

Organizers

Program Co-chairs   Gianluca Moro
Dept. of Electronics, Computer Science and Systems,
University of Bologna, Italy

Claudio Sartori
IEIIT-BO-CNR, University of Bologna, Italy

Munindar P. Singh
Dept. of Computer Science,
North Carolina State University, USA

Panel Chair   Aris M. Ouksel
Dept. of Information and Decision Sciences,
University of Illinois at Chicago, USA

Steering Committee

The steering committee consists of the above plus the following people:

Karl Aberer, EPFL, Lausanne, Switzerland

Sonia Bergamaschi, Dept. of Science Engineering,
University of Modena and Reggio-Emilia, Italy

Manolis Koubarakis, Dept. of Electronic and Computer Engineering,
Technical University of Crete

Paul Marrow, Intelligent Systems Laboratory,
BTexact Technologies, UK

Program Committee

Karl Aberer, EPFL, Lausanne, Switzerland
Sonia Bergamaschi, University of Modena and Reggio-Emilia, Italy
M. Brian Blake, Georgetown University, USA
Rajkumar Buyya, University of Melbourne, Australia
Ooi Beng Chin, National University of Singapore, Singapore

Sponsors

This workshop would not have been possible without the generous support from our sponsors, UNI.TU.RIM S.p.A., Fondazione Cassa di Risparmio di Rimini, and Microsoft. To these we express our gratitude.

Table of Contents

Information Acquisition Through an Integrated Paradigm: Agent + Peer-to-Peer

Beng Chin Ooi[1], Wee Siong Ng[2], Kian-Lee Tan[1], and AoYing Zhou[3]

[1] Department of Computer Science,
National University of Singapore, Singapore
{ooibc, tankl}@comp.nus.edu.sg
[2] Singapore-MIT Alliance,
National University of Singapore, Singapore
smangws@nus.edu.sg
[3] Department of Computer Science and Engineering,
Fudan University, Shanghai, P.R. China
aoying@fudan.edu.cn

Abstract. Agent computing provides developers with a way to define problem-solving computation at an abstract level, whereas, the key strength of current P2P development centers on resource gathering and defining efficient resource discovery strategies. Integration of the two paradigms is required for the development of self-evolving, open and scalable systems. In this paper, we first investigate varieties of P2P facilities that could benefit agent development and discuss broadly different ways of integration of the two paradigms. Second, we present a prototype system, BestPeer, that exploits both agent and P2P computing. In P2P environments, the schema is typically not given in advance or it might be implicit in the data. Consequently, it is notably challenging to acquire, manage and analyze data in order to produce meaningful information for decision-making. We next present PeerDB that is built on top of BestPeer to facilitate data sharing without a global schema.

1 Introduction

Agent and Peer-to-Peer (P2P) are two paradigms that realize the real power of computing through autonomous, distributed and dynamic systems. These systems are becoming increasingly popular as they enable users to exchange digital information and share in problem-solving by participating in complex networks. In particular, many researchers consider the agent system as an autonomous problem-solving entity while P2P provides support for pooling resources together. Merging these two disciplines by adopting the best of each approach could potentially provide an ultimate solution that is inexpensive, easy to use, self-learning and modifying, highly scalable and needing no central administration.

In order to deal with the autonomous, scale and dynamism that characterize P2P and agent systems, a merged paradigm is required that includes

G. Moro, C. Sartori, and M.P. Singh (Eds.): AP2PC 2003, LNAI 2872, pp. 1–12, 2004.

self-organization, adaptation and automated information matching, and support discovering as intrinsic properties. In this paper, we first define different approaches on merging infrastructures from these two disciplines. Second, we present BestPeer [1,11], a system that integrates both paradigms to support fast and easy P2P application development. Our solution incorporates a self-configurable mechanism whereby a node in the BestPeer network can dynamically reconfigure itself to have direct (logical) connections with peers that benefit it most.

Finally, we elaborate on an interesting issue based on the integrated paradigm: how can an agent perform information acquisition in the P2P system without relying on global knowledge? We present our experience in addressing this problem in the context of PeerDB, a full-fledged data management system that supports fine-grain content-based searching with the help of agent technologies. Our solution incorporates Information Retrieval (IR) techniques which enable peers to share data without shared schema. PeerDB employs a name-based matching technique that matches schema elements by relying on the user to supply additional information (metadata) in order to reduce mismatch. PeerDB primarily concerns itself with the online information exploration. Online information exploration is different from traditional data translation and schema integration strategies. In the former, results are transient and users are more tolerant of mismatch candidates. Schema integration, on the other hand, needs to ensure certain degree of consistency and accuracy, which in turn, requires more complicated approaches. PeerDB provides a simple and yet effective approach for information acquisition in environments with heterogeneous data sources.

2   The Infrastructures

In this section, we shall discuss the strategies for merging infrastructures from P2P and agent computing.

2.1   Facilities Provided by P2P

The P2P community has contributed much to the development of efficient resource discovery and routing strategies. Clearly, an efficient resource discovery strategy together with query routing strategy forms fundamental problems of resource sharing. Earlier efforts such as Napster adopt a centralized model of resource sharing. Here, the central server maintains a master list of all the metadata of peers in the network. This metadata is being used for describing data housed in peers and it might include file name, IP address, line speed and so on. However, the data is located in the peers. In this case, the servers are simply playing the role of answering queries and indexing the meta-information submitted by connecting peers. Perhaps this centralized architecture is most similar to existing development of multi-agent systems [7,6,22,14]. Agents are required to contact a centralized resource manager for locating the services. However, such an approach has several limitations. First, there is a single point of failure. In additional, maintaining a unified view is computationally expensive and scaling up can be a serious problem. More recently, several routing mechanisms in pure decentralized environment have been proposed. For example the Breadth-First-Traversal [4] (BFT) and distributed hash table (e.g., Chord [21] and CAN [16]). These facilities may potentially to be reused in agent development for developing a truly autonomous and decentralized system.

2.2   Merging of Infrastructures: P2P and Agent

There are three broad approaches for merging the two technologies. One is based on integrating P2P technology to underlying agent systems (the left image of Figure 1). For instance, a DHT-based [16,21,2] routing strategy could be integrated into an existing agent system for efficient agent routing. This approach is agent-oriented since it defines P2P as a subset of tools to facilitate efficient routing of agents. The second approach is a P2P-oriented merging strategy, where the main idea is to build a proprietary software agent on top of an existing P2P system (the right image of Figure 1). The third approach operates on three tiers, with a middleware in between the agent and P2P layers (the centre image of Figure 1).

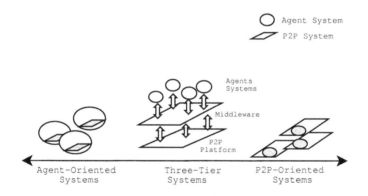

Fig. 1. Infrastructure of P2P and Agents

Most of the existing agent systems provide support for agent collaboration and communication but are not native to P2P technology. The development of P2P applications based on these platforms would require a longer and more costly effort. There are several reasons that suggest the limitation of applying a traditional agent system in a P2P model. First, traditionally, mobile search agents perform search operations by moving themselves to the site containing the target information and executing a given task. The agent's path is either predefined or the agent has knowledge of where to find the services. For example, in order to find the cheapest airfare, a travel agent is given a set of sites that provide airfare query services. The agent's programmers have to know where the agent needs to go and where the next destination is after the task at a site is completed. However, this may require a pre-defined knowledge of the environment – which is not always feasible, e.g., there may not exist any pre-defined knowledge of who is offering a particular service and where. The problem may be solved by integrating P2P query routing strategies into agent systems to form agent-oriented systems. Obviously, the main drawback concerns the extensibility of the system to upgrade the services, e.g., incorporating new routing strategies or new P2P services into the system will cause a major disruption of the system. Moreover, the whole architecture may possibly become "fatter", which may in return result in unpredictable behavior. Also, there may exist several agent systems with P2P supports but which are unable to communicate with each other. This may be due to the fact that they employ either different agent communication languages or different P2P protocols. In apparent recognition of this problem, the agent community has started to standardize agent communication languages such as KQML [3] and FIPA ACL [20]; meanwhile, P2P is still evolving. The details of the agent computing roadmap can be found in [17].

P2P-oriented system have inherited similar issues that are faced by the agent-oriented approach. This paradigm may be useful in a specific corporate environment where the predefined protocol and languages have been set up as in the agent-oriented approach. The two approaches that have just been discussed tend to be closed systems rather than sustainable ones that could adapt to future publicly-advertised standards.

The alternative solution – which is the third approach to the merger of agent and P2P technologies – operates at the following three tiers: 1) an agent system running on the peer to provide application-related services, 2) a P2P platform to handle communication and the necessary message routing strategy, and 3) a middle tier that handles the communication between the agent and P2P layers. Each tier focuses exclusively on its assigned tasks. For example, when a new P2P routing strategy is invented, only the P2P layer needs to be updated. Similarly, to accommodate large numbers of participants, only the middle tier needs to be scaled by employing industry agreed protocols and languages. Such an approach would help to develop a fully open and truly scalable distributed data sharing system that supports dynamic networking and heterogeneity in the data environment.

Figure 2(a) depicts the three-tier system. Middleware platform provides general-purpose agent's behavioral functions, such as sending and receiving messages, repository for data storing and retrieving. It also offers negotiation and coordination management among peers. These functions are commonly needed for any kind of agent systems and regardless of the applications domains. Domain specific behaviors, on the other hand, are provided by the specific agent systems. In general, middle layer is a generic agent platform which provides common skeletons and basic agents functionalities. The purpose is to allow agents from different systems to cooperate. Agents from different systems can be transformed to a common agent that operates in middleware layer and vice versa.

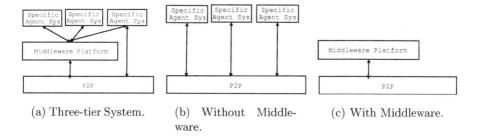

(a) Three-tier System.   (b) Without Middle-ware.   (c) With Middleware.

Fig. 2. Variant of Three-tier System.

Since the middleware platform itself is an agent platform (with limited agent capabilities), there are two possible variances of the three-tier system: without middleware platform (Figure 2(b)) and with middleware platform (but without any specific agent systems) (Figure 2(c)). A three-tier system without the middleware platform is more functionalities-rich but it is a platform dependency approach, since each of the agents may be created based on APIs provided by different platform vendors. The different interaction protocol of each vendor makes coordination among peers from different agent systems difficult. In contrast, a system with only middleware platform has limited functionalities, but facilitates easy interaction.

3   The BestPeer Approach

As mentioned earlier, agent systems designers could have benefited from connections with P2P disciplines. A good evaluation of work on combining P2P and agent paradigms can be found in [10]. In this section, we shall discuss a working prototype of integrated agent-P2P system developed for serving as a platform on which P2P applications can be developed easily and efficiently based on agent technologies.

The BestPeer [1,11] project was initiated in the year 2000 at the National University of Singapore to study how P2P technologies can be employed for distributed applications, such as collaborative caching, information retrieval, distributed data management, etc. It is a three-tier architecture with an agent layer at the top of the hierarchy, middleware layer that resides in between the underlying P2P layer on the one hand and the agent layer on the other. The P2P layer is the lowest layer of the hierarchy for supporting low-level communication, resource sharing capabilities amongst nodes and self-network reconfiguration.

In BestPeer, the P2P technology provides resource sharing capabilities amongst nodes, while mobile agents technology further extends the functionalities. In particular, since agents can carry both code and data, they can effectively perform any kind of functions. With mobile agents, BestPeer not only provides files and raw data, but processed and meaningful information. For example, in

BestPeer, an agent can be sent to a peer with the data file to "digest" its content and to generate reports for the requester. In another word, in contrast to existing P2P systems, i.e., Gnutella, Napster, that provide only file level sharing (i.e., sharing of the entirety of a file), BestPeer supports for content-based search with the help of agent technologies.

In BestPeer, we have implemented our own Java-based agent system instead of using existing systems (e.g., [9]). Like existing systems, both the agent and its class have to be present for the agent to resume execution at the destination engine. Thus, if the class is not already at the destination node, the class has to be transmitted also. For the moment, we have adopted a purely "code-shipping" strategy where a node will always perform its operation at the destination node (where the data reside). This is a reasonable approach as it exploits parallelism by enabling all peers to operate on their data simultaneously; otherwise, the node will become a bottleneck.

More importantly, the use of agents allows BestPeer nodes to collect information (e.g., what files/content are sharable, statistics, etc.) on the BestPeer network, and this can be done offline. This allows a node to be better equipped to determine who should be its directly connected peers or who can provide it better service.

BestPeer is self-configurable (P2P layer), i.e., a node can dynamically optimize the set of peers that it can communicate directly with based on some optimization criterion. By keeping peers that provide most information or services in close proximity (i.e, direct communication), the network bandwidth can be better utilized and system performance can be optimized.

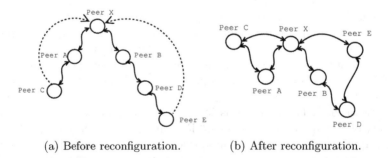

(a) Before reconfiguration.   (b) After reconfiguration.

Fig. 3. Example on BestPeer's Reconfigurable Feature.

Figure 3 illustrates an example of BestPeer's reconfigurable feature. In Figure 3(a), Peer X is the base node that initiates a request. Here, Peer X initially has two directly connected peers - Peers A and B. However, only Peer C and Peer E contain objects that match Peer X's current query. Peer X can then obtain the results from Peer E and Peer C directly. At the same time, Peer X determines that Peer C and Peer E are not its direct peers and they benefit it most. As such, Peer X will keep these two peers as its directly connected peers (assuming Peer X can keep at least 4 directly connected peers), resulting in the new network layout shown in Figure 3(b).

Our approach is to keep promising peers as close as possible with no (or little) information exchange between peers. This is to keep the nodes as autonomous as possible. Moreover, since nodes can redefine the number of direct peers it would like to have and implement their own reconfiguration strategies, any tight form of "collaboration" will be complicated to realize and maintain. In BestPeer, three default reconfiguration strategies have been designed and deployed (see [12] for the details).

4   Knowledge Acquisition in BestPeer

The initial research activities in P2P systems have been focused on designing resource discovery mechanisms. However, recent trends are focusing on research on semantics issues for integrating heterogeneous data sources. For example, K. Aberer et al. [18] focus on semantic interoperability in a P2P network with a gossiping technique. Other works, such as Semantic Web [19] and P2P data management systems [15,8,5] have also been proposed. In this section, we shall present the PeerDB which is a full-fledged data management system that supports fine-grain content-based searching. PeerDB [13] employs Information Retrieval (IR) techniques to allow peers to share data without relying on a global shared schema.

4.1   Scenario Overview

To motivate the importance of heterogeneity data sources management, we present the following scenario. In a hospital, each specialist has a group of patients that are solely under his care. While some patient data are stored in a centralized server of the hospital (e.g., name, address, etc), other data (e.g., X-rays, prescription, allergy to drugs, history, reaction to drugs, etc) are typically managed by the specialist on his personal PC. For most of these patients, the specialist is willing to share their data, but there are always some cases where he is unwilling to share for different reasons (e.g., part of his research program on a new drug, etc). By making the sharable patient data available to other specialists, it allows them to look for other patients who may have similar symptoms as their own patients, and hence can help them in making better decisions on the treatment (e.g., drugs to prescribe, reactions to look out for, etc).

In a typical P2P data sharing environment: (1) any specialist can join/leave the network; (2) the answers need not be complete (i.e., missing data from some specialists is not critical), (3) nodes have to search for content from geographically distributed and autonomous information sources. (4) the schema defined by each specialist may be different.

4.2   Architecture of a PeerDB Node

Arising from the mentioned scenario of the issues of P2P data management system, we note that to provide automated support for matching the large number of heterogeneous representation of schemas is one of the most fundamental problems. Thus, the prime objective of the PeerDB is to provide automated matching strategy that allows user to retrieve relevant information from heterogeneous data sources without shared global schemas.

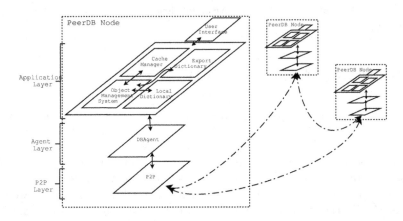

Fig. 4. PeerDB node architecture

PeerDB is built on top of BestPeer platform. It is based on agent technologies to facilitating the acquisition and evaluation of the different schemas on distributed information sources. Figure 4 illustrates the internals of a PeerDB node. There are essentially four components that are integrated and implemented on the middleware layer. The first component is a data management system that facilitates storage, manipulation and retrieval of the data at the node. We note that the interface of the data management system is essentially an SQL query facility. Thus, the system can be used on its own as a stand alone DBMS outside of PeerDB.

The next two components are related to data sharing management. For each relation that is created (through the PeerDB interface), the associated meta-data (schema, keywords, etc) are stored in a **Local Dictionary**. There is also an **Export Dictionary** that reflects the meta-data of relations that are sharable to other nodes. Thus, only relations that are exported can be accessed by other nodes in the network. We note that the meta-data associated with the Export Dictionary is a subset of those found in the Local Dictionary, and the distinction here is a logical one. The last component is a cache manager. We are dealing with caching remote meta-data and data in secondary storage, and the cache manager determines the caching and replacement policies.

In the agent layer, there is a database agent system called DBAgent. DBAgent provides the environment for mobile agents to operate on. Each

PeerDB node has a *master agent* that manages the query of the user. In particular, it will clone and dispatch *worker agents* to neighboring nodes, receive answers and present them to the user.

Finally, we have the routing strategy, network management and messages management at the P2P layer. These services are provided by BestPeer platform. It also monitors the statistics and manages the network reconfiguration policies.

4.3   Schema Mapping

In PeerDB, an Information Retrieval (IR) based approach is employed for schema mapping. For each relation that is created by the user, meta-data are maintained for each relation name and attributes. These are essentially keywords/descriptions provided by the users upon creation of the table, and serve as a kind of synonymous names. DBAgents are sent out to the peers to find out potential matches and bring the corresponding meta-data back. By matching keywords from the meta-data of the relations, PeerDB is able to locate relations that are potentially similar to the query relations.

Peer	Names	Keywords
P1	Kinases	protein, human
	SeqID	key, identifier, ID
	length	length
	proteinSeq	sequence, protein sequence
P2	Protein	protein, annexin, zebrafish
	SeqNo	number, identifier
	len	length
	sequence	sequence
P3	ProteinKLen	protein, kinases, length
	ID	number, identifier
	seqLength	length
	ProteinKSeq	protein, sequence
	ID	number, identifier
	sequence	sequence
P4	Protein	protein, kinases, annexin, ...
	name	name
	char	characteristics, features, functions

Fig. 5. Keywords for the relations/attributes names.

We illustrate the strategy with an example. Suppose we have four peers that share genomic data. Peer P1 defines a relation Kinases(SeqID, length, proteinSeq). Peer P2 defines a relation Protein(SeqNo, len, sequence). Peer P3 defines two relations ProteinKLen(ID, seqLength) and ProteinKSeq(ID, sequence). Peer P4 defines a relation Protein(name, char). Figure 5 shows the keywords defined for these relations by the various peers. Suppose the user at peer P1 (he knows his own schema but not the schema of other peers) issues the following SQL query to look for kinases sequences that are longer than 30 base pairs: `SELECT SeqId, proteinSeq FROM Kinases WHERE length > 30`. Now, since one of the keywords for Kinases (relation name) is protein, and protein is also a keyword for P2's relation `Protein` and P3's relations `ProteinKLen` and `ProteinKSeq`, these relations match the query relation. Similarly, we find that the attributes `SeqID`, `proteinSeq` and `length` all have matching keywords in P2 and P3. For P3, we note that the query may have to be turned into a join query when evaluated there. For P4, we only have a match in relation name but not in the attributes. Thus, P4 will be ranked lower than P2 and P3. Semantically, we note that P2's data are not actually those that P1 is interested in (since they are not Kinases data). As such, it is important to have the meta-data and additional information returned to the users before fetching the data.

4.4 Agent Assisted Query Processing

In PeerDB, we adopt a two-phase agent-assisted query processing strategy. In the first phase, the relation matching strategy (as described above) is applied to locate potential relations. These relations (meta-data, database name, and location) are then returned to the query node for two purposes. One, it allows user to select the more relevant relations. This is to minimize information overload when data may be syntactically the same (having the same keywords) but semantically different. That is, different schemas are mediated. Moreover, this can minimize transmitting data that are not useful to the user, and hence better utilizes the network bandwidth. Two, it allows the node to update its statistics to facilitate future search process. Phase two begins after the user has selected the desired relations.

In phase two, the queries will be directed to the nodes containing the selected relations, and the answers are finally returned (and cached). The two phases are completely assisted by agents. In fact, it is the agents that are sent out to the peers, and it is the agent that interacts with the DBMS. Moreover, a query may be rewritten into another form by the DBAgent (e.g., a query on a single relation may be rewritten into a join query involving multiple relations).

4.5 Preliminary Results

To evaluate PeerDB's performance, we conducted several sets of experiments (see [13] for the details). We summarize our findings here.

- IR based approach is effective, but still limited. We used the standard IR measures, *Precision* and *Recall*, as performance metrics to measure the approach's effectiveness on relation matching. Our results show that when the threshold value is large (resulting in a large number of relations accepted as matching), *Recall* is low because of the large number of irrelevant relations that share common keywords. However, *Precision* is high showing that most of the retrieved relations are indeed relevant to the query. This result is consistent with typical IR applications, and demonstrated the effectiveness of our approach.
- Self-configuration is important. We study two versions of PeerDB: one with the reconfiguration feature turned off, the other with the reconfiguration feature turned on. From the experiment, we find that the reconfigurable one is more superior than the non-reconfigurable one both in initial response time and in the number of answers returned within a given time, which demonstrates that self-configuration is important for performance improvement.

With the ability to reconfigure the network, relevant nodes will move "closer" and thus queries will always be directed to the more promising node first.
- Caching is helpful for reducing response time. Though many open issues are involved in P2P caching, we did some controlled experiments to evaluate the effect of caching on the performance by varying the storage capacity of each peer. We observe that as the storage capacity of each node increases, the response time decreases. This is expected as more tuples can be found in local and neighboring peers. Meanwhile, by caching previous query results, duplicate work and data movement can be avoided.

5   Conclusion

The objective of this paper is to investigate varieties of P2P facilities that could benefit agent development. We have addressed several common problems and discuss broadly different ways in the integration of agent and P2P. Furthermore, we have introduced BestPeer, a prototype system that have integrated the best of agent and P2P technologies. BestPeer allows data sharing in ad-hoc P2P systems without strong control over the topology of the network and the contents of each peer. In addition, BestPeer employs a simple methodology where every BestPeer node maintains a statistic log of its environment. These logs are updated each time after some query results are obtained. Based on the statistics, optimization such as self-reconfiguring the network to achieve better performance for subsequent queries is applied. Finally, we presented PeerDB, a peer-based data management system that employs IR techniques to handle data sharing amongst heterogeneous data sources. Each PeerDB peer is allowed to define its schemas without any global constraints. Meta-data is used to resolve the conflict of different semantic objects with different syntactic presentations.

References

1. *BestPeer Project Home Page*, http://xena1.ddns.comp.nus.edu.sg/p2p/.
2. P. Druschel and A. Rowstron, *Pastry: Scalable, Distributed Object Location and Routing for Large-Scale Peer-to-Peer Systems*, IFIP/ACM International Conference on Distributed systems platforms (Middle ware), 2001, pp. 329–350.
3. T. Finin, R. Fritzson, D. McKay, and R. McEntire, *KQML as an Agent Communication Language*, 3rd International Conference on Information and Knowledge Management (CIKM), 1994, pp. 456–463.
4. Gnutella Development Home Page, *http://gnutella.wego.com/*.
5. A. Y. Halevy, Z. G. Ives, D. Suciu, and I. Tatarinov, *Schema Mediation in Peer Data Management Systems*, International Conference on Data Engineering (ICDE), 2003.
6. G. Karjoth, D.B. Lange, and M. Oshima, *A Security Model for Aglets*, IEEE Internet Computing **1** (1997), no. 4.
7. N. Karnik and A. Tripathi, *Agent Server Architecture for the Ajanta Mobile-Agent Systems*, International Conference on Parallel and Distributed Processing Techniques and Applications, 1998.

8. A. Kementsietsidis, M. Arenas, and R. J. Miller, *Mapping Data in Peer-to-Peer Systems: Semantics and Algorithmic Issues*, ACM SIGMOD International Conference on Management of Data, 2003.
9. D. Lange and M. Oshima, *Programming and Deploying Java Mobile Agents with Aglets*, Addison-Wesley, 1998.
10. G. Moro, A. M. Ouksel, and C. Sartori, *Agents and Peer-to-Peer Computing: A Promising Combination of Paradigms*, Springer-Verlag (LNAI 2530), 2003, pp. 1–14.
11. W. S. Ng, B. C. Ooi, and K. L. Tan, *BestPeer: A Self-Configurable Peer-to-Peer System*, Poster in International Conference on Data Engineering (ICDE), 2002, p. 272.
12. W. S. Ng, B. C. Ooi, and K. L. Tan, *Bestpeer: A Self-Configurable Peer-to-Peer System*, Technical Report, http://xena1.ddns.comp.nus.edu.sg/p2p/bestpeer.pdf, 2002.
13. W. S. Ng, B. C. Ooi, K. L. Tan, and A. Y. Zhou, *PeerDB: A P2P-based System for Distributed Data Sharing*, International Conference on Data Engineering (ICDE), 2003, pp. 633–644.
14. H. S. Nwana, D. T. Ndumu, L. C. Lee, and J. C. Collis, *ZEUS: A Toolkit and Approach for Building Distributed Multi-Agent Systems*, International Conference on Autonomous Agents (Agents) (Seattle, WA, USA), 1999, pp. 360–361.
15. B. C. Ooi, K. L. Tan, A. Y. Zhou, C. H. Goh, Y. G. Li, C. Y. Liau, B. Ling, W. S. Ng, Y. F. Shu, X. Y. Wang, and M. Zhang, *PeerDB: Peering into Personal Databases*, ACM SIGMOD International Conference on Management of Data (Demo), 2003.
16. S. Ratnasamy, R. Francis, M. Handley, R. Krap, J. Padye, and S. Shenker, *A Scalable Content-Addressable Network*, ACM SIGCOMM, 2001.
17. M. Luck, P. McBurney and C. Preist, *Agent Technology: Enabling next generation computing: a roadmap for agent based computing*, Agentlink, 2003.
18. K. Aberer, P. Cudré-Mauroux and M. Hauswirth, *A Framework for Semantic Gossiping*, SIGMOD Record, 31(4), 2002.
19. Semantic Web Home Page, *www.w3.org/2001/sw/*.
20. I. A. Smith and P. R. Cohen, *Toward a Semantics for an Agent Communications Language Based on Speech-Acts*, 13th National Conference Artificial Intelligence, (AAAI Press), 1996.
21. I. Stocia, R. Morris, D. Karger, M. F. Kaashoek, and H. Balakrishnan, *Chord: A Scalable Peer-to-Peer Lookup Service for Internet Applications*, ACM SIGCOMM, 2001.
22. R. Vincent, B. Horling, and V. Lesser, *An agent infrastructure to build and evaluate multi-agent systems: The java agent framework and multi-agent system simulator*, Lecture Notes in Artificial Intelligence: Infrastructure for Agents, Multi-Agent Systems, and Scalable Multi-Agent Systems., vol. 1887, Wagner & Rana (eds.), Springer,, January 2001.
23. B. Y. Zhao, J. Kubiatowicz, and A. Joseph, *Tapestry: An Infrastructure for Fault-tolerant Wide-area Location and Routing.*, Technical report, UCB/CSD-01-1141, University of California, Berkeley, 2001.

Robustness Challenges in Peer-to-Peer Agent Systems

Onn Shehory

IBM Research Labs in Haifa
Haifa University, Mount Carmel, Haifa
31905 Israel
onn@il.ibm.com

Abstract. Peer-to-peer systems, and in particular peer agent systems within organizations and in open electronic markets, have a promise for improved distribution of information and services and increasing overall performance and fault-tolerance. Nevertheless, these advantages come at a price. The complexity of communication, and in time of computation, increases. Further, failure of weak nodes running agents, which can be addressed by the peer-to-peer architecture, introduces another overhead. In addition to complexity issues, peer-to-peer networks, be their members agents or humans, lack in their ability to enhance trust and security, and are vulnerable to attacks. These shortcomings of peer-to-peer agent systems must be addressed to promote the adoption of such systems. This paper discusses advantages and weaknesses of peer-to-peer agent systems, and the effect these have on overall system robustness. Some solution directions are pointed at as well.

1 Introduction

The peer-to-peer (P2P) paradigm introduces a fundamental change in system architecture. It contrasts two major architectures: the centralized monolithic system architecture, and the distributed, client-server system architecture. The most prominent change that this new architecture introduces is the distribution of control (and responsibility): in P2P systems there is no single point of control, and the responsibility for system functionality is distributed among its members. Such a paradigm shift requires an infrastructure to enhance this new type of interaction among computer systems. Peer-to-peer interaction protocols were implemented early-on in several multi-agent systems (e.g., RETSINA [1]). Those early implementations, however, did not provide a generic infrastructure to be used by others for developing P2P systems. The DARPA CoABS project [2] advanced the state of the art in multi-agent systems towards a generic P2P infrastructure. Yet, only the FIPA specification[3] has formally defined generic agent P2P interaction protocols, and a variety of FIPA implementations (e.g., JADE [4], FIPA-OS [5]) support such P2P interaction.

On a parallel track, the immense growth of the web and the use of the MPEG-1 layer 3 [6] compression algorithm, and the corresponding MP3 audio file format,

G. Moro, C. Sartori, and M.P. Singh (Eds.): AP2PC 2003, LNAI 2872, pp. 13–22, 2004.
© Springer-Verlag Berlin Heidelberg 2004

have lead to an extensive exchange of music files among users. This file exchange activity (in many cases violating copyrights) was performed among peers using file sharing protocols, most prominently Napster. The Napster protocol requires a server where files can be searched for, yet the files themselves are located at the clients and are transferred directly between peers. Thus, the exchange is done in a peer-to-peer manner. A later, serverless, file sharing protocol, is Gnutella [7], where each peer holds a local directory of peers. Using Gnutella, search is performed by querying peers and, when the sought files are not found at the peers' directories, delegating the query to their peers, iterating the delegation to some predefined depth. Several other serverless P2P protocols (e.g., Freenet [8], Morpheus [9]) exist.

Following the P2P file sharing market push, researchers have developed several P2P overlays (e.g., CAN [10], Chord [11], Pastry [12]). These provide an infrastructure for large scale P2P applications, expanding beyond file sharing. The advantage of these over earlier P2P systems is that they were more carefully designed and analyzed, to increase efficiency and scalability. Hence, multi-agent systems, in which interactions are inherently P2P, could benefit from such overlays. Several attempts to do exactly this were performed by agent researchers. Yet in many cases, multi-agent systems differ from classical P2P systems. In particular, classical P2P systems usually assume that peers are either users or applications, whereas in multi-agent systems peers are usually autonomous (possibly intelligent) computational entities. Additionally, in many cases multi-agent systems require location mechanisms beyond a simple directory service (e.g., brokering, matchmaking [13]). Further, agents may be self-interested, thus selfishly exploit the P2P system to increase their gains (e.g., use remote cache, but provide no cache on local host). Selfish behavior is exhibited by humans in P2P systems as well, however due to their computational capabilities, agents might be able to excel in selfishness, negatively affecting overall performance of the system.

These properties of peer-to-peer agent systems may have an effect on the robustness of such systems, thus on their acceptance as a generic approach to system design. In this paper we discuss these robustness concerns. We start by comparing the P2P architecture to other system architectures (Section 2). We then briefly introduce multi-agent systems, referring to their P2P properties (Section 3). The advantages of P2P systems are presented in Sections 4.1 and 4.2, and their weaknesses are discussed in Section 4.3. Section 5 concludes the paper.

2   P2P Versus Client-Server

Both P2P and client-server are distributed system architectures. In a client-server architecture, multiple clients are connected to a single server, requesting services from that server. The server is typically a dominant machine on which shared resources are located and shared applications run. The control over resource and service provision is at the server machine. Clients do not directly

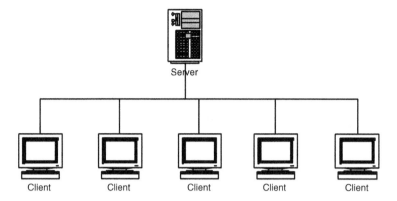

Fig. 1. Client-server architecture

interact among themselves, nor do they provide services or resources to one another. In a client-server system, clients must know the server, an be able to communicate with it, in order that the system function. In some client-server architectures, though not in all, new clients may be added dynamically to the system. The client-server architecture is depicted in Figure 1.

In a peer-to-peer architecture, each node in the system serves both as a client and as a server. Thus, no single node assumes control of the system. Rather, each node requests some resources and services from other nodes, and provides other nodes with services and resources. A node fully controls its own activity, however it has no control over remote activity. Typically in P2P architectures, unlike client-server architectures, the relationship among peers is symmetric,[1] i.e., no peer dominates the interaction. In P2P systems, there is a need for a mechanism that would allow peers to locate the resources or the services they seek. Such a mechanism can be provided via a centralized directory server, or by each peer maintaining a local directory, typically relatively small. Service location is performed by searching the local directory, then directories of peers, and so forth up to some search depth. The members of a P2P system do not necessarily know one another, and membership in the system can change dynamically, each peer deciding for itself whether (and when) it should join or leave the system. A peer-to-peer architecture is depicted in Figure 2.

3   Multi-agent Systems

Multi-agent systems are systems in which multiple agents, distributed over a network, interact. Such interaction can be facilitated both via a client-server architecture and via a P2P architecture. Yet, for open multi-agent systems in

---

[1] Several recent P2P architectures have introduced super-peers, which are peers that contribute more resources to the system. Such peers may asymmetrically have more rights within the P2P system compared to regular peers.

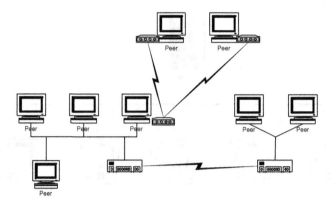

Fig. 2. A typical peer-to-peer architecture

which agents can join an leave at any time, and where member agents are fully autonomous, a P2P architecture is preferable. Hence, not surprisingly, the communication module of autonomous agents in such open multi-agent systems supports symmetric communication [14]. That is, an agent in such systems can take the role of a client, a server, or both. Thus, an agent is a peer in a P2P agent system. Unlike P2P systems in which applications interact to request and provide services, agents are usually assumed to be autonomous, self-interested reasoning computational entities. As such, they may misbehave, manipulate, or even deceive, to reach their goals. Such behaviors can also be found among human peers in P2P systems. Yet, within a networked, computerized system, agents may have an advantage over humans in computational power and speed. Thus, multi-agent systems (which are inherently P2P systems) may intensify problems which already arise in other P2P systems.

4   P2P Advantages and Disadvantages

Comparing P2P systems to client server systems, and further to a fully-centralized monolithic system (e.g., a mainframe), we can identify several properties in which P2P system are clearly better than the others. Distribution is an example of such a property. Such properties are discussed in Section 4.1. With respect to several other properties, it is believed that P2P can be better than, or at least as good as, other architectures. Such properties are discussed in Section 4.2. However, P2P is not the ultimate solution, and with respect to some properties it is clearly inferior. These weaknesses are discussed in Section 4.3. Note that most of the properties referred to in this section are applicable to both P2P systems and P2P multi-agent systems.

4.1   Prominent Advantages

P2P architectures are, by design, distributed, and peers are free to join and leave the system. They further do not require explicit identity disclosure. This results in the following advantages of P2P systems over others:

- **Distribution**
  P2P systems are highly distributed. This property is manifested in the system being serverless: peers do not need a central server to locate remote peers, resources and services, nor are they controlled externally by a server. Peers can reside on any machine across a network, each peer having a local, limited view of the system.
- **Emergent Behavior**
  Monolithic and client-server systems are designed to address a set of specific problems, given a set of resources and services. In P2P systems, the design usually refers to the interaction protocols, however not necessarily to the resources, services and functionality available within the system. The openness and the dynamism of P2P systems result in problems arriving at the system being resolved in an emergent, ad-hoc manner. That is, resources and services required for solving the problem are searched for among peers, and once located they are used for the solution. In that sense, the system exhibits emergent behavior. Since new nodes that arrive at the system may add new resources and services, its actual capabilities may be beyond those planned for initially.
- **Scalability**
  Requiring no central point for interaction and control, P2P systems appear highly scalable. One should recall, however, that in P2P systems, locating resources and services comes at a cost, and this cost increases with the size of the system. Although in the worst case the increase in location costs will be linear in the size of the system, the average cost is logarithmic [15], and is quasi-constant for practical cases. Client-server systems scale up well too, however scaling is confined by the limited capability of the server (or several servers) to support the clients at an acceptable quality of service. Scalability of client server systems comes at the economic cost of increasing server capabilities.
- **Autonomy**
  A P2P system comprised of software components is loosely coupled, in the sense that each peer provides resources and performs tasks at its own discretion. This is in particular typical in multi-agent systems, where peer agents are inherently autonomous entities. Although such autonomy is not always beneficial for overall system behavior, it is advantageous for addressing the goals of the peer agents and the users on behalf which these agents might be acting. Such a property is not provided by client-server systems, let alone monolithic systems.
- **Economic Efficiency**
  The economic advantages of P2P systems are threefold. Firstly, the cost

of ownership incurred by each pear is low. Each peer can use multiple resources and services, however it needs to own only a small subset thereof. Secondly, the system scales at virtually no cost. In contrast, client-server and monolithic systems require costly investments in hardware and software for scaling them up. Thirdly, in open, market-like environments, where services and resources are traded, rational behavior among peer agents should result (given a sufficiently large market), in an efficient market. That is, the market should arrive at an efficient allocation of resources among the agents. Hence, for such environments the P2P approach is economically advantageous.

4.2   Probable Advantages

In addition to the above properties, which are, at least under some condition, prominent advantages of P2P systems over other systems, there are several properties of P2P systems that seem advantageous, but are not always so. These are listed below.

- **Self-Organization**
  Self-organization and dynamic adaptation of systems introduces a combinatorial coordination problem. Self-organization has been studied extensively for monolithic as well as client-server systems. Implementations of such system behavior succeeds in some cases however exhibits less success in others. Self-organization in P2P systems, and in particular of multi-agent systems, was studied to some extent, however there is no clear evidence that self-organization in P2P systems arrives at better (or worse) results compared to other systems. Although adaptation could be beneficial, its computational cost may prove too high. This cost may increase in unstructured, P2P systems, as locating, selecting, and re-organizing peers is costly in such systems.
- **Protocol Simplicity**
  Peer-to-peer protocols are usually very simple. However, client-server protocol are not complex either. Monolithic system do not require an interaction protocol whatsoever. Hence, compared to other architectures, the advantage of simple protocols is limited. Further, P2P protocols that properly address security issues introduce an additional complexity.
- **Fault-Tolerance**
  It is widely agreed that redundancy increases fault-tolerance. Since in P2P systems multiple nodes may be providing similar resources and services, and since the systems is highly distributed, failure of a single node, or a single communication line, should have little effect on overall system behavior. Client-server systems which are distributed too can fail when the central server fails. In contrast, there is no central server in P2P systems, thus such a failure will not occur. Yet, monolithic systems as well as client server systems (to a lesser extent) are engineered and optimized to minimize failures. Some of these systems are embedded with redundant components for high system availability. Therefore, the advantage of P2P systems in fault-tolerance is limited, and is applicable mainly to large-scale, aggregate systems.

– **Performance**
P2P systems may have access to large quantities of resources and services. They should hence be able to perform diverse and complex computational tasks. P2P systems can also distribute tasks among multiple nodes, thus increasing timely performance of tasks. Yet, monolithic and client-server systems, unlike P2P systems, are usually optimized for their tasks and for using their resources. The sub-optimal computation within P2P systems may thus prove inferior to other systems' computation. Additionally, P2P systems run on top of network infrastructure and topology which may be shared by other systems and poorly designed and configured. Thus, P2P systems are vulnerable to severe network latencies.

– **Anonymity**
P2P protocols usually do not require that peers disclose their identity (they do require some internal ID, though). Hence, peers can gain access to resources and be serviced yet keep their anonymity. Anonymity is out of scope in monolithic systems, and in client-server systems anonymity is not assumed. However, in the latter systems, users can run anonymizers on clients, thus gaining anonymity. In both P2P and client-server systems, running sniffers on network nodes can reveal identities for which anonymity was initially sought. Hence, Anonymity is not unique to, and can be violated in, P2P systems.

4.3 Weaknesses

Thus far we have presented advantages, or at least probable advantages, of P2P systems. It is important to note that P2P systems have several weaknesses as well. The distribution of peers and the type of interaction among them expose P2P systems to several risks. These are detailed below.

– **Usage patterns:** In similarity to web usage patterns [16], resources and services within a P2P network are prone to the "Tragedy of the Commons" [17] as well. That is, free access to resources may result in their extensive usage by some peers, which will in turn over-congest the nodes providing the resources and eventually deem them unreachable to all peers. Several studies have shown that this phenomenon is exhibited in file sharing P2P systems. Another usage pattern is the unequal contribution of peers to the system. That is, some nodes contribute very little, if any, resources, whereas other contribute a lot. This difference in contribution levels may result from fundamental differences between the nodes on which the peers run (e.g., a weak desktop machine vs. a high-end server machine), however it may also result from selfish behavior of a peer. A partial remedy to the latter problem is afforded by the introduction of super-peers into the P2P system. These are already in use in some P2P systems however are not common in multi-agent systems.
– **Security:** Peer-to-peer systems, distributed over an open network, are vulnerable to multiple security problems typical in such networks. These include:

lack of confidentiality; no authentication and access control mechanism; no guaranties on data and service integrity; exposure to denial-of-service attacks; and others. In market-based P2P and agent systems, impersonating others and repudiating transactions are expected as well. Many of the above problems can be solved using cryptographic techniques. Using such techniques, researchers have introduced both agent security and P2P security solutions [18,19,20]. Yet, these solutions complicate the interaction protocol and impose computation and communication overheads, thus reflecting on system performance.

– **Privacy and trust:** Privacy and trust, although in times referred to as security issues, are different aspects of peer and agent interaction. Privacy refers to the confidentiality of information disclosed to other parties *after* this information was disclosed to those. To date, no mechanism provides for a peer to guarantee that such information is kept confidential. The P3P protocol [21] only suggests ways to express privacy policies and preferences, but it does not provide means for enforcing these policies. Thus, a peer that seeks privacy relies on its trust in another peer for keeping its private information confidential.

There are multiple definitions for trust, yet the major result of trust is the willingness of and agent or a peer to delegate responsibility (e.g., for task execution) to others. Security mechanisms can increase trust, for instance, because they can prevent impersonation. However, they cannot guarantee that a trusted peer will prove trustworthy as expected. Reputation mechanisms (e.g., [22]) can increase trust too, but they do not provide guarantees as well.

Peer-to-peer systems are usually based on some level of trust among the peers. Among humans, likely due to societal codes, the majority of peers appear trustworthy, at least within the scope of the P2P system. For multi-agent systems, however, such trust is not guaranteed, and mechanisms should be devised to enhance trust to an acceptable level.

– **Quality of service:** In P2P systems, the openness and the anonymity of the system result in peers offering services at diverse levels of quality. Thus, even when one peer trusts another one to provide a resource or a service, in current P2P protocols there are no explicit mean to specify the requested quality. Further, even if the request states the requested quality, there are no means to guarantee that such a quality will be provided. This deems P2P systems, to some extent, unreliable.

– **Manipulative and malicious behavior:** Unreliability is may result from peers proactively acting in a manipulative or malicious behavior. Such phenomena intensify in market-based agent systems, where self-interested agent attempt to maximize their gains. A simple example for such a behavior is a case where an agent has requested a service from another agent and paid for it; following, the payee has performed the service, however to reduce its costs the payee has performed the service at a very low quality. This case may be extended to a case where the payee reports that it has performed the task allocated to it, although it may have never actually performed it.

There is a vast array of possible manipulative behaviors, of which many can be addressed by designing preventive mechanisms using methods from game theory. Nevertheless, the cost of implementing such mechanisms may be very high, it times prohibitive to practical system implementation.

The above are prominent weaknesses of P2P systems, and within multi-agent systems some do intensify. Additional weaknesses exist, some of which were referred to in Section 4.2, when assessing probable advantages.

5 Conclusion

As we show, P2P systems, including P2P agent systems, introduce an array of advantages which are not provided by other system architectures. However, the weaknesses of P2P systems, of which some are intensified in multi-agent systems, cannot be ignored. These weaknesses suggest that P2P agent systems may significantly luck in their robustness when compared to other, less distributed and more structured, systems.

P2P systems are vulnerable to multiple attacks of which only some have solutions known in the art. They rely on trust and privacy, and these are only partly enhanced by technological solutions. They are further exposed to manipulative behavior, for which solutions may be too complex. And, at the computational level, they introduce both communication and computation overheads in terms of location protocols, caching requirements and security mechanisms.

Thus, although P2P systems, and even more so multi-agent systems, present a shift of paradigm in system architecture, and although several advantages of P2P systems place them by far ahead of competing systems, their success as a generic solution for system design depends, to a large extent, on the success of the P2P and Agents research communities to overcomes P2P weaknesses and increase its robustness.

References

1. Sycara, K., Paolucci, M., van Velsen, M., Giampapa, J. The RETSINA MAS infrastructure. Autonomous Agents and MAS **6** (2003)
2. CoABS: http://coabs.globalinfotek.com/
3. FIPA: http://www.fipa.org/repository/index.html
4. JADE: http://sharon.cselt.it/projects/jade/
5. FIPA-OS: http://www.emorphia.com/research/about.htm
6. MP3: http://www.iis.fraunhofer.de/amm/techinf/layer3/
7. Gnutella: http://www.gnutella.com
8. Freenet: http://freenet.sourceforge.net/
9. Morpheus: http://www.morpheus.com/
10. Ratnasamy, S., Francis, P., Handley, M., Karp, R., Shenker, S. A scalable content-addressable network. In Proceedings of ACM SIGCOMM'01. (2001) 161–172
11. Stoica, I., Morris, R., Karger, D., Kaashoek, F., Balakrishnan, H. Chord: A scalable peer-to-peer lookup service for internet applications. In Proceedings of ACM SIGCOMM'01. (2001) 149–160

12. Rowstron, A., Druschel, P. Pastry: Scalable, distributed object location and routing for large-scale peer-to-peer systems. In Proceedings of IFIP/ACM International Conference on Distributed Systems Platforms. (2001) 329–350
13. Klusch, M., Sycara, K. 8: Brokering and Matchmaking for Coordination of Agent Societies: A Survey. In Coordination of Internet Agents. Springer (2001) 197–224
14. Shehory, O., Sycara, K. The RETSINA communicator. In Proceedings of Autonomous Agents. (2000) 199–200
15. Shehory, O. A scalable agent location mechanism. Intelligent Agents VI **LNAI 1757** (2000) 162–172
16. Huberman, B. The Laws of the Web. MIT Press (2001)
17. Hardin, G. The tragedy of the commons. Science **162** (1968) 1243–1248
18. Wong, H.C., Sycara, K. Adding security and trust to multi-agent systems. Applied Artificial Intelligence **14** (2000) 927–941
19. Mass, Y., Shehory, O. Distributed trust in open multi-agent systems. In Proceedings of AA'00 workshop on Trust, Fraud and Deception. (2000)
20. Castro, M., Druschel, P., Ganesh, A., Rowstron, A., Wallach, D.S. Security for structured peer-to-peer overlay networks. In Proceedings of OSDI'02. (2002)
21. P3P: http://www.w3.org/p3p/
22. Yu, B., Singh, M.P. Small-world reputation management in online communities. CIA2000 **LNAI 1860** (2000) 154–165

Bayesian Network Trust Model in Peer-to-Peer Networks

Yao Wang and Julita Vassileva

Computer Science Department, University of Saskatchewan at 1C101 Eng. Bldg.,
57 Campus DR., Saskatoon, SK S7N 5A9,Canada
{yaw181, jiv}@cs.usask.ca

Abstract. In this paper, we propose a Bayesian network-based trust model in peer-to-peer networks. Since trust is multi-faceted, even in the same context, peers still need to develop differentiated trust in different aspects of other peers' behaviors. The peer's needs are different in different situations. Depending on the situation, a peer may need to consider its trust in a specific aspect of another peer's capability or in a combination of multiple aspects. Bayesian networks provide a flexible method to represent differentiated trust and combine different aspects of trust.

1 Introduction

In heterogenous open P2P systems, some peers might be buggy and some might be malicious and provide bad services. Since there is no centralized node to serve as an authority to supervise peers' behaviors and punish peers that behave badly, malicious peers have an incentive to harm other peers to get more benefit because they can get away with their bad behaviors. Mechanisms for trust and reputation can be used to help peers distinguish potential benevolent partners from potential malicious partners and thus provide protection for both consumers and providers of services.

Trust and reputation mechanisms have been proposed for large open environments in e-commerce, distributed computing, recommender systems. Agents are often used to manage and reason about trust and reputation on the behalf of users. In this situation, trust is defined as an agent's belief in attributes such as reliability, honesty and competence of the trusted agent. The reputation of an agent defines an expectation about its behavior, which is based on other agents' observations or information about the agent's past behavior within a specific context at a given time. They are used to help agents make decisions on whether a potential partner is trustworthy to interact with. Here the interaction refers to the activity occurring when an agent gets service from another agent.

Some of the literature on trust and reputation treats the two concepts interchangeably or ambiguously. The two concepts are related, but different. Agent A's trust in agent B is the accumulation of evaluations that agent A has of its past interactions with B. It reflects agent A's subjective viewpoint of B's capability. The reputation of agent B, from agent A's perspective, is the collective

G. Moro, C. Sartori, and M.P. Singh (Eds.): AP2PC 2003, LNAI 2872, pp. 23–34, 2004.

evaluation based on other agents' evaluations of B. It is an objective measure for agent B's capability, resulting from the evaluations of many other agents.

2   Bayesian Network-Based Trust Model

We will use a peer-to-peer file sharing application as an example to describe our approach, however this approach is general and can be applied to other domains, like web-services, e-commence, recommender systems or peer-to-peer distributed computing. In peer-to-peer file sharing applications, this approach can also be integrated with current file sharing protocols, such as Gnutella.

In file sharing systems in peer-to-peer networks, each peer plays two roles, the role of file provider offering files to other peers and the role of user using files provided by other peers. In order to distinguish the two roles of each peer, in the rest of the paper, when a peer acts as a file provider, we call it file provider; otherwise, we call it simply agent. An agent builds two kinds of trust. One is the trust in file providers' competence in providing services. The other is the trust in another agent's reliability in providing recommendations about file providers. Here the reliability includes two aspects: whether the agent is truthful in telling its information and whether the agent is trustworthy or not. Since agents are heterogeneous, they judge other agent's behavior by different criteria. If their criteria are similar, one agent can trust another agent. If their criteria are different, they cannot trust each other even if both of them tell the truth. We assume all the agents are truthful in telling their evaluations. So we only take care of the situation where agents have different ways of judging issues, which reflects different user types.

2.1   Trust in a File Provider's Competence in Providing Files

In a peer-to-peer network, file providers' capabilities are not uniform. For example, some file providers may be connecting through a high-speed network, so they are able to send files to other agents at a fast speed. Some file providers might like music, so they share a lot of music files. Some may be interested in movies and share some movies. Some may be very picky in file quality, so they only keep and share files with high quality. Therefore, the file provider's capability can be presented in various aspects, such as the download speed, file quality and file type (see Figure 1). The agent's needs are also different in different situations. Sometimes, it might want to know the file provider's overall capability. Sometimes it might only be interested in the file provider's capability in some particular aspect. For instance, an agent wants to download a music file from a file provider. At this time, knowing the file provider's capability in providing music files is more valuable for the agent than knowing the file provider's capability in other aspects. Agents also need to develop differentiated trust in file providers' capabilities. For example, the agent who wants to download a music file from the file provider cares about whether the file provider is able to provide the music file with good quality at a fast speed, which involves the file provider's capabilities in two aspects, quality and speed. How does the agent combine its two trust representations, the trust in the file provider's capability in providing music files with good quality and the trust in the file provider's capability in providing a fast download speed, in order to decide if the file provider is trustworthy?

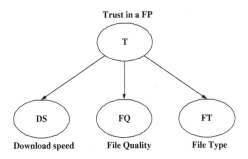

Fig. 1. A bayesian network model

A Bayesian network provides a flexible method to solve the problem. A Bayesian network is a relationship network that uses statistic methods to represent probability relationships between different elements. Its theoretical foundation is the Bayes rule [1].

$$p(h|e) = \frac{p(e|h).p(h)}{p(e)} \tag{1}$$

$p(h)$ is the prior probability of hypothesis h; $p(e)$ is the prior probability of evidence e; $p(h|e)$ is the probability of h given e; $p(e|h)$ is the probability of e given h.

A naive Bayesian network is a simple Bayesian network. It is composed of a root node and several leaf nodes. We will use a naive Bayesian network to represent the trust between an agent and a file provider.

Every agent develops a naive Bayesian network for each file provider that it has interacted with. Each Bayesian network has a root node T, which has two values, "satisfying" and "unsatisfying", denoted by 1 and 0, respectively. $p(T = 1)$ represents the value of agent's overall trust in the file provider's competence in providing files. It is the percentage of interactions that are satisfying and measured by the number of satisfying interactions m divided by the total number of interactions n. $p(T = 0)$ is the percentage of not satisfying interactions.

$$p(T = 1) = \frac{m}{n}, \text{where } p(T = 1) + p(T = 0) = 1 \tag{2}$$

The leaf nodes under the root node represent the file provider's capability in different aspects. Each leaf node is associated with a conditional probability table (CPT). The node, denoted by FT, represents the set of file types. Suppose it includes five values, "*Music*", "*Movie*", "*Document*", "*Image*" and "*Software*".

Table 1. The CPT of node FT

	$T = 1$	$T = 0$
Music	$p = (FT = "Music"|T = 1)$	$p = (FT = "Music"|T = 0)$
Movie	$p = (FT = "Movie"|T = 1)$	$p = (FT = "Movie"|T = 0)$
Document	$p = (FT = "Document"|T = 1)$	$p = (FT = "Document"|T = 0)$
Image	$p = (FT = "Image"|T = 1)$	$p = (FT = "Image"|T = 0)$
Software	$p = (FT = "Software"|T = 1)$	$p = (FT = "Software"|T = 0)$

Its CPT is showed in Table 1. It includes two columns of values. Each column follows one constraint, which corresponds to one value of the root node. The sum of values of each column is equal to 1.

$p(FT = "Music"|T = 1)$ is the conditional probability with the condition that an interaction is satisfying. It measures the probability that the file involved in an interaction is a music file, given the interaction is satisfying. It can be computed according to the following formula:

$$p(FT = "Music"|T = 1) = \frac{p(FT = "Music", T = 1)}{p(T = 1)} \tag{3}$$

$p(FT = "Music", T = 1)$ is the probability that interactions are satisfying and files involved are music files.

$$p(FT = "Music", T = 1) = \frac{m1}{n} \tag{4}$$

$m1$ is the number of satisfying interactions when files involved are music files.

$p(FT = "Music"|T = 0)$ denotes the probability that files are music files, given interactions are not satisfying. The probabilities for other file types in Table 1 are computed in a similar way.

Node DS denotes the set of download speeds. It has three items,"*Fast*", "*Medium*" and "*Slow*", each of which covers a range of download speed.

Node FQ denotes the set of file qualities. It also has three items, "*High*", "*Medium*" and "*Low*". Its CPT is similar to the one in Table 1.

Here we only take three aspects of trust into account. More relevant aspects can be added in the Bayesian network later to account for user preferences with respect to service.

Once getting nodes' CPTs in a Bayesian network, an agent can compute the probabilities that the corresponding file provider is trustworthy in different aspects by using Bayes rules, such as $p(T = 1|FT = "Music")$ - the probability that the file provider is trustworthy in providing music files, $p(T = 1|FQ = "High")$ - the probability that the file provider is trustworthy in providing files with high quality, $p(T = 1|FT = "Music", FQ = "High")$ - the probability that the file provider is trustworthy in providing music files with high quality. Agents can set various conditions according to their needs. Each probability represents trust in an aspect of the file provider's competence. With the Bayesian networks, agents can infer trust in the various aspects that they need from the corresponding probabilities. That will save agents much effort in building each trust separately, or developing new trust when conditions change.

2.2 Evaluation of an Interaction

A search request in file sharing peer-to-peer applications usually results in a long list of providers for an identical file. An agent can arrange the list according to its trust in these file providers. Then the agent chooses the most trusted file providers in the top of the list to interact with. Agents update their corresponding Bayesian networks after each interaction. If an interaction is satisfying, m and n are both increased by 1 in Formula 4. If it is not satisfying, only n is increased by 1. Two main factors are considered when agents judge an interaction, the degree of their satisfaction with the download speed s_{ds} and the degree of their satisfaction with the quality of downloaded file s_{fq}. The overall degree of agents' satisfaction with an interaction is computed as the following:

$$s = w_{ds} * s_{ds} + w_{fq} * s_{fq}, \text{ where } w_{ds} + w_{fq} = 1 \tag{5}$$

w_{ds} and w_{fq} denote weights, which indicate the importance of download speed and the importance of file quality to a particular agent (depending on the user's preferences). Each agent has a satisfaction threshold s_t. If $s < s_t$, the interaction is unsatisfying; otherwise, it is satisfying.

2.3 Handing Other Agents' Recommendations

If an agent is not sure about the trustworthiness of a file provider, it can ask other agents to make recommendations for the file provider. The agent can send various recommendation requests according to its needs. For example, if the agent is going to download a movie, it may care about the movie's quality. Another agent may care about the speed. So the request can be "Does the file provider provide good quality movies?". If the agent cares both about the quality and the download speed, the request will be something like "Does the file provider provide good quality files at a fast download speed? ". When other agents receive these requests, they will check their trust-representations, i.e. their Bayesian networks, to see if they can answer such questions. If an agent has downloaded movies from the file provider before, it will send recommendation that contains the value $p(T = 1|FT = "Music", FQ = "High")$ to answer the first request or the value $p(T = 1|FT = "Music", FQ = "High", DS = "Fast")$ to answer the second request. The agent might receive several such recommendations at the same time, which may come from the trustworthy acquaintances, untrustworthy acquaintances, or strangers. If the references are untrustworthy, the agent can discard their recommendations immediately. Then the agent needs to combine the recommendations from trustworthy references and from unknown references together to get the total recommendation for the file provider:

$$r_{ij} = w_t * \frac{\sum_{l=1}^{k} tr_{il} * t_{lj}}{\sum_{l=1}^{k} tr_{il}} + w_s * \frac{\sum_{z=1}^{g} t_{zj}}{g}, \text{ where } w_t + w_s = 1 \tag{6}$$

r_{ij} is the total recommendation value for the jth file provider that the ith agent gets. k and g are the number of trustworthy references and the number of unknown references, respectively. tr_{il} is the trust that the ith user has in the lth trustworthy reference. t_{lj} is the trust that the lth trustworthy reference has in j^{th} file provider. t_{zj} is the trust that the zth unknown reference has in j^{th} file provider. w_t and w_s are the weights to indicate how the user values the importance of the recommendation from trustworthy references and from unknown references. Since agents often have different preferences and points of view, the agent's trustworthy acquaintances are those agents that share similar preferences and viewpoints with the agent most of time. The agent should weight the recommendations from its trustworthy acquaintances higher than those recommendations from strangers. Given a threshold θ, if the total recommendation value is greater than θ, the agent will interact with the file provider; otherwise, not.

If the agent interacts with the file provider, it will not only update its trust in the file provider, i.e. its corresponding Bayesian network, but also update its trust in the agents that provide recommendations by the following reinforcement learning formula:

$$tr_{ij}^{t+1} = \alpha * tr_{ij}^{t} + (1 - \alpha) * e_{\alpha} \qquad (7)$$

tr_{ij}^{t} denotes the trust value that the ith agent has in the jth reference after t recommendations of the jth reference; α is the learning rate - a real number in the interval [0,1]. e_{α} is the new evidence value, which can be -1 or 1. If the value of recommendation is greater than θ and the interaction with the file provider afterwards is satisfying, e_{α} is equal to 1; in the other case, since there is a mismatch between the recommendation and the actual experience with the file provider, the evidence is negative, so e_{α} is -1.

Another way to find if an agent is trustworthy or not in telling the truth is the comparison between two agents' Bayesian networks relevant to an identical file provider. When agents are idle, they can "gossip" with each other periodically, exchange and compare their Bayesian networks. This can help them find other agents who share similar preferences more accurately and faster. After each comparison, the agents will update their trusts in each other according the formula:

$$tr_{ij}^{t+1} = \beta * tr_{ij}^{t} + (1 - \beta) * e_{\beta} \qquad (8)$$

The result of the comparison e_{β} is a number in the interval [-1, 1]. β is the learning rate - a real number in the interval [0,1] which follows the constraint $\beta > \alpha$. This is because the Bayesian network collectively reflects an agent's preferences and viewpoints based on all its past interactions with a specific file provider. Comparing the two agents' Bayesian networks is tantamount to comparing all the past interactions of the two agents. The evidence e_{α} in Formula 7 is only based on one interaction. The evidence e_{β} should affect the agent's trust in another agent more than e_{α}.

How do the agents compare their Bayesian networks and how is e_β computed? First, we assume all agents have the same structure of Bayesian networks. We only compare the values in their Bayesian networks. Suppose agent 1 will compare its Bayesian network (see Figure 1) with the corresponding Bayesian network of agent 2. Agent 1 obtains the degree of similarity between the two Bayesian networks by computing the similarity of each pair of nodes (T, DS, FQ and FT), according to the similarity measure based on Clark's distance [2], and then combining the similarity results of each pair of nodes together.

$$e_\beta = 1 - 2 * \sum_{i=1}^{4} (w1_i * c_i), \text{ where } w1_1 + w1_2 + w1_3 + w1_4 = 1 \qquad (9)$$

$$c_1 = \sqrt{\frac{(v1_{11} - v2_{11})^2}{(v1_{11} + v2_{11})^2} + \frac{(v1_{12} - v2_{12})^2}{(v1_{12} + v2_{12})^2}} \qquad (10)$$

$$c_i = \frac{\sum_{j=1}^{2} \sqrt{\sum_{l=1}^{h_i} \frac{(v1_{ijl} - v2_{ijl})^2}{(v1_{ijl} + v2_{ijl})^2}}}{2}, \text{ where } i = 2, 3, 4 \qquad (11)$$

$w1_1, w1_2, w1_3$ and $w1_4$ are the weights of the node T, DS, FQ, and FT, respectively, related to agent 1, which indicate the importance of these nodes in comparing two Bayesian networks. c_1, c_2, c_3 and c_4 are the results of comparing agent 1 and agent 2's CPTs about node T, DS, FQ and FT. Since the node T is the root node and it has only one column in its CPT, while other nodes (DS, FQ, FT) are the leaf nodes and have two columns of values in theirs CPTs, we compute c_1 differently from c_2, c_3, and c_4. h_i denotes the number of values in the corresponding node. $h_1 = 3$; $h_2 = 3$; $h_3 = 5$. $v1_{11}$ and $v1_{12}$ are the values of $p(T = 1)$ and $p(T = 0)$ related to agent 1. $v2_{11}$ and $v2_{12}$ are the values of $p(T = 1)$ and $p(T = 0)$ related to agent 2. $v1_{ijl}$ and $v2_{ijl}$ are the values in agent 1's CPTs and agent 2's CPTs, respectively.

The idea of this metric is that agents compute not only their trust values, their CPTs, but also take into account their preferences (encoded as the weights, $w1_1, w1_2, w1_3, w1_4$). So agents with similar preferences, such as the importance of file type, quality, download speed, will weight each other's opinions higher.

3   Evaluation

We evaluate our approach in a simulation of a file sharing system in a peer-to-peer network developed on the JADE 2.5.

3.1   Experimental Setup

For the sake of simplicity, each node in our system plays only one role at a time, either the role of a file provider or the role of an agent. Every agent only knows other agents directly connected with it and a few file providers at the beginning.

Every agent has an interest vector. The interest vector is composed of five elements: *music, movie, image, document and software*. The value of each element indicates the strength of the agent's interests in the corresponding file type. The files the agent wants to download are generated based on its interest vector. Every agent keeps two lists. One is the agent list that records all the other agents that the agent has interacted with and its trust values in these agents. The other is the file provider list that records the known file providers and the corresponding Bayesian networks representing the agent's trusts in these file providers. Each file provider has a capability vector showing its capabilities in different aspects, i.e. providing files with different types, qualities and download speeds.

Our experiments involve 10 different file providers and 40 agents. Each agent will gossip with other agents periodically to exchange their Bayesian networks. The period is 5, which means after each 5 interactions with other agents, the agent will gossip once. $w_{ds} = w_{fq} = 0.5; \alpha = 0.3; \beta = 0.5; wl_1 = wl_2 = wl_3 = wl_4 = 0.25$. The total number of interactions is 1000.

3.2   Results

The goal of the first experiment is to see if a Bayesian network-based trust model helps agents to select file providers that match better their preferences. Therefore we compare the performance (in terms of a percentage of successful recommendations, which is the number of successful recommendations over the number of positive recommendations) of a system consisting of agents with Bayesian network-based trust models and a system consisting of agents without Bayesian networks (BN) that represent general trust, not differentiated to different aspects. Successful recommendations are those positive recommendations (obtained based on Formula 6) when agents are satisfied with interactions with recommended file providers. If an agent gets a negative recommendation for a file provider, it will not interact with the file provider. We have two configurations in this experiment:

•Trust and reputation system with BN (*TRBN*): the system consists of agents with Bayesian networks-based trust models that exchange recommendations with each other;

•Trust and reputation system without BN (*TR*): the system consists of agents that exchange recommendations, but don't model differentiated trust in file providers.

Figure 2 presents the means and standard deviations of percentages of successful recommendations in the two systems for 10 runs. It shows that the system using Bayesian networks performs slightly better than the system with general trust both in means and in standard deviations.

The goal of the second experiment is to see if the exchange of recommendation values helps agents to achieve better performance (defined as the percentage of successful interactions with file providers, which is the number of successful interactions divided by the total number of interactions). This is in fact a measure of confidence in peers' forecast, since peers interact with a file provider only

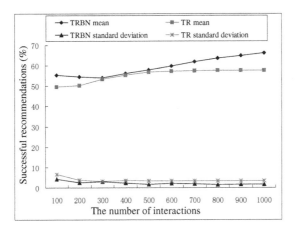

Fig. 2. Trust and reputation system with BN vs. without BN

if their trust exceeds a threshold or they get a positive recommendation. For the reason, we compare four configurations:
•Trust and reputation system with BN;
•Trust and reputation system without BN;
•Trust system with BN: the system consists of agents with Bayesian networks-based trust models, which don't exchange recommendations with each other;
•Trust system without BN: the system consists of agents that have no differentiated trust models and don't exchange recommendations with each other.

Figure 3 shows that the two systems, where agents share information with each other, outperform the systems, where agents do not share information. The trust system using Bayesian networks is slightly better than the trust system without using Bayesian networks. There is an anomaly in the case when agents do not share recommendations, since in the end of the curve the system without BN perform better than the system with BN. This could be explained with an imprecise BN due to insufficient experience.

In some sense, an agent's Bayesian network can be viewed as the model of a specified file provider from the agent's personal perspective. In our experiments, we use a very simple naive Bayesian network, which can not represent complex relationships. In the real file-sharing system, the model of file providers might be more complex and required the use of a more complex Bayesian network. Our Bayesian network only involves three factors.

4 Discussion and Related Work

How many Bayesian networks can an agent afford to maintain to represent its trust in other agents in the networks? It depends on the size of the network and the likelihood that agents have repeated interactions. Resnick [3] empirically shows that 89.0% of all seller-buyer pairs in eBay conducted just one transaction during a five-month period and 98.9% conducted no more than four. The

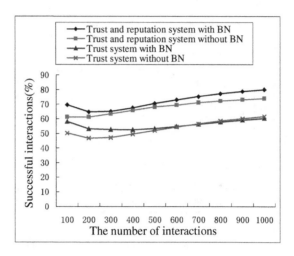

Fig. 3. The comparison of four systems

interactions between the same seller and the same buyer are not repeatable. The buyer's trust in a seller is only based on one direct interaction. The seller's reputation is mostly built on the buyers' having a single experience with the seller. This situation often happens in a very large network or in large e-commence sites. Since there are a large number of sellers and buyers, the chance that a buyer meets the same seller is rare. But if the kind of goods being transacted is only interesting to a small group of people, for example, collectors of ancient coins, the interactions about this kind of goods happen almost exclusively in a small group. So the probability that sellers and buyers have repeated interactions will be high, and they will be able to build trust in each other by our method.

Our approach is useful in situations where two agents can repeatedly interact with each other. In a small-size network, there is no doubt that our approach is applicable. For a large network, our approach is still suitable under the condition that the small-world phenomenon happens. The small-world phenomenon was first discovered in the 1960ies by social scientists. Milgram's experiment showed that people in the U.S. are connected by a short (average length of 6) chain of intermediate acquaintances. Other studies have shown that people tend to interact with other people in their small world more frequently than with people outside. The phenomenon also happens in peer-to-peer networks. Jovanovic [4] shows that the small-world phenomenon occurs in Gnutella. It means that agents are inclined to get files from other agents from a small sub-community. This small sub-community often consists of agents that have similar preferences and viewpoints.

Our approach also requires that agents have compatible ontologies, i.e. their "understanding" of the elements of the Bayesian networks have to be identical or similar at comparision. Although this is a strong assumption, it is feasible if peers are designed by the same person or group or they have similar perferences.

Abdul-Rahman and Hailes [5] capture the most important characteristics of trust and reputation and propose the general structure for developing trust and reputation in a distributed system. Most of the later works in the area follow their ideas, but in different application domain, such as [6], [7], [2], Sabater and Sierra's work [8] extends the notion of trust and reputation into social and ontological dimensions. Social dimension means that the reputation of the group that an individual belongs to also influences the reputation of the individual. Ontological dimension means that the reputation of an agent is compositional. The overall reputation is obtained as a result of the combination of the agent's reputation in each aspect. Our approach integrates these two previous works [5], [8], and applies them to file sharing system in peer-to-peer networks. Another difference between our work and Sabater and Sierra's work is that we use Bayesian networks to represent the differentiated trust at different aspects, other than the structure of ontology. Another difference is that we don't treat the differentiated trusts as compositional. Usually the relationship between different aspects of an agent is not just compositional, but complex and correlative. Our approach provides an easy way to present a complex and correlative relationship. Our approach is also flexible in inferring the trust of an agent for different needs. For example, sometimes we care about the overall trust. Sometimes we only need to know the trust in some specific aspect. This bears parallel with work on distributed user modeling and purpose-based user modeling [9], [10].

Yu and Singh [11], [12] focus on how to use social networks to gather information to compute agents' reputation. They do not deal with differentiated trust and reputation. Cornelli's work [7] is on the area of file sharing in peer-to-peer networks. However, it concentrates on how to prevent the attacks to the reputation system and does not discuss how agents model and compute trust and reputation.

5   Conclusions

In this paper, we propose a Bayesian network-based trust model. Bayesian networks provide a flexible method to represent differentiated trust in different aspects of each other's capability and combine different aspects of trust. We evaluated our approach in a simulation of a file sharing system in a peer-to-peer network. Our experiments show that the system where agents communicate their experiences (recommendations) outperforms the system where agents do not communicate with each other, and that a differentiated trust adds to the performance.

Future work includes adding more aspects in the Bayesian networks, trying to find the key parameters that influence the system performance, and testing the system under other performance measures, for example, how fast an agent can locate a trustworthy service provider. Applying this approach to peer-to-peer systems for computational services is particular promising.

References

1. Heckerman, D.: A tutorial on learning with bayesian networks. Technical report, Microsoft (1995)
2. Montaner, M., López, B., de la Rosa, J.L.: Opinion-based filtering through trust. In: Cooperative Information Agents VI — Proceedings of the 6th International Workshop, CIA 2002. (2002) 164–178
3. Resnick, P., Zeckhauser, R.: Trust among strangers in internet transactions: Empirical analysis of ebay's reputation system. (In: NBER Workshop on Empirical Studies of Electronic Commerce)
4. Jovanovic, M.A.: Modeling large-scale peer-to-peer networks and a case study of gnutella. Master's thesis, University of Cinicnnati (2001)
5. Abdul-Rahman, A., Hailes, S.: Supporting trust in virtual communities. In: Proceedings of the Hawai'i International Conference on System Sciences, Maui, Hawaii (2000)
6. Azzedin, F., Maheswaran, M.: Evolving and managing trust in grid computing systems. In: IEEE Canadian Conference on Electrical & Computer Engineering. (2002)
7. Cornelli, F., Damiani, E., di Vimercati, S.D.C., Paraboschi, S., Samarati, P.: Implementing a reputation-aware gnutella servent. Lecture Notes in Computer Science **2376** (2002) 321
8. Sabater, J., Sierra, C.: Regret: a reputation model for gregarious societies. (In: 4^{th}Workshop on Deception, Fraud and Trust in Agent Societies)
9. Niu, X., McCalla, G., Vassileva, J.: Purpose-based user modelling in a multi-agent portfolio management system. In: Proceedings of User Modeling UM03, Johnstown, PA (2003)
10. Vassileva, J., McCalla, G., Greer, J.: Multi-agent multi-user modeling. User Modeling and User-Adapted Interaction (2003)
11. Yu, B., Singh, M.P.: A social mechanism of reputation management in electronic communities. In: Proceedings of Fourth International Workshop on Cooperative Information Agents. (2000) 154–165 36% acceptance rate.
12. Yu, B., Singh, M.P.: Searching social networks. In: Proceedings of the Second International Joint Conference on Autonomous Agents and Multiagent Systems (AAMAS'03), (ACM Press) 65–72

Agent-Based Social Assessment of Shared Resources*

Matthias Nickles and Gerhard Weiß

Department of Computer Science, Technical University of Munich
D-85748 Garching bei München, Germany, {nickles,weissg}@cs.tum.edu

Abstract. Prior to the access to decentralized resources like web services and shared files in peer-to-peer networks, the user needs to be provided with accurate information about these resources. While some of them can be specified impartially, other descriptions might be biased by individual preferences or subjective utility, for example quality ratings or content synopsizes. Unfortunately, such assessments of distributed resources usually either solely reflect the requirements, opinion and preferences of the resource providers or single users, or they consist of plain, often overgeneralized ratings obtained from voting-based recommender systems. In contrast to these approaches, we propose an agent-based framework for the distributed assignment and social weighting of rich, multidimensional and possibly *inconsistent* resource descriptions obtained from the conflicting opinions of communicating agents, which compete in the assertion of individual resource assessments.

Keywords: Open Systems, Peer-to-Peer Computing, Semantic Web, Multidimensional Rating, Collaborative Filtering.

1 Introduction

In the context of resource sharing in large, open and heterogenous peer-to-peer networks like Gnutella, eDonkey or KaZaA, and public internet resources like web sites and web services, a well-known problem is constituted through the notorious lack of reliable, impartial descriptions (especially ratings) of such resources. If a resource description (RD) is available, in most cases the description is provided by the original resource provider, which makes it in general as useless as any other kind of advertisement. In contrast, recommendation systems [1] based on the evaluation of access statistics, voting or resource content analysis try to ascertain the "objective" value of resources. E.g., collaborative filtering recommendation systems provide filtering criteria for site classification, which classify the rated object in terms of "appropriate/inappropriate" or "interesting/uninteresting", based on the assumed interests of a more or less homogenous group of users with a common profile, or on implicitly majority voting algorithms like Google's *PageRank* [2]. As a supplement or as a competing approach, content-based filtering recommendation systems try to analyze the content of documents (usually by means of keyword counting) and compare these results with the interest profiles of the potential users [3]. The main drawback of such filtering systems is their limitation to

* This work is supported by DFG (German National Science Foundation) under contracts no. Br609/11-2 and MA759/4-2.

G. Moro, C. Sartori, and M.P. Singh (Eds.): AP2PC 2003, LNAI 2872, pp. 35–40, 2004.

one-dimensional descriptions (amounting to *"like/dislike"*) grounded in the presumed predilections of predefined or computationally demarcated interest groups. This approach does not provide much help for the process of interest forming, which should in fact *precede* any filtering. Likewise, *trust networks* like PeopleNet [4] don't help much in case there is no trust yet regarding a specific rater, topic or object. Another problem is the apparent black-box character of many (commercial) recommendation methods, which on the one hand provides some protection against manipulation, but on the other hand seriously restricts their trustability. Balanced descriptions (i.e. the weighting of the opinions of multiple users and groups) which are in addition reliable and unrestricted can currently only be provided by humans, for example journalists and experts, or through discussion forums (e.g., newsgroups and threaded message boards like *Slashdot* [5]). Another disadvantage of this kind of approach is the absence of a machine readable encoding of the results, which makes it almost impossible for information agents like web spiders to analyze such descriptions. Although the Semantic Web effort addresses the problem of missing machine-understandability of web site descriptions, it currently focusses primarily on the specification of languages and tools for the syntactical representation of semantics and ontologies, not on the process of information gathering and rating itself, and it is just beginning to take into consideration phenomena like social RD impact [6], conflicting opinions, information biasing by commercial interests, and inconsistent or intentionally incorrect information. In contrast to traditional approaches, our goal is to provide a framework for the emergence of so-called *social resource descriptions* (social RDs) with the following properties:

Recognition of controversies. A high amount of RDs are subjectively biased quality judgements with a high conflict potential. Competitive descriptions, represented by software agents, shall *enable* such controversies, and social resource descriptions shall make them *explicit* and available to information agents.

Pro-active opinion representation. The competitive descriptions which contribute to social descriptions are no single "passive" statements like votes for an opinion poll, but shall instead continuously be represented by social agents which support them actively in a dynamic social process, e.g. by means of argumentation or conflicting behavior.

Complexity and hybridity. Due to the size, the heterogeneity and the openness of the world wide web and public peer-to-peer networks, the agent-supported description of resources is a highly complex task. Socially obtained descriptions increase the complexity of hybrid information-rich environments because they make human sociality "behind" the technical infrastructure visible. Nevertheless, to overcome the idea of a web consisting of unrelated (or only syntactically related) information pieces, the enabling of computational social structures is inalienable in our opinion.

Unveiling of social intentions. Even an individual description does not only assert the rated resource, but makes an implicit statement about the actor that is responsible for the description [6].

2   Architecture

As an approach to the described issues, we outline a multiagent system consisting of the following components. For lack of space, we cannot go into technical details.

1. Self-interested *description agents* which are able to deliberatively describe resources in accordance with the opinions, criteria and interests of their clients, and to represent their individual descriptions in a discourse with other description agents[1]. They act either as representatives for existing RDs (therefore in some sense the pro-active "incarnations" of RDF documents), or of peer agents, user communities, source creators (e.g., web sites owners or media providers), or private and public organizations. Every description agent supports a certain opinion and announces, asserts and probably defends it in an open discussion *forum* which is assigned to the rated resource (usually a web site) or a peer-to-peer client (e.g., a file sharing application). These forums are public whiteboards, on which the agents put their messages addressed to other agents and receive responses - very much like people do in newsgroups and message boards. Every forum has its own description vocabulary which could be assembled by the agents themselves via some ontology negotiation technique.

2. A technical instance (*Social Resource Description System* (SRDS)) for the technical facilitation of description agents communication and for the derivation of social RDs from these communication. It is a software component which observes the forums and continuously derives from the forum communication so-called *social expectation structures* [7,8]. These structures are distilled to social RDs. Together with the rated web page, the descriptions are presented to the user (e.g. to the web surfer through a special HTML frame within the browser window or via some user agent), and to information agents, for example the web spiders of internet search machines like Google or Altavista. The description agents will also obtain these information, since such knowledge is considered to be important for the agents to let them intentionally avoid or achieve conflicting or collaborative behavior in respect to other agents and social norms, and to find appropriate allies and opponents.

3   Social Resource Descriptions

In terms of the RDF standard (the XML-based *Resource Description Framework* [9], a successor of the internet rating language PICS [10]), the description of a certain (web) resource is a finite set of statements (*elementary resource descriptions*) together with a description vocabulary. Each statement describes the properties of the respective resource (which can be virtually any kind of object like web site attributes, documents or web services, but also other statements) by means of meta data, according to a vocabulary of property types or classes (sometimes called an "ontology" or "schema"). Technically, such an elementary resource description is defined as a proposition of the form $(resource, propertyType, value)$, in which $resource$ denotes an object with an unique identifier (i.e., a Uniform Resource Identifier (URI) or a locator

---

[1] *Voting* is considered to be a simple kind of such discourse participation.

like $ed2k : //\backslash file|filename.mp3)$. $propertyType$ is the described attribute of the resource (an element of the given description vocabulary), and $value$ is its assigned value. Elementary RDs can be expressed through a formal description language, for example RDF or DAML/OIL [11]. A simple example for a description with boolean property type is
($\mathtt{www.SomeCompany.com}$, $MinorOrientation, True$). $value$ can also be a resource by itself, and thus the description vocabulary can form a hierarchy of (meta-) property types (e.g., $Author$ and $Trustability$ in
$\{\mathtt{www.somesite.com}, Author, John), (John, Trustability, high)\}$.
Social RDs are based on *expectations* regarding social agent behavior and derived from graphical *expectation networks* [7,8][2]. They are sets of expectations regarding the anticipated utterance of elementary RDs in a certain discourse context, inductively learned by the SRDS from the observation of agent communications. Each element of a social resource description is the expectation of a certain *reply* to a question regarding the *agreement* with an elementary RD, directed to agents (or, in a generalized way, to social agent *roles*) which currently participate in the observed forum. The calculation of social RDs regarding resource properties from expectations regarding communications makes use of the fact that an elementary RD is equivalent to a set of meta descriptions, i.e. "descriptions of descriptions" with a common property type "$Assent$": From a multidimensional description ($resource, propertyType, value$) as in RDF we can generate meta-descriptions in the form of ($propertyType = value, Assent, degree\,of\,assent$), where the first element of this tuple is the content (logical proposition) of an assertive speech act, the second element denotes the property type corresponding to the speech act performative "$Assert$"[3]. The omitted resource $resource$ is provided implicitly through the forum topic. The social amount of agreement or dissent, respectively, can then simply be measured as the probability that a certain RD agent (or a role subsuming a set of agents) utters the message "$Actor_1 \rightarrowtail Actor_2 :'\ Assert(propertyType = value)'$".
E.g., a SRDS query regarding the assessment of the SomeCompany site by a set of agents A would look like ($\mathtt{www.SomeCompany.com}$, $MinorOrientation, ?x$) (where $?x$ is an existentially quantified variable with instances v_i), which could be transformed into the speech acts "$B \rightarrowtail A :'\ Query(MinorOrientation =?v)'$ or "$B \rightarrowtail A :'\ Request(Assert(MinorOrientation = v_i))'$.
The social RD is then simply a set of expectabilities (the expectation *strengths*, denoted as probabilities in a range of 0 to 1) of the potential reactions to such a request, together with attributes for expectation *normativity* and *deviancy*[4]. E.g., the resulting values for answers asserting
($\mathtt{www.SomeCompany.com}$, $MinorOrientation, True(= v_1)$) could be
$strength = 0.9, normativity = 0.7, deviancy = 0.01$

---

[2] Note that *trust* is a special kind of such social expectation.

[3] or what ever performative the respective communication agent language provides to signal consent.

[4] Informally, *normativity* = long-term stability of social expectations, in a range from 0 to 1, and *deviancy* = difference between a highly normative, long-term expectation and the actual probability of the respective speech act occurrence obtained from short-term observations. Please see [8,7] for details.

and $strength = 0.1$, $normativity = 0.7$, $deviancy = 0.01$ for
(www.SomeCompany.com, $MinorOrientation, False(= v_2))$[5] (i.e., these agents assert in a quite normative way that SomeCompany is highly minor-oriented).

We denote (unconditioned) social RDs as sets of terms having the form
$Actor : (resource, propertyType, (value, expectability, normativity, deviancy))$,
where $Actor$ can denote an agent or a social role.

The query results are obtained from the expectation network, either directly if the expectation network already contains expectations for the respective
$Query/Request(...) \rightarrow Assert/Agree/Deny(...)$ speech act trajectories, or by means
of an SRDS query on the forum directed to the RD agents. In the latter case, the query
introduces the required expectation network paths, and then the SRDS observes the subsequent agent communications to obtain expectabilities which reflect the agent opinions
along these paths. Besides this example, expectation networks allow for the obtainment
of a large variety of other kinds of social RDs, e.g.:

- *Single agent RD*, obtained from
  "$B \rightarrowtail SingleAgent :' Query(PropertyType =?v)'$" $\rightarrow$
  "$SingleAgent \rightarrowtail B :' Assert(PropertyType = v_i)'$"
- *Social role RD*[6], obtained from
  '$B \rightarrowtail Role :' Query(PropertyType =?v)'$" $\rightarrow$
  "$Role \rightarrowtail B :' Assert(PropertyType = v_i)'$"
- *Public RD* (provided that the substitution list for role *All* contains every agent within
  the forum), obtained from
  '$B \rightarrowtail All :' Query(PropertyType =?v)'$" $\rightarrow$
  "$All \rightarrowtail B :' Assert(PropertyType = v_i)'$"
- *Conditioned social RD*, obtained from
  $Prefix \rightsquigarrow$ "$B \rightarrowtail A :' Query(PropertyType =?v)'$" $\rightarrow$
  "$A \rightarrowtail B :' Assert(PropertyType = v_i)'$"
  Here, "$Prefix \rightsquigarrow$" denotes a sequence of messages (or message templates) which
  has to precede the Query/Answer pattern. For example, an agent might commit himself to a certain RD that has been requested from another agent only if the other
  agent agrees with a certain RD by himself (behavioral *reciprocity* of self-interested
  agents).
  Since an expectation network can model virtually any kind of interaction pattern,
  Prefix could denote highly complex conditions, e.g. auctions for the selling of web
  site ratings for the purpose of commercial advertising (i.e., the agents commit themselves to agree with the opinion of the auction winner).

3.1 Embedding Social Resource Descriptions Within RDF Documents

To provide a machine-readable format for (simple) social RDs taking the form
$\{Actor : (resource, propertyType, (value, expectability, normativity, deviancy))\}$,
it seems reasonable to extend a well-established XML-based RD language like the

---

[5] Uttered using a "*Deny*" performative, for example.
[6] Although social roles usually group similarly behaving agents, in our formal framework [7], a
single role can generalize different inconsistent opinions.

RDF. This can basically be done by means of a replacement of the description parts of statements with lists of probabilistically annotated propositions. The description vocabulary for the following example is implicitly given as an XML namespace "V" , provided by some fictitious rating organization "description.org", and through a "Social Resource Description Rating Meta Language" namespace called SRDML:

```
<rdf:Description about='http://www.SomeCompany.com'
    xmlns:s='http://description.org/schema'>
        <V:MinorOrientation>
            <SRDML:disjunctive>
                <SRDML:boolean strength=0.9 normativity=0.7 deviancy=0
                    agent='Entertainment industry'>True</SRDML:boolean>
                <SRDML:boolean strength=0.1 normativity=0.7 deviancy=0
                    agent='Entertainment industry'>False</SRDML:boolean>
                <SRDML:boolean strength=0.3 normativity=0.7 deviancy=0.6
                    agent='User community 6'>True</SRDML:boolean>
                <SRDML:boolean strength=0.7 normativity=0.7 deviancy=0.6
                    agent='User community 6'>False</SRDML:boolean>
            </SRDML:disjunctive>
        </V:MinorOrientation>
</rdf:Description>
```

References

1. Delgado, J.: Agent-based Recommender Systems and Information Filtering on the Internet. PhD thesis, Nagoya Institute of Technology (2000)
2. http://www.google.com.
3. J. Delgado, N. Ishii, T.U.: Content-based collaborative information filtering: Actively learning to classify and recommend documents. In: Cooperative Information Agents II. Learning, Mobility and Electronic Commerce for Information Discovery on the Internet. LNAI. Springer-Verlag, Berlin (1998)
4. http://peoplenet.stanford.edu.
5. http://www.slashdot.org.
6. http://www.w3.org/2001/sw/meetings/tech-200303/social-meaning/.
7. Nickles, M., Rovatsos, M., Brauer, W., Weiß, G.: Communication Systems: A Unified Model of Socially Intelligent Systems. In Fischer, K., Florian, M., eds.: Socionics: Its Contributions to the Scalability of Complex Social Systems. Volume XXXX of LNCS. Springer-Verlag, Berlin (to appear 2003)
8. Brauer, W., Nickles, M., Rovatsos, M., Weiß, G., Lorentzen, K.F.: Expectation-Oriented Analysis and Design. In: Proceedings of the 2nd Workshop on Agent-Oriented Software Engineering (AOSE-2001) at the Autonomous Agents 2001 Conference. Volume 2222 of LNAI., Montreal, Canada, Springer-Verlag, Berlin (2001)
9. http://www.w3.org/RDF/.
10. http://www.w3.org/PICS/.
11. http://www.daml.org/.

A Passport-Like Service over an Agent-Based Peer-to-Peer Network

Shi-Cho Cha, Yuh-Jzer Joung, and Yu-En Lue

National Taiwan University, Taipei, Taiwan
csc@mba.ntu.edu.tw, joung@ccms.ntu.edu.tw, eric@yuenlue.com

Abstract. We propose *Personal Data Backbone* (*PDB*) to provide Passport-like services over an agent-based peer-to-peer network. The main objective is to bring the control of personal data back to their owner. By applying technologies in agents and in peer-to-peer networks, PDB enables flexible and secure personal data acquisition in a spontaneous network formed by participating users.

1 Introduction

Many information services and applications need personal data for authentication and other application-specific purposes when users sign on their systems. As more and more Web-based services are offered, personal data are stored among different service providers and data repositories. It then takes time and efforts for both users and services to build mutual understanding, as data are spread over many different places. Moreover, the lack of accumulation and aggregation of these information often limits the capability of services to adapt and personalize into user's preferences.

To relieve users from maintaining copies of personal data at different places, the so-called *Single-Sign On* (*SSO*) services have been developed to allow a user to access different application services with only a single action of authentication and authorization. An SSO acts as the single authority to provide personal profile of each user to applications. Such services can usually be implemented by Network Information Service (NIS) within a local area network, or X.500 and LDAP directory services within an organization. As the popularity of Web-based applications spreads all over the world, the heterogeneity of applications and the diversity of personal profiles needed by them increase. Hence, the need of Internet-wide SSO services merges. For example, Microsoft's *.NET Passport* allows a person to use a single Passport account to traverse all participating services seamlessly.

However, both users and service providers may feel uncomfortable leaving their data to a single authority. One such concern could be if their actions will be tracked by the service secretly, or if they will be forced to use another service or buy another product for such service. Moreover, service providers may not wish their customers' data to be managed by another company (especially when the company may be or may become their competitor). Furthermore, while the operation of such service can bring up commercial profits and competition advantages, several similar services may emerge. Consequently, we could end up again in having to maintain personal data at different SSO services. For example, a person may have a Passport account to use Passport participating services,

G. Moro, C. Sartori, and M.P. Singh (Eds.): AP2PC 2003, LNAI 2872, pp. 41–46, 2004.
© Springer-Verlag Berlin Heidelberg 2004

and have another account at Liberty Alliance (http://www.projectliberty.org/) or AOL's Magic Carpet [1] for similar purposes.

In light of the above problems, one may wonder why not just let people themselves provide such service? In fact, some simple form of SSO can be easily implemented on individuals' computers. For example, current Web browsers can remember IDs and passwords of the users. When a person wants to login a Web service, he needs only to input a few alphabets, which then invoke a local procedure to interact with the Web service to auto-fill the user's identity and password for the Web service. However, such local-side implementation makes profile roaming very expensive to implement since the user's computer has to be online at any time. Furthermore, the use of a person's information must be controlled. A certain form of contractual agreement between users and the application service providers must be established. Finally, personal data covers many aspects, from a person's photos to his current geographic position. Sophisticated handling of these data is required for a new generation of information services.

Therefore, we propose *Personal Data Backbone* (*PDB*), which makes use of both agent and peer-to-peer technologies to provide Passport-like services. By using peer-to-peer technology, people can collaborate with one another to achieve better performance, scalability, availability and reliability of the SSO services. With personal agents, users of PDB can set their own privacy policies and access rules on using their personal data, and then have their agents establish privacy and data usage agreements with service providers even if they are not online. The whole PDB system is currently under implementation. Here we present its architecture pertaining to SSO services and main design concepts.

2   The System

2.1   Overview

The system architecture at each peer, shown in Fig. 1, is composed of three layers: *Application Service Layer*, *System Service Layer*, and *Base Layer*. The latter two constitute our peer-to-peer platform (henceforth referred to as *MyP2P*), over which applications can be built. In our design, applications are implemented as mobile agents [2, 3] in the Application Service Layer. Mobility allows them to replicate and/or migrate across different MyP2P platforms to cope with network failures and load balancing. The agent nature injects autonomy into programs so that they can act asynchronously and autonomously, and adapt dynamically to the execution environment.

Although our design philosophy on MyP2P is to make it a general-purpose platform to accommodate various applications, we will focus here only on passport-like services on top of it. These services are implemented by *PDB Service* agents and *Personal Data Management (PDM)* agents. In general, each PDM agent handles one user's 'passport'. For performance and fault tolerance issues, however, there may be 'clones' of a PDM agent residing at different peers. Likewise, there may be more than one PDM agent on top of a MyP2P platform at each peer to handle different user's personal data. To manage these PDM agents, each peer launches one PDB Service agent. The PDB Service agent provides bindings between users and their PDM agents and manages the PDM agents to offer the PDB service.

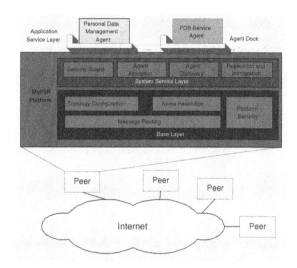

Fig. 1. System Architecture.

The System Service Layer provides four main services for application agents: *Security Guard*, *Agent Allocation*, *Replication and Immigration*, and *Agent Discovery*. Security Guard prevents application agents from improper access to underlying resources, as well as protects them from being attacked by other (resident and nonresident) application agents. Agent Allocation mechanism allocates other MyP2P platforms for application agents (by communicating with the corresponding mechanism in the destination platforms) when they need to be replicated and migrated. The Replication and Immigration mechanism deals with the actual replication and movement of the agents. It also accepts replication and immigration requests from other MyP2P platforms, and provides an 'agent dock' to host each incoming agent. (*Agent docks* are the places agents reside in the Application Service Layer.) The Agent Discovery mechanism searches for target agents requested by application agents.

The Base Layer provides services for forming and accessing to the peer-to-peer network. Similar to Tapestry [4] and Pastry [5], the main design of the Base Layer is based on the randomized object access scheme proposed by Plaxton et al. [6]. It has the following main components: *Topology Configuration*, *Name Resolution*, *Message Routing*, and *Platform Security*. Topology Configuration maintains a given topology for MyP2P platforms in the network in the presence of node failures. Name resolution provides distributed name lookup services issued from the Agent Allocation and Agent Discovery mechanisms. Message Routing delivers messages to destination agents in the Application Service Layer, or routes them to the next MyP2P platform. Finally, Platform Security ensures the integrity of the platform.

2.2   PDB Services

PDB service provides the following four main functions. The *opt-in* procedure is invoked when a person wants to use an ISA (Information Service and Application) through PDB

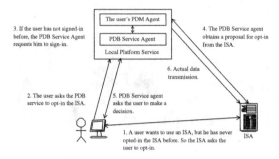

Fig. 2. An opt-in scenario.

at the first time. Thereafter, he needs to *login* the ISA for authentication every time he wishes to use its service. The *administration service* allows a person to set and modify his personal data. Finally, the *data service* allows ISAs to request data from the backbone.

Before a user can use PDB service, a MyP2P platform must be installed in his local host, and a PDB Service agent must be launched on top of the platform. In order for the PDB Service agent to know whom the user is, the user needs to 'sign-in' the PDB service. We call this procedure 'sign-in' to distinguish it from the above login function of PDB. In the sign-in procedure, the PDB Service agent requests the user to input his account name and password for authentication. The PDB Service agent then calls the *Agent Discovery* module in the System Service Layer to find the user's PDM agent. Recall that PDM agents may migrate and replicate themselves over the peer-to-peer network. So if no PDM agent of the user is on the platform (from which the user signs-in), a nearby clone of the user's PDM agent will be located and migrated/replicated to the platform. When the user's PDM agent is located on the platform, the PDB Service agent uses the data stored in the PDM agent to authenticate the user.

The opt-in function can be depicted in Fig. 2. After receiving a user's opt-in request, an ISA asks the user to request his local PDB Service agent to complete the opt-in process. This step can be done transparently by redirecting the ISA's request to the user's local platform service, which consists of the user's PDM agent and a PDB Service agent on the local peer. When the PDB Service agent receives the opt-in request, the PDB Service agent checks if the user has signed-in the PDB service. If not, the PDB Service agent requests the user to sign-in the PDB service as described above. Then, the PDB Service agent retrieves an opt-in proposal from the ISA. The proposal is based on the *Platform for Privacy Preferences* (*P3P*) [7], which is designed to let a Web site disclose its privacy preference about what personal data is required by this site and for what purpose. The PDB Service agent can generate an opt-in page from this proposal, and sends the page to the user to let him confirm the opt-in process. By reviewing the opt-in page, the user can decide whether or not to opt-in the ISA. If he decides to opt-in, the personal data required to complete the opt-in process will be sent to the ISA by the PDB Service agent, and thereafter he can start using the services provided by the ISA.

In the above scenario, the PDB Service agent may also complete the opt-in process automatically if the proposal sent by the ISA matches the preferences set by the user in his PDM agent, and the user has authorized the PDB Service agent to skip over the confirmation step in this situation. Furthermore, licenses of using the user's data can be issued to the ISA [8,9].

The login process of PDB is similar to the opt-in process, but simpler. When a user wishes to login an ISA, the PDB Service agent need only tell the ISA the identity of the user so that the ISA can authenticate the user with the identity. Moreover, when a user needs to set or modify his personal data and preferences, he can invoke the administration function of the PDB service. After verifying the identity of the person, the PDB Service agent modifies the data stored in the person's PDM agent to serve the update requests.

In the above functions, the PDB Service agent uses personal data stored in a user's PDM agent to fulfill the user's request. ISAs, on the other hand, may request a person's personal data actively from PDB, even if the person is not online. This function is also useful when some personal data may be updated frequently, and the newest version is required.

2.3   Security

When a PDB Service agent needs a person's data for operation, it must request a key from the person (during the sign-in process). 'Raw' personal data can then be decrypted with the key and be used for further operations. **For a successful operation of PDB, some trust must be assumed.** To a person, we say that a computer is *trusted* if he is sure that the computer is not hacked and all platform components function correctly in the computer. The platform correctness in turn can prevent frauds in the Application Service Layer by letting the Security Guard in the System Service Layer detect whether or not an application agent can be trusted. This can be done using *signatures*. More specifically, when an application agent is developed, a standard hash algorithm is used to generate a *code signature* from the program code of the agent. To increase the trust, the program code can also be verified and certified by a consortium.

So we make the following assumption in the system:

Trust Assumption: *When a user is using the PDB service, to the user there is at least one trusted computer in the network (e.g., the computer he signs in).*

Such an assumption is reasonable and, in fact, crucial to every secure systems. No information system can function correctly and securely if there is no trusted computer a user can use to access the system. Based on the assumption, a user can always find a trusted peer to request for PDB service. He need not worry about his personal data being accessed by other unauthorized person while the data are processed because operations of a PDB Service agent only occur in his trusted computer.

Recall that we wish PDB to offer persistent data service by allowing ISAs to access a person's data even if the person is not online or his own computer is not available. Clearly, data replication and/or migration can be used to facilitate such service. Let us call a copy (clone) of a PDM agent at a trusted peer *primary*. The above trust assumption ensures that there is at least one primary copy of a PDM agent when the user's own computer is powered on. To facilitate persistent data service, the primary copy must be replicated or migrated to another peer while the underlying computer is to be powered off. This is done by the Agent Allocation mechanism in the System Service Layer of MyP2P.

A fundamental problem behind the replication/migration scheme is that: *How does a peer determine whether or not another peer is trusted?* Without a centralized manager, this problem is considerably difficult, and is still one of the main challenges in peer-to-peer networks. Our goal here is not to solve the problem. Rather, we assume a trust determination function for solving the problem, and use it for our replication/migration scheme in between MyP2P platforms. Such a function need only satisfy a sound requirement, namely, if it determines that a peer is trusted, then the peer is indeed trusted. A very weak trust determination function is to declare all other peers untrusted. In practice, with the help of some centralized mechanisms, we can usually design a stronger function for the problem.

In the presence of a trust determination function, if the Agent Allocation mechanism in a MyP2P platform finds another trusted peer, then the Agent Allocation mechanism can send the primary copy of a PDM agent to the destination peer, and the data service on the PDM agent can continue even if the first peer is down. Even if no trusted peer can be found and no primary copy of a PDM agent is available, we can still allow a limited support of data service by replicating a portion of the data in a PDM agent to an untrusted peer. Recall that data stored in a PDM agent are grouped and imposed with different security control according to their confidential level. For low and non-confidential data, they can be replicated to an untrusted peer to increase data availability. The partial clones of a PDM agent in our system are referred to as *secondary*, and are assumed to be less critical when under security attacks. In any case, full data service will be reinstalled when trusted computer(s) are back to the line and the primary copies are restored.

References

1. Newell, C.: AOL quietly launches magic carpet. In: eWeek.com. (2002) Retrieved from http://www.eweek.com/article2/0,3959,113131,00.asp.
2. Fuggetta, A., Picco, G.P., Vigna, G.: Understanding Code Mobility. IEEE Transactions on Software Engineering **24** (1998) 342–361
3. Lange, D.B., Oshima, M.: Seven good reasons for mobile agents. Communications of the ACM **42** (1999) 88–89
4. Zhao, B.Y., Kubiatowicz, J., Joseph, A.D.: Tapestry: An infrastructure for fault-tolerant wide-area location and routing. Technical Report UCB/CSD-01-1141 , UC Berkeley (2001)
5. Rowstron, A., Druschel, P.: Pastry: scalable, decentralized object location and routing for large-scale peer-to-peer systems. In: Proceedings of the 18th IFIP/ACM International Conference on Distributed Systems Platforms (Middleware). (2001)
6. Plaxton, C.G., Rajaraman, R., Richa, A.: Accessing nearby copies of replicated objects in a distributed environment. MST: Mathematical Systems Theory **32** (1999)
7. Cranor, L., Langheinrich, M., Marchiori, M., Presler-Marshall, M., Reagle, J.: Platform for Privacy Preference (P3P). In: W3C Recommendations. (2002)
8. Cha, S.C., Joung, Y.J.: Online Personal Data Licensing. In: Proceedings of the 3rd International Conference of Law and Technology (LAWTECH2002), (2002) 28–33
9. Cha, S.C., Joung, Y.J.: From P3P to OPDL. In: Proceedings of the 3rd Workshop on Privacy Enhancing Technologies (PET2003) (2003)

A Robust and Scalable Peer-to-Peer Gossiping Protocol*

Spyros Voulgaris[1], Márk Jelasity[2], and Maarten van Steen[1]

[1] Department Computer Science, Faculty of Sciences, Vrije Universiteit Amsterdam,
The Netherlands
{spyros,steen}@cs.vu.nl
[2] Department of Computer Science, University of Bologna, Italy
jelasity@cs.unibo.it

Abstract. The newscast model is a general approach for communication in large agent-based distributed systems. The two basic services—membership management and information dissemination—are implemented by the same epidemic-style protocol. In this paper we present the newscast model and report on experiments using a Java implementation. The experiments involve communication in a large, wide-area cluster computer. By analysis of the outcome of the experiments we demonstrate that the system indeed shows the scalability and dependability properties predicted by our previous theoretical and simulation results.

1 Introduction

The popularity of peer-to-peer systems in the last couple of years illustrates how the Internet is gradually shifting toward a distributed system that supports more than only client-server applications. A key issue in peer-to-peer systems is that distribution of data and control across processes is symmetric. Moreover, this distribution is done in such a way that processes are highly autonomous and independent of each other. The important advantage of this approach is scalability. A well-designed peer-to-peer system can easily scale to millions of processes, each of which can join or leave whenever it pleases without seriously disrupting the system's overall quality of service.

A crucial aspect of large-scale peer-to-peer systems is that they are easy to manage. Any system that attempts to centrally manage how processes connect to each other and distribute data and control will fail, notably when processes join and leave all the time. Instead, it should be a property of the design itself that the distribution of data and control takes place in an automated fashion that requires no global management at all. In effect, we are looking at the design of self-managing systems.

There are many different types of peer-to-peer systems. In most cases, these systems can be divided into two separate layers. The lowest layer consists of protocols for handling group membership and communication, whereas the highest

* This work was partially supported by the Future & Emerging Technologies unit of the European Commission through Project BISON (IST-2001-38923).

G. Moro, C. Sartori, and M.P. Singh (Eds.): AP2PC 2003, LNAI 2872, pp. 47–58, 2004.
© Springer-Verlag Berlin Heidelberg 2004

layer implements the required functionality for a specific application. The lowest layer thus forms the core of the peer-to-peer system. Roughly speaking, there are three types of core systems.

The first, and most popular type is designed to efficiently support content-based searching. In many cases, these systems operate with centralized index servers that keep track of where content is located. The index servers are often constructed dynamically in the form of super peers [15]. Examples include Gnutella and KaZaa. The second type aims at efficiently routing a request to its destination through an overlay network formed by the collection of peers. Examples of such systems are Chord [12], Pastry [11], Tapestry [16], and CAN [10]. A third type deploy epidemic protocols [3]. In these systems, the goal is not so much enabling point-to-point communication between peers, but rather the rapid and efficient dissemination of information. Examples in this class include Scamp [6], and probabilistic reliable broadcasting [4,5,9].

In this paper, we concentrate on information-dissemination based systems that deploy epidemic protocols. A crucial element in an epidemic protocol is that a participating peer can randomly select another peer to exchange information. Traditional protocols supported this random selection by providing a list of all other participating peers. Clearly, such an approach cannot scale to large networks. As an alternative, approaches such as described in [4,7] ensure that a peer always has a list that represents an independent and randomly selected sample from the entire set of peers.

We have recently developed an epidemic protocol for disseminating information in large, dynamically changing sets of autonomous agents. This, so-named, *newscast protocol* solves two problems inherent to large sets of agents: (1) information dissemination, and (2) efficient membership management. The main distinction in comparison to similar epidemic-based solutions, is that agents can join and leave at virtually no cost at all, and without affecting the information-dissemination properties of the protocol.

The associated model of *newscasting*, that is, the model of information dissemination and membership management as presented to agents, is described in detail in a separate paper [8], along with theoretical analyses partly based on simulations. To better substantiate our claims regarding scalability, we have implemented the newscast protocol (in Java). We subsequently used this implementation to conduct a series of experiments that *emulate* large-scale agent-based applications on a real network. In particular, we set up a series of experiments with 128,000 agents scattered across a hierarchically organized cluster of 320 processors. These processors, in turn, are geographically spread over four different sites in the Netherlands.

An important and interesting aspect of these experiments is that the underlying communication network is heterogeneous. It includes interprocess communication facilities on a single workstation, point-to-point local-area high-speed links, as well as wide-area links. In this way, we are better able to measure the effect that a real communication infrastructure has on the properties of our dissemination model.

In this paper, we describe the newscast protocol and report on our experiments involving emulation of large networks of agents. We show that the theoretical results, which are based on an idealized underlying communication infrastructure, still hold when dealing with a realistic infrastructure, thus further substantiating our claims that newscasting is a highly robust and scalable model for information dissemination in large and rapidly changing sets of agents. In the following we discuss our protocol, the experimental setup, and the results of our experiments, to end with conclusions.

2   The Newscast Protocol

In our implementation of the newscast model, a large group of agents is connected through a simple peer-to-peer data exchange protocol. The protocol is extremely simple: each agent knows only a (continuously changing) small set of peers of which one is randomly chosen to exchange information. In this section, we start with explaining how the protocol works, after that we explore some remarkable theoretical properties of its emerging behavior. These properties are further investigated in Section 3 when we report on our large-scale emulation experiments.

2.1   Principal Operation

The two main building blocks of our newscast model are a *collective of agents* and a *news agency*, as shown in Figure 1. The basic idea is that the news agency asks all agents regularly for *news* by means of a callback function getNews(). In addition, the news agency provides each agent with news about the other agents in the collective, again through a callback function newsUpdate(news[]).

The definition of what counts as news is application dependent. The agents simply live their lives (perform computations, listen to sensors and the news, etc.) and based on the computations they have completed and the information they have collected they must provide the news agency with news when asked.

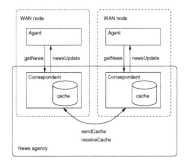

Fig. 1. The organization of a newscast application.

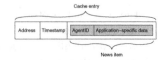

Fig. 2. The format of news items and cache entries.

The model itself can be fully specified in terms of the functional and statistical properties of the operations getNews() and newsUpdate(news[]). Instead of this definitial style of specification, we take a much simpler approach in this paper by describing the semantics of the model in terms of the newscast protocol, of which we have shown that it meets the model's specifications [8].

Each agent has an associated *correspondent* that runs on the same machine hosting the agent. The correspondents jointly form the distributed implementation of the news agency. Each correspondent maintains a *fixed-sized* cache of c news items. Whenever an agent passes a news item to its correspondent, the latter timestamps the item, adds its own network address, and subsequently caches the item. A news item itself consists of an agent identifier and the actual news as provided by the agent, as shown in Figure 2.

Correspondents regularly exchange caches as follows. Omitting specific details (which are found in [8]), each correspondent executes the following five steps once every ΔT time units (ΔT is referred to as the *refresh interval*).

1. Request a fresh news item from the local agent by calling getNews(). Add the item to the cache.
2. Randomly select a peer correspondent by considering the network address of other (and available) correspondents as found in the cache.
3. Send all cache entries to the selected peer, and, in turn, receive all the peer's cache entries. Merge the received entries into the local cache.
4. Pass the received cache entries from the peer agent to the local agent by calling newsUpdate().
5. The correspondent now has $2c$ cache entries; it subsequently throws away the c oldest ones.

The selected peer correspondent executes the last three steps as well, so that after the exchange both correspondents have the same cache. Note, however, that as soon as any of these two correspondents executes the protocol again, their respective caches will most likely be different again.

The protocol does not require that the clocks of correspondents are synchronized, but only that the timestamps of news items in a single cache are mutually consistent. We assume that the communication time between two correspondents is negligible in comparison to ΔT (which is generally in the order of minutes). When a correspondent A passes its cache to B, it also sends along its current local time, T_A. When B receives the cache entries, it subsequently adjusts the timestamp of each entry with a value $T_A - T_B$, effectively normalizing the time of each new entry to those already cached.

2.2   Properties of Newscasting

As it turns out, this simple model of communication has desirable statistical properties. To understand the behavior of newscasting, we consider the communication graphs G_t at different time instants t that are induced by maintaining caches at each correspondent. Each such graph is constructed from a corresponding directed graph D_t as follows. The vertex set V_t of D_t contains the correspondents. For correspondents a and b in V_t we have the link $a \to b$ if and only if the address of b is in the cache of a at time t. The cache-exchange algorithm leads to a series of directed graphs, given an initial directed graph D_0. The communication graph G_t is now simply constructed by dropping the orientation in D_t. G_t expresses the possibility of cache exchanges.

Now consider the series of graphs $G_0, G_{\Delta T}, G_{2\Delta T}, \ldots$. Note that during a time interval ΔT each correspondent initiates the cache-exchange algorithm. In other words, after ΔT time units, all correspondents will have fetched a news item from their agent, exchanged caches with at least one of their neighbors (and possibly more), and have passed c news items to their agent. We say that a *communication cycle* has completed.

We have conducted simulations with up to 50,000 correspondents, assuming an idealized communication infrastructure with no communication delays and packet losses. Our simulations show that even for relatively small cache sizes (say, $c = 20$) each graph $G_{k\Delta T}$ stays connected. Moreover, it turns out that the average length of each shortest path between two nodes is small, as shown in Figure 3(a).

In fact, further investigations revealed that the induced communication graphs have many properties in common with what are known as *small worlds* [1, 14]. An important property of these types of networks is that they show a relatively high *clustering coefficient*, which, for a given node, is the ratio of the number of edges between the neighbors of the node and the number of all possible edges between the neighbors. For example, in a complete graph all nodes have

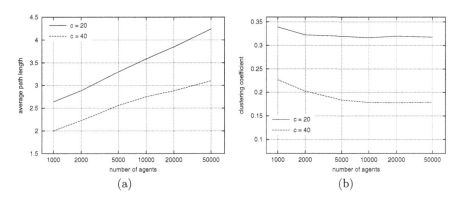

(a)   (b)

Fig. 3. (a) Average shortest path length between two nodes for different cache sizes. (b) Average clustering coefficient taken over all nodes.

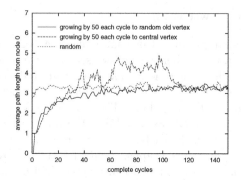

Fig. 4. Average shortest path length while adding 50 agents every cycle until 5000 agents have been added.

a clustering coefficient of 1 while in random graphs this coefficient is typically small (if our graphs were random, the clustering coefficient would be expected to be c/n). Figure 3(b) shows the clustering coefficient for different cache sizes c and communication graphs $G_{k\Delta T}$.

Simulations also show that we need only an extremely simple way of handling membership, which is an important improvement in comparison to other epidemic models. Consider the worst solution to handling membership that could possibly disrupt the emergent behavior of our protocol: an agent contacts a well-known central server and simply initiates the cache-exchange protocol with that server. This approach systematically biases the content of caches, which now all depend on what is stored at the central server.

We conducted a simulation experiment in which we admitted 50 new agents at every communication cycle until 5000 agents had joined the network, after which no new agents were allowed to join. When measuring the average path length again, we obtain the results shown in Figure 4. What is seen, is that shortly after the last 50 agents have been added (i.e., after 100 completed cycles), the average path length quickly converges to the one we would expect in a stable graph. We can conclude that even this worst-imaginable membership protocol does not affect the properties of newscasting. In effect, when a node wants to join, it needs to know only the address of a single other node and can simply start with executing the newscast protocol. Leaving is done by simply stopping communication.

3   Validation of the Newscast Protocol

Using theoretical analyses and simulations, we are able to show that the statistical properties of the protocol meet the specifications of the newscast model. However, in the world of large-scale systems, theory and practice often diverge. Therefore, to investigate how the protocol would behave in practice and to further substantiate our claims, we conducted a series of *emulation* experiments.

Emulation, as opposed to simulation, involves implementing the protocol and conducting experiments on a real network of computers. In our case, we carried out experiments with a collective of up to 128,000 agents distributed across a 320-node wide-area cluster of workstations.

3.1   The Implementation

In order to experiment with the newscast model described earlier, we implemented its underlying protocol. Java was chosen for portability reasons, allowing us to easily execute the protocol in heterogeneous environments. Our implementation is organized as three modules: the core, the application, and the utility module. The *core module* implements a correspondent materializing the epidemic protocol described in Section 2.1. The core module has no dependencies on the other two modules. It is a self-contained implementation of the newscast protocol. All communication is based on UDP. Multiple instances of the core module can coexist in a single Java virtual machine, behaving as separate, independent correspondents.

The *application module* provides the implementation of an agent. One instance of the core module has exactly one associated instance of the application module. Our experiments were focused on the properties of the epidemic protocol itself without considering any particular application. Therefore the agent we defined has only basic functionality. It returns empty content in the getNews() operation, and ignores any content delivered to it through the newsUpdate(news[]) operation.

The *utility module* serves the specific needs of our experiments, such as batch running, coordinating the experiments, and logging. Exactly one utility module instance exists in each virtual machine. In particular, the utility module takes care of starting multiple agent-correspondent pairs each running on a separate thread within the same Java virtual machine to allow emulation of a large network. It coordinates with utility modules running on other Java virtual machines (possibly on remote hosts) to determine initial connection addresses for the correspondents. The utility module also contains logging functionality. It periodically freezes the agent-correspondent pairs running in the Java virtual machine, logs their state, and then resumes operation. Utility modules coordinate to ensure that freezing and resuming for logging occur simultaneously on all the Java virtual machines spread across the different hosts.

3.2   The DAS-2

We conducted our experiments on the *Distributed ASCI Supercomputer* (DAS-2), a wide-area distributed cluster-based system consisting of five clusters of dual-processor PCs located at different sites across the Netherlands. The cluster at the Vrije Universiteit consists of 72 nodes, while the other clusters consist of 32 nodes each, giving a total of 200 nodes (400 processors). Each node has two 1-GHz Pentium-III processors, and at least 1GB of RAM.

Nodes within a single cluster are connected by a Fast Ethernet (100Mbps) network dedicated to their cluster. Clusters, in turn, communicate over wide-area links, which are shared for all traffic between the universities and which have shown to support an aggregated bandwidth of 20 Mbps.

3.3   Experimental Setting

We carried out experiments with a network of 128,000 agents distributed across 160 dual-processor nodes on four of the five DAS-2 clusters. We recorded and analyzed the behavior of the newscast model for three different cache sizes c: 20, 30 and 40. In all three cases the refresh interval ΔT was 10 seconds.

The presented series of experiments was conducted to examine the possible impact of the underlying network's heterogeneity on the operation of the newscast model. It is, therefore, worth describing the deployment of agents across the DAS-2 nodes. We used 160-dual processor nodes, selecting 64 nodes from the cluster at the Vrije Universiteit, and 32 nodes out of three other DAS-2 clusters. We executed two Java virtual machines per node (one per processor), each Java virtual machine running 400 agents.

The deployment of agents described above presents a desirable property for our experiments: network heterogeneity. Four different types of communication were involved, depending on the relative location of the agents communicating:

- *Intraprocess* communication for agents running in different threads within the same Java virtual machine.
- *Interprocess* communication for agents run by separate Java virtual machines, but on the same DAS-2 node.
- *Local-area* (or *intracluster*) communication for agents residing on different nodes, but within the same cluster. These agents were communicating through a 100Mbps Fast Ethernet network.
- *Wide-area* (or *intercluster*) communication for agents belonging to different clusters. This type of communication was carried out over the wide-area links shared with other wide-area traffic.

This diverse environment (with respect to networking) provided us with a valuable testbed for studying the newscast model.

It is important to observe that even though 800 agents run within each DAS-2 node, more than 99% of the communication between agents is either across wide-area or local-area links. For any given agent, 799 other agents run on the same node, and 127,200 run on other nodes, which account for 0.6% and 99.4% of the total 128,000 agents respectively. As we observed in our experiments, the items in an agent's cache are randomly distributed over *all* the participating agents, irrespective of their location. Therefore we expect only 0.6% of the total communication to be within or between processes on the same node, and all the rest to be across local-area or wide-area links. In particular, agents in the three 32-node clusters are expected to experience 80% wide-area and 19.4% local-area traffic, while agents in our 64-node cluster are expected to have 60% wide-area and 39.4% local-area traffic.

Another parameter of our experiments that is worth noting, is the *bootstrapping* mechanism. By bootstrapping we refer to the procedure of providing agents with the information required to jump-start the newscast network's formation. In principle, a new agent joins by contacting *any* existing agent and exchanging caches. When the whole network starts from scratch, a systematic way has to be present to provide one or more initial communication points to each agent. In our experiments this task was handled by the utility module. All agents were provided with the single address of one selected agent. Providing agents with a choice of (possibly random) agents to connect to initially, enhances the randomness of the network in the early cycles. However, a bootstrapping mechanism as simple and centralized as the one we chose further substantiates our claims of the protocol's convergent behavior, as discussed in the following section.

4 Results

This section presents a thorough analysis of the output of our three large-scale experiments with 128,000 correspondents using cache sizes of 20, 30, and 40, respectively. We will often compare the emerging communication graphs to random graphs. In all cases, the random graphs we refer to are generated by selecting exactly c undirected edges randomly for each node. For example, in such a graph each node has at least c edges (but usually more).

4.1 Statistical Properties of the Communication Graph

Figure 5 illustrates the two most important properties of the emergent communication graphs. The number of cycles actually performed was over 5000, however, only the initial cycles are depicted because the values remain the same throughout the experiment indicating a convergent behavior.

The *average path length* from a node is defined as the average of the minimal path lengths of that node to all other nodes. To get a finite value we have to

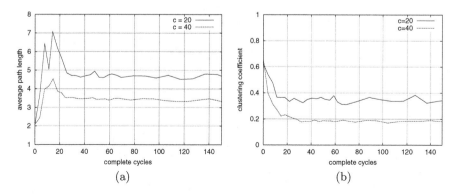

Fig. 5. (a) The evolution of average path length from a node. (b) Clustering coefficient.

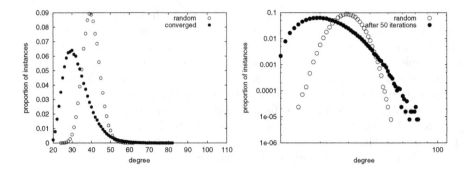

Fig. 6. Degree distribution on (a) linear and (b) log-log scale using the same range. The depicted values belong to a single converged communication graph with $n = 128000$ and $c = 20$ (converged) and a graph with c random edges generated for each vertex (random).

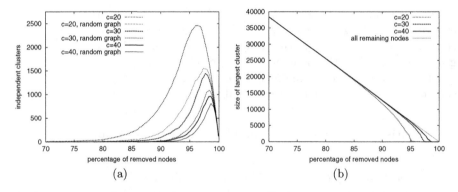

Fig. 7. Partitioning of the communication graph as a function of the percentage of removed random nodes (node failures). The curves belong to a single graph. The largest clusters of random graphs are omitted for clarity; their relationship to the communication graphs is similar to the relationship in the case of the number of clusters.

have a connected graph. We can observe very low average path lengths which coincide with the expected lengths after extrapolation of the simulation data shown in Figure 3(a). The initial peak is explained by the applied bootstrapping mechanism described in Section 3. This mechanism results in an initially unbalanced neighborhood structure. However, after all correspondents get connected to the collective, the average path length converges quickly to its final value.

The *average clustering coefficient* taken over all nodes is shown in Figure 5(b), and again corresponds to our simulation results. Together with the values found for average path lengths, we can indeed conclude that our communication graphs are *small-world* graphs.

Small-world graphs come in very different flavors however. One interesting property to investigate is whether our graphs are *scale free* or not. The degree of a random node defines a random variable. If this variable is exponentially distributed (linear on the log-log scale) then the graph is scale free. Figure 6 shows the distribution of the node degree for the case of $c = 20$ which deviates the most from the random case.

It can be seen clearly that our communication graph is not scale free. From a dependability point of view this is an advantage since scale-free graphs are sensitive to the removal of highly connected nodes (even though they are less sensitive to random node removal). The effect of node removal in our graphs is discussed next.

4.2   Robustness to Node Removal

Figure 7 shows the effect of node removal to the connectivity of the communication graph. Note that the number of clusters decreases when approaching 100% removal because the remaining graph itself becomes small. The graph shows very similar behavior to a random graph, especially if the cache is large. These results indicate considerable robustness to node failures especially considering the size of the largest cluster which indicates that most of the clusters are in fact very small and most of the nodes are still in a single connected cluster.

5   Conclusions

In this paper we presented experiments with a Java implementation of the news-cast model. The experiments involved 128,000 agents communicating with each other over a wide-area, large-scale heterogeneous cluster of processors.

The outcome of these experiments is particularly valuable since it represents the real implementation of our model as opposed to previously conducted simulations, yet the size of the system is comparable with the scale of typical simulation results as well. The results are in complete agreement with the theoretical predictions and simulations presented in [8] providing practical evidence concerning the correctness of our algorithm and of the statistical properties of the emerging communication graphs.

As we demonstrated, the series of the communication graphs show stable small-world properties which make it a dependable and effective device for information dissemination and membership management. Most importantly, these properties are not maintained explicitly, but they are emergent from the underlying simple epidemic-style information exchange protocol.

References

1. R. Albert and A.-L. Barabasi. "Statistical Mechanics of Complex Networks." *Reviews of Modern Physics*, 74(1):47–97, Jan. 2001.
2. M. Castro, P. Druschel, Y. C. Hu, and A. Rowstron. "Exploiting Network Proximity in Peer-to-Peer Overlay Networks." Technical Report MSR-TR-2002-82, Microsoft Research, Cambridge, UK, June 2002.

3. A. Demers, D. Greene, C. Hauser, W. Irish, J. Larson, S. Shenker, H. Sturgis, D. Swinehart, and D. Terry. "Epidemic Algorithms for Replicated Database Management." In *Proc. Sixth Symp. on Principles of Distributed Computing*, pp. 1–12, Aug. 1987. ACM.

4. P. Eugster, R. Guerraoui, S. Handurukande, A.-M. Kermarrec, and P. Kouznetsov. "Lightweight Probabilistic Broadcast." In *Proc. Second Int'l Conf. Dependable Systems and Networks*, pp. 443–452, June 2001. IEEE Computer Society Press, Los Alamitos, CA.

5. P. T. Eugster and R. Guerraoui. "Probabilistic Multicast." In *Proc. Int'l Conf. Dependable Systems and Networks*, June 2002. IEEE Computer Society Press, Los Alamitos, CA.

6. A. Ganesh, A.-M. Kermarrec, and L. Massoulié. "Scamp: Peer-to-Peer Lightweight Membership Servic for Large-Scale Group Communication." In *Proc. Networked Group Communication Workshop*, volume 2233 of *Lect. Notes Comp. Sc.*, pp. 44–56, Nov. 2001. Springer-Verlag, Berlin.

7. A. Ganesh, A.-M. Kermarrec, and L. Massoulié. "Peer-to-Peer Membership Management for Gossip-based Protocols." *IEEE Trans. Comp.*, 52(2):139–149, Feb. 2003.

8. M. Jelasity and M. van Steen. "Large-Scale Newscast Computing on the Internet." Technical Report IR-503, Vrije Universiteit, Department of Computer Science, Oct. 2002.

9. A.-M. Kermarrec, L. Massoulié, and A. Ganesh. "Probabilistic Reliable Dissemination in Large-Scale Systems." *IEEE Trans. Par. Distr. Syst.*, 14(3):248–258, Mar. 2003.

10. S. P. Ratnasamy. *A Scalable Content Addressable Network.* PhD thesis, University of California at Berkeley, Oct. 2002.

11. A. Rowstron and P. Druschel. "Pastry: Scalable, Distributed Object Location and Routing for Large-Scale Peer-to-Peer Systems." In R. Guerraoui, (ed.), *Proc. Middleware 2001*, volume 2218 of *Lect. Notes Comp. Sc.*, pp. 329–350, Nov. 2001. Springer-Verlag, Berlin.

12. I. Stoica, R. Morris, D. Karger, M. F. Kaashoek, and H. Balakrishnan. "Chord: A Scalable Peer-to-peer Lookup Service for Internet Applications." In *Proc. SIGCOMM*, Aug. 2001. ACM.

13. I. Stoica, R. Morris, D. Liben-Nowell, D. R. Karger, M. F. Kaashoek, F. Dabek, and H. Balakrishnan. "Chord: A Scalable Peer-to-peer Lookup Protocol for Internet Applications." *IEEE/ACM Trans. Netw.*, 2003. To appear.

14. D. J. Watts. *Small Worlds, The Dynamics of Networks between Order and Randomness.* Princeton University Press, Princeton, NJ, 1999.

15. B. Yang and H. Garcia-Molina. "Designing a Super-Peer Network." In *Proc. 19th Int'l Conf. Data Engineering*, Mar. 2003. IEEE Computer Society Press, Los Alamitos, CA.

16. B. Y. Zhao, J. Kubiatowicz, and A. D. Joseph. "Tapestry: An Infrastructure for Fault-tolerant Wide-area Location and Routing." Technical Report CSD-01-1141, Computer Science Division, University of California, Berkeley, Apr. 2001.

Group Formation Among Peer-to-Peer Agents: Learning Group Characteristics

Elth Ogston, Benno Overeinder, Maarten van Steen, and Frances Brazier

Department of Computer Science, Vrije Universiteit
Amsterdam de Boelelaan 1081a,
1081 HV Amsterdam The Netherlands
{elth, bjo, steen, frances}@cs.vu.nl

Abstract. This paper examines the decentralized formation of groups within a peer-to-peer multi-agent system. More specifically, it frames group formation as a clustering problem, and examines how to determine cluster characteristics such as area and density in the absence of information about the entire data set, such as the number of points, the number of clusters, or the maximum distance between points, that are available to centralized clustering algorithms. We develop a method in which agents individually search for other agents with similar characteristics in a peer-to-peer manner. These agents group into small centrally controlled clusters which learn cluster parameters by examining and improving their internal composition over time. We show through simulation that this method allows us to find clusters of a wide variety of sizes without adjusting agent parameters.

1 Introduction and Background

Forming groups of similar agents can serve many purposes within a multi-agent system. Group membership can provide an alternative to directory services when performing associative matching, and the process of coalition formation requires a manner of identifying preliminary groups. Clustering is the abstract problem of dividing a set of data into groups of like items. The clustering problem, however, has been primarily studied in the centralized case of grouping items that have been gathered together in a database. In the context of multi-agent systems, on the other hand, we consider large groups of distributed agents [5] [8]. These agents ideally require only peer-to-peer interactions to perform their basic operations in order to achieve scalability, flexibility and independence of components. Centralized clustering is a difficult problem because clusters can have many unknown characteristics, such as size and shape, which make them difficult to define. Decentralized clustering is even more problematic because global information such as the size or range of a data set is unavailable. In previous work [6] we discussed a method by which agents could perform decentralized clustering, provided that we could predefine the desired number of items in a cluster. In this paper we consider a manner in which agents can learn cluster area and density, thus allowing them to perform on a much broader range of data sets without having to adjust parameters. We demonstrate, through simulation experiments, collections of agents representing two dimensional points grouping themselves. Initial experimental results show that these agents, without

G. Moro, C. Sartori, and M.P. Singh (Eds.): AP2PC 2003, LNAI 2872, pp. 59–70, 2004.

changing experimental parameters, can identify clusters or varying density with between 20 and 250 points.

The clustering problem has been widely studied [2], however it is usually assumed that points in the data set can be compared by some central "clusterer". In peer-to-peer systems, on the other hand, data is distributed widely over a network and this assumption no longer holds. Further, in multi-agent systems the notion of agent autonomy can exclude the use of a single central comparison function. By decentralizing clustering we thus exacerbate the problem of how to tell a computer the characteristics of the clusters that we wish to find. One of the great difficulties encountered when designing clustering algorithms is defining the term "cluster" in a way that a computer can interpret. Intuitively a cluster can be seen as a connected dense region of points, surrounded by a less dense region. Finding clusters is thus finding boundaries between density regions. Because these boundaries are generally fuzzy, computer algorithms need a more concrete definition. To achieve this additional restrictions are used to make clusters calculable.

The K-means algorithm [4], for instance, fixes the number of clusters in the data set and, hidden in its total error squared measure, makes the assumption that clusters are roughly spherical. Given this information, clusters will extend to their natural boundaries, provided that centoids are chosen correctly. The k-means passes and various starting heuristics are methods of estimating the "correct" centroids.

Hierarchical algorithms [2], (we will use the top down minimal spanning tree algorithm as an example), split clusters along the largest existing edge between points to obtain each level. By doing this they in essence say "if there is a density boundary, this edge must cross it". This method identifies boundaries nicely, but leaves the problem of choosing which level of the tree contains the correct clustering. By basing this on some statistic, like the total error squared or the number of clusters, additional assumptions are introduced that are, again, dependant on the data set.

Density based clustering specifically looks for density boundaries by walking through a data set from point to nearest point. Here it is clear to see that a definition of a boundary is required. DBSCAN [1] specifically says that clusters are areas with at least a given density. DBSCLADS [9] makes the assumption that clusters are of roughly uniform density, with a parameter to define "roughly."

Overall, the standard data set dependant "clues" used by clustering algorithms include:

- the number of clusters, or analogously, the expected cluster size,
- the minimum gap between clusters,
- the minimum density of clusters.

Each of these gives a global standard for the data set, but can be used in decision functions locally. This allows centralized clustering algorithms to be parallelized, provided that global information about the data set can be shared between processing units [7]. P-CLUSTER [3] for instance parallelized k-means by distributing each k-means pass and synchronizing centroid information between passes.

In [6] we showed how clustering could be performed by a *decentralized* multi-agent system, provided that we could set beforehand the maximum size of the clusters we wished to obtain. In fact, knowing any of the above clues makes the form of decentralized clustering that we studied fairly easy, as it gives clusters an indication of when they have reached their boundaries. The real challenge occurs when these clues are absent, or do not hold for all clusters in the data set.

In this paper we show how clusters that lack any central coordination between them can learn cluster parameters by watching their internal composition over time. This allows them to find clusters with varying cluster sizes and densities, and even to identify clusters with widely differing characteristics within the same data set. Whereas in [6] we study the problem of clustering in a fully decentralized way across possibly large networks and the speed of convergence of this clustering, in this paper we study the problem of dynamically determining when to continue or to stop clustering.

Section 2 of this paper summarizes our base peer-to-peer clustering algorithm from previous work. Section 3 discusses the information available to an agent cluster when attempting to discover correct data cluster parameters. We then describe how this can be used, given that clusters themselves are centrally controlled and assuming that a cluster can correctly detect when it internally contains more than one data cluster. Section 4 then describes a method for doing this detection without needing to know the complete details of the data held by the agents in the cluster, and provides some experimental results exploring the range of data sets that the resulting method can handle.

2 The Basic Decentralized Agent Clustering Method

When defining our agent grouping method we consider very large systems with at least thousands of agents, like the internet, which must be distributed because their data cannot be collected centrally for reasons of size, privacy or dynamics. We thus specify that our agents must communicate in a decentralized manner, though we allow some cooperative group operations to be done by a central elected member of the group. For this reason we consider agent groups that are much smaller then the system as a whole, containing tens to hundreds of agents. We assume a global addressing system exists, allowing agents to send a message to any other agent, but limit the memory available to agents to store addresses so that they only know of the existence of a few neighbors at any one time.

The problem of grouping similar agents is, in the abstract, a clustering problem. Clustering in general considers a set of data items, S that must be partitioned into subsets, $s_1, s_2... s_k$, such that items within each subset have more in common with each other then they do with points in other subsets. In the agent domain we consider each agent as an item with particular characteristics, and with the goal of finding other like agents. We depict these agents as having a main "attribute" which describes its overall properties, and a number of "objectives" which describe its current short term goals for which a "matching" objective in a partner agent must be found. For instance, our agents could represent documents where an agent's attribute would be the document text, its objectives could be what it currently considers to be keywords for that text, and matches could be based on the distance between keywords in a given ontology. To group our agents we allow them to independently find matches using a peer-to-peer search protocol. We then choose some of the stronger matches that are formed to link agents into clusters of cooperating agents. Over time these clusters update their agents' choice of matches and their own membership, based on better matches that are encountered through the search

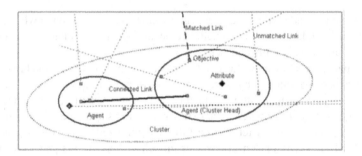

Fig. 1. A diagram of two clustered agents.

protocol. This process results in agents self organizing into clusters that approximate underlying clusters within their data. Figure 1 diagrams two clustered agents.

To create measurable experiments with these agents we consider the simple case where agents represent a set of two-dimensional points, generated to contain underlying data clusters. We initiate an experiment by creating one agent for each data point in the set. Each agent is given five elementary objectives, that are simply the data point. These objectives each use a matching function that measures the Euclidean distance between their point and that of a potentially matching objective. This distance is compared to a value learned over time indicating how small a distance represents a good match. To initiate an experiment we randomly pair up objectives, creating a graph in which the agents are nodes, each with five random edges to other agents. We call these edges "links." Links represent communication paths between agents. They can be of one of three types: "unmatched links" between two objectives that have nothing in common, "matched links" between two objectives that have agreed that they are similar, and "connected links" between strongly matched objectives. Initially each agent is considered to be an individual cluster.

Clusters simultaneously carry on two cycles of operations. The first is shuffling unmatched links to give objectives new potential matches. The second is making matched links into connections and breaking weaker connections so as to be able to replace them with better ones. Groups of agents that are joined by a path of connected links are defined as being a single cluster. They elect one member of the cluster as the cluster head, which keeps a map of the cluster composition and is thus able to make decisions that require an overview of the cluster as a whole. The cluster head is the only agent that knows the cluster composition, all other agents know only the address of the cluster head and the address of the five objectives that they are linked to in other agents.

The search for new matches is performed independently by the agents' objectives. This search is done by objectives first testing initial unmatched links to determine if a match should be formed. If an objective finds a match it informs its cluster head. Otherwise one objective in the link pair sends its neighbor's address to its own cluster head. The cluster head collects these rejected addresses, and after a time shuffles them, returning new addresses to the waiting unmatched links, who can then begin the process over again. During this search we maintain the invariant that any objective at any time has only one neighbor whom it can contact an who can contact it.

When two objectives agree on a match, they both inform their cluster head of the new matched link along with the Euclidean distance between their points. The cluster heads stores a list with details of all matched links in the cluster. It considers matches with a shorter distance to be better then longer ones.

The creation and breaking of connected links, which changes cluster composition, occurs "every now and then", based on some internal timing in the cluster head. A cluster head first selects its best matched link and attempts to make it into a connected link by sending a request through the link to the neighboring cluster head. If the request is accepted, a new connection is agreed, one cluster head surrenders its data to the other, forming a single cluster, and the cycle ends. Clusters, however, have a maximum size that limits how many agents they can contain. If a connection request is refused because the resulting cluster would be too large both clusters consider operations to change their size. This involves checking if they want to break one of their connected or matched links. The cluster head chooses one of its longer links to break. Breaking a matched link does not effect cluster size, but leaves objectives free to find better matches. Breaking a connected link requires the cluster head to calculate a new cluster map. If this no longer forms a connected graph the cluster head appoints a new second head and sends it the information for the new cluster to be broken off.

The process above is described formally in our previous work [6]. In that paper we found that clusters will grow to their maximum size and over time consolidate to contain most of the points in an contiguous area. If the maximum size is set to be as large as a real data cluster and smaller than two neighboring data clusters, then the agent clusters will correspond to data clusters. Thus agents can self organize to find data clusters, with the limitation that the maximum size of the agent clusters must be set correctly beforehand. Most centralized clustering algorithms contain similar limitations, and thus we found that decentralized clustering compared favorably. The size of data clusters is, however, a parameter that can change for each data set, and even between clusters in a data set. Moreover, it is something that intelligent agents might be able to learn, giving an important advantage to agent clustering methods.

3   Growing Clusters

In order to be able to discover natural clusters in data, our agent clusters need a way to determine when they should increase or decrease their maximum size. To understand the operations open to an agent cluster we must first consider what data it has available. Imagine ourselves as a cluster, looking over the data landscape. Our entire view of the world is composed of our internal data and links to a few outside objectives. Agents in a cluster each know their own data point, and for each matched and connected link the length of that link. We should not assume that agents know the data point of the agent on the other end of a link since points may be complex or private collections of data.

From this picture a cluster as a whole knows:

- The density of the 'found' points for its region, i.e. the internal agents' points.
- Possibly, the existence of some external points that suggest if its surroundings are of equal density, indicated by matched links of a short length.

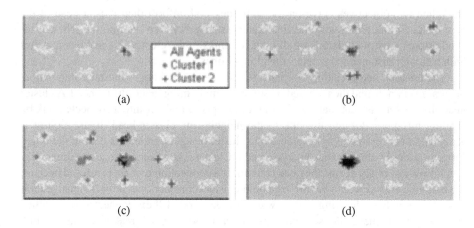

(a)   (b)

(c)   (d)

Fig. 2. The development of two clusters.

A cluster however does not know:

- The actual density of the area it covers, as there could be points in that area that have not yet been found.
- The actual density of its surroundings, since if a cluster only has distant matches, it does not mean that nearby ones do not exist.

From this information a cluster can compare its internal density to the density of its neighbors in the peer-to-peer system. However, unless this area of the system contains most of the relevant points form the data set, this tells us nothing about the data clusters. Luckily we can also assume that the majority of nearby points in the data set will group together. Our base procedure changes clusters by creating and breaking connections, favoring shorter connections, and thus naturally forms compact clusters over time. Figure 2 is a series of 4 time shots showing a system with data clusters containing 50 points each, being clustered by agents with a maximum cluster size of 25. We see how two agent clusters that end up splitting a data cluster grow over time. The last frame of figure 2 shows that a too small maximum cluster size results in a large data cluster being split into smaller regions. From this we may assume that an agent cluster contains most of the points in the area it covers after some time has passed and its composition has become stable. On the other hand, we can never be absolutely certain that this is the case since (i) we cannot be certain that cluster composition is stable at any point in time and (ii) in very large systems finding all the points in an area can take a long time. We will, however, use this assumption to grow the maximum cluster size, and make up for mistakes by shrinking clusters again should they become too large.

Figure 2 is a birds-eye view, not the actual picture seen by the cluster. To make cluster-wide decisions, including growing, we collect, in the cluster head, data from the individual agents. For the basic clustering algorithm the cluster head needs to store a map of the cluster which includes the addresses of agents in the cluster, the length of the matched links currently held those agents, and the length of the connected links between those agents. Figure 4(b) shows the ordered series of connected link lengths for the cluster whose data points are pictured in figure 4(a). This, along with a similar list with the length of the matched links, is the view of the world available to the cluster head.

Let us hypothesize that we have a function, shouldSplit(), that returns either that a cluster is a good size, or that certain links should be broken to form better, smaller clusters. We could then regulate cluster growth as follows: when considering a size change clusters first call this function to determine if they are currently too big. If so they spilt, resetting the maximum sizes of the resulting clusters. If not they should possibly be larger. To check this they call the shouldSplit() function again, this time also considering their best match as part of the cluster. If this still results in a good cluster we assume that there are other points that could belong to this cluster but do not because it is too small, and increase the maximum size.

The shouldSplit() function essentially calculates if an agent cluster's data belongs to one or more data clusters. Thus, given the data points in the cluster and the external data point for potential connections, in theory we should be able to use any existing clustering algorithm to implement it. Because the function is only used internally in relatively small clusters it is acceptable to use any of the centralized algorithms.

To test this method of cluster growth we ran some experiments with the resulting agent algorithm, using a "perfect" shouldSplit() function. This "perfect" function was given the minimum gap between clusters for a data set, and returned that any connected links longer then this gap should be broken. We generated 20 data sets using the the generation algorithm in [6], each containing 25 clusters with a fixed radius of 1, a gaussian internal distribution of points, and 20 to 200 points. We clustered these data sets, giving agents an initial maximum cluster size of 15. Measuring cluster stability to determine when to check for growth is difficult, and thus we simply guessed that after a long enough period the cluster will be about stable. Thus, we added to the algorithm in section 2 that every 10 times a cluster gets to the point where it checks if it should be breaking a link, it instead checks to see if it should change its maximum size, using the shouldSplit() function as described above. Figure 3 shows the resulting agent clusters for 15 of these data clusters. The majority of data clusters were found correctly. At point A an agent cluster has been incorrectly split into two. This occurs because the connections within a cluster are only an approximation of the minimal spanning tree for the cluster. These cluster will most likely rejoin after a time. At point B we see an agent cluster that has grown too large and now consists of two data clusters. Again, over time this mistake should also be corrected. Of the 500 clusters we generated we observed 23 incorrectly split clusters, and 15 too large clusters after running the algorithm for a fixed amount of time. We choose this time to be about twice as long as it takes clusters to initially grow to the correct size, thus giving them some time to improve. From this data we conclude that the above method is valid way of learning cluster size, provided that we can come up with a adequate real implementation of the shouldSplit() function.

4   Determining When a Cluster Is Too Large

As we discussed in the previous section, if we know some information about the data set, like cluster density or size, the shouldSplit() function is relatively simple to implement,

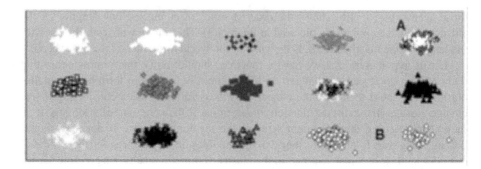

Fig. 3. Example clustering, given a perfect shouldSplit() function

we only need to check if the current cluster conforms to the known criteria. Without this information a cluster essentially needs to run a clustering algorithm internally to decide if it should be one or more clusters. However, this isn't as easy as it sounds. Agents' attributes can be large or complex data points, such as entire text documents or user profiles, which would be expensive to store in the cluster head where shouldSplit() is calculated. Furthermore, when checking for cluster growth we also considered the nearest matched data point. This is data from an agent in another cluster, and might be private. For these reasons, in this section we experiment with a shouldSplit() function that only uses the data already available to the cluster heads.

In order to run the basic clustering algorithm cluster heads need to store some summary information about their matched and connected links: the lengths of those links. For estimating cluster density this information might be sufficient. Instead of clustering the data points themselves to implement shouldSplit(), as we suggested above, we could cluster the length of the connected links. Assuming that connected links are between nearby agents (in the data space), this would determine if the connected links form one set, indicating a continuous cluster density, or two (or more) sets, indicating that some links are over a larger gap between two data clusters. If two sets are found breaking all of the longer connections should split a large cluster into two (or more) good clusters. Clustering link lengths in this manner has the further advantage that it considers lower dimensional data, and is thus less computationally intensive.

Clustering link lengths, however, requires that we can tell the difference between longer links between clusters and random fluctuations in link length, due to the random placement of points and the fact that connections are only an approximation of the minimum spanning tree between points. The examples in figures 4 and 5 show two clusters, one of the correct size, and one that should be split. These data clusters were created to have a random gaussian distribution of points, according to the algorithm described in [6]. Frame (a) of the figures shows the data points in the clusters, frame (b) shows the the lengths of each of the connected links in the clusters, sorted from largest to smallest. A comparison of the two figures shows that a large change between two consecutive links indicates that a cluster that should be split. However, graph 4(b) shows that the good cluster also contains relatively large changes in link length. We have found, though experimentation, that it is not enough to simply consider the ratio between the

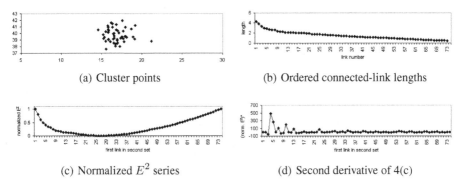

(a) Cluster points

(b) Ordered connected-link lengths

(c) Normalized E^2 series

(d) Second derivative of 4(c)

Fig. 4. A good agent cluster.

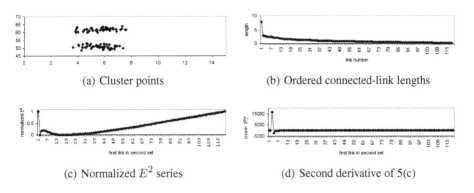

(a) Cluster points

(b) Ordered connected-link lengths

(c) Normalized E^2 series

(d) Second derivative of 5(c)

Fig. 5. An agent cluster that contains two data clusters.

largest drop and the average drop. Any value for this ratio high enough to avoid splitting the majority of good clusters, also failed to recognize some large clusters, eventually allowing the system to conglomerate into a single cluster.

In place of considering only the distance between consecutive lengths, we need a measure that takes into account all lengths when contemplating a split. To do this we assume that the ordered link lengths form two sets, those that are too long, and those that are good. Our task now is to determine where to divide the link length series into these two sets. We create a series of all the possible divisions, first with all lengths in the same set, then with the highest value in the first set and all others in the second, next with the two highest values in the first set, and so forth. Considering each of these groupings as a clustering of the lengths, we calculate a measure of the goodness of these clusterings, the total error squared used in the k-means algorithm . Total error squared is defined as:

$$E^2 = \sum_{i=1}^{k} \sum_{x \in C_i} \|x - m_i\|^2.$$

given k clusters $C_1, \ldots, C_k$, where C_i has a mean value m_i for $1 \leq i \leq k$. E^2 sums the square of the distance between the vector of points in each cluster, and the average vector for that cluster, thus indicating how far a clustering is from a perfect clustering. Figures 4(c) and 5(c) show the resulting E^2 series from the example clusters.

A correct clustering of a data set has a lower E^2 value than an incorrect clustering. However, a clustering into two clusters will also have a lower E^2 then a clustering with one cluster. For this reason we cannot simply choose the partition of lengths with the lowest E^2. We also need to determine if an E^2 graph indicates that our lengths form one group or two. Consider the length series $\{1000, 1000, 1000, 1, 1, 1\}$. The correct partition $\{1000, 1000, 1000\}, \{1,1,1\}$ will have an E^2 of 0, while the incorrect partitions to either side of it in the E^2 series, $\{1000, 1000, 1000, 1\}, \{1,1\}$ and $\{1000, 1000\}$, $\{1000, 1, 1\}$ will have high E^2 values. This results in a discontinuity in the E^2 series. On the other hand, while the E^2 series for the length set $\{1000, 999, 998, 997, 996, 995\}$ also falls and rises, it does so gradually. Thus we calculate the second derivative of the E^2 series, $E^{2"}$, depicted in 4(d) and 5(d). Large changes in length result in peaks in the second derivative. We use the approximation for the second derivative for an equidistant series of points: $f"(x) = (y_2 - 2y_1 + y_0)/h^2$. For the distance between points, h, we use $1/N$ where N is the number of connected links in the cluster. This scales the calculation by the size of the cluster.

A large agent cluster made up of two perfect data clusters each containing an infinite number of identical points and placed an infinite distance apart will exhibit a peak of infinity in the $E^{2"}$ curve described above, while two correct agent clusters for this data will have a constant $E^{2"}$ curve with value 0. We, however, do not have perfect clusters, and thus the large peaks in bad agent clusters will be well below infinity, while good agent clusters will still display small peaks. There are several reasons for this: data points within a cluster are spread out, clusters are close together, and our clusters have small numbers of data points making our estimate for the second derivative imperfect. On the other hand, all that is important is that we can find a cutoff value that distinguishes between too-high low values, and too-low high values. For the clusters in figures 4 and 5 any value between 500 and 15,000 would do. By normalizing the E^2 curve between 0 and 1 we make this cutoff value independent of the radius of the data clusters. However, the number of data points in a cluster does effect it. Small clusters with randomly placed points will show more variation in their strength values, raising the height of peaks that should be 0. Less data points will also result in a cruder estimate of discontinuities in the $E^{2"}$, lowering the height of peaks. From this we observe that small clusters are much harder to distinguish then larger ones, and that a cutoff that works for small clusters should also be sufficient for larger ones.

In experiments with a range of data set we find that a cutoff of 175 consistently produces good clusters. This value is fairly low, and sometimes results in links within good clusters being broken. However, as these links are usually the long ones that reach across the cluster breaking them still leaves a connected graph of shorter links intact. Agent clusters that have grown to include more than two data clusters can contain more then the assumed two sets of link strengths, resulting in several peaks in the $E^{2"}$ series. A cutoff value of 175 however is low enough that it usually detects the last peak, splitting the cluster correctly. Due to the scaling of E^2, an extremely large link strength can

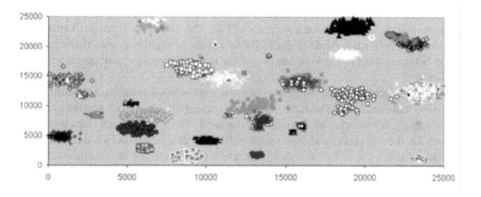

Fig. 6. Example clustering, using the shouldSplit() function form Section 4.

overshadow other large link strengths, however, since the clusters repeatedly check if they are too large, a cluster that is not completely split at one time will be split the next time round.

Figure 6 shows the resulting algorithm run on 36 randomly placed clusters, with radii between 1 and 1000, and 20 to 250 points. We see some of the same mistaken joins and splits seen in the more even clusters in figure 3. Overall, however, we find that our clustering algorithm does a good job of identifying the clusters, even when they are of very different size and density, and even in some cases where two such clusters are not well separated. This is a large improvement over our original agent algorithm which would have been unable to cluster this data due to the fact that the clusters have largely varying numbers of points.

5   Discussion and Conclusions

Overall, we have replaced a very data dependant clustering parameter, the expected maximum cluster size, with a cutoff parameter measuring sudden changes in link density, that allows agents to detect a much larger range of clusters with different areas and densities. We have shown some initial experiments indicating that this method is effective. However, we still need to fully explore the range of clusters that it can handle.

Ideally we would like agents to find clusters, within the same data set, independent of the number of points they contain, their density and the distance between them. The method we presented in this paper is dependant on the number of points, because of of our estimate of E^{2}". However, our clusters are even more limited in size by their internal communication, meaning that we only need to be able to deal with clusters with up to a few thousand points.

The method in this paper is also dependant on the ratio of the distance between points within a cluster and the distance between clusters themselves. Two clusters that are overlapping will look like the same cluster to most algorithms. Two clusters that are close together can also look the same to our algorithm since it doesn't consider all of the spatial data available. Thus we find a chaining effect where a string of points between two clusters will lead to them being considered as one. This is a common problem in density based clustering. Our algorithm will also be unable to distinguish small gaps between clusters whose density gradually decreases, as small increases in the length of links between clusters can look like part of the natural increase in link length within the cluster.

Finally, our method of cluster boundary detection is also dependant on the distribution of points within a cluster. The experiments here presented clusters with a random gaussian distribution, showing that we can deal with smoothly changing distances between cluster points. On the other hand, sudden changes will be detected as gaps between clusters. Such sudden changes can occur in very regular clusters, for instance in clusters with points that are placed evenly on a grid. All of the above issues require further experimentation to determine the exact range of clusters that our agents can now handle.

References

1. Ester, M., Kriegel, H., Sander, J., and Xu, X.: A Density-Based Algorithm for Discovering Clusters in Large Spatial Databases with Nose. Second International Conference on Knowledge Discovery and Data Mining (1996) 226–231
2. Jain, A.K., Murty M.N., Flynn, P.J.: Data Clustering: A Review. ACM Computing Surveys, Vol 31, No. 3, September (1999). 264-322
3. Judd, D., McKinley, P., and Jain A.: Large-Scale Parallel Data Clustering. IEEE Transactions on Pattern Analysis and Machine Intelligence. Vol 20, No. 8. August (1998). 871-876
4. Kaufman, L. and Rousseeuw, P. Finding Groups in Data: an Introduction to Cluster Analysis, John Wiley and Sons (1990)
5. Klusch, M. and Gerber, A.: Dynamic Coalition Formation Among Rational Agents. IEEE Intelligent Systems. Vol 17, No. 3 (2002) 42-47
6. Ogston, E., Overeinder, B., Van Steen, M., and Brazier, F.: A Method for Decentralized Clustering in Large Multi-Agent Systems. Second International Joint Conference on Autonomous Agents and Multi-Agent Systems (2003) To be published
7. Olson, C.: Parallel Algorithms for Hierarchical Clustering. Parallel Computing 21, (1995) 1313-1325
8. Shehory, O. and Kraus, S.: Task Allocation via Coalition Formation among Autonomous Agents. Proceedings of the Fourteenth International Joint Conference on Artificial Intelligence (1995) 655-661
9. Xu, X., Ester, M., Kriegel, H., and Sander, J.:A Distribution-Based Clustering Algorithm for Mining in Large Spatial Databases. Proceedings of the 14th International Conferece on Data Engineering (1998) 324-332

A Pheromone-Based Coordination Mechanism Applied in Peer-to-Peer

Kurt Schelfthout and Tom Holvoet

Department of Computer Science, Katholieke Universiteit Leuven
Celestijnenlaan 200A,
3001 Leuven, Belgium
{Kurt.Schelfthout, Tom.Holvoet}@cs.kuleuven.ac.be

Abstract. In this paper, we discuss the principle of synthetic pheromones, which we view as a high level coordination mechanism suitable for scalable, distributed systems, such as peer to peer systems. We present a software abstraction for the application of synthetic pheromones, building on an existing coordination mechanism, objectspaces. The coordination principle is evaluated on the problem of search in a file-sharing P2P system.

1 Introduction

Some distributed systems have very stringent requirements concerning decentralization, scalability and robustness. For example, a peer to peer system needs to deal with a very large number of peers, joining or leaving the system at will, preferably operating without a central component. Other examples include active networks [1](networks that are able to dynamically reconfigure themselves in response to faults or changing quality of service requirements) and manufacturing control [2](where it is difficult to gather and plan centrally because information may be outdated very rapidly).

These systems seem like a natural application domain for multi-agent systems (hereafter written MAS). An agent is a problem solving entity, that is *situated* in a local environment (i.e. is no global or centralized component and has no complete view of the system), and is naturally able to adapt itself to harsh circumstances.

Our interest is in the development of a coordination infrastructure for multi-agent systems. A coordination infrastructure provides mechanisms by which agents can coordinate their activities in a concurrent and distributed world. A typical example is the division of work among autonomous agents, and the reconstruction of the end result after the work is done. Coordination is especially important in the kind of systems mentioned above, since they are inherently composed out of multiple distributed entities that need to cooperate for the system to function.

Our main focus is on achieving coordination through environment-mediated communication - this means that there is no *direct* interaction between agents,

G. Moro, C. Sartori, and M.P. Singh (Eds.): AP2PC 2003, LNAI 2872, pp. 71–76, 2004.
© Springer-Verlag Berlin Heidelberg 2004

instead agents communicate or interact *indirectly* by changing their environment. This change can be noted by other agents, who are then able to react appropriately. This is interesting because agents thus become highly *decoupled*: in order to communicate, the sending agent does even not need to be alive when the receiving agent gets the message.

An existing approach for coordinating agents is the tuplespace approach, first introduced for concurrent computing in Linda [3], and later on refined and varied upon, notably for object-oriented and distributed computing (Objective Linda [4], CO^3PS[5] ...). It remains an active research area, with notable recent variants being MARS [6] and Lime [7].

Presented here is an extension of objectspaces with support for synthetic pheromones, the virtual variant of substances ants (among others) use to achieve a coordinated behavior on the colony level. This is discussed in detail in Section 2. In the following section, we elaborate on our implementation of synthetic pheromones, that is build on top of an existing objectspace architecture, CO^3PS[5], augmented with a meta-layer [8] that makes it easier to extend the objectspace with new mechanisms. We indicate some design and implementation issues. Furthermore, the new principles are evaluated on a file-sharing Gnutella-like [9] P2P system.

2   Pheromones as Dynamic Objects

The underlying principle of synthetic pheromones [10] is based on the mechanism ants (among others) use to find food. A pheromone is a chemical substance an ant can drop in the environment. The pheromone then propagates (by Brownian motion) through the environment, as well as evaporates over time. Ants for example use it to build a path from the nest to a food source, by laying pheromone trails to the food.

These trails are governed by two important dynamics. The first is the propagation of pheromones: the stronger the trail, the further it propagates, and the more it attracts other ants (from distances further away). While there is food remaining, ants keep on reinforcing the trail, attracting even more ants. The second important dynamic is the evaporation of the trail: once the food is gone, no more ants are reinforcing the trail, and all pheromones eventually evaporate, thus stop "misleading" ants. Evaporation is a "forgetting" factor for the system. This keeps the system responsive to changes. This scheme appears to be very robust and scalable in practice. Therefore, we would like to apply it as a coordination mechanism in software, as for example in [10].

A pheromone in our (software) system is represented as a passive object in an objectspace. Pheromones can thus be read from and put into the objectspace. Also, our ants (agents) live in a graph environment, each node being an objectspace, connected to its neighbors using link objects (a special kind of passive objects).

The data structure to represent a synthetic pheromone is fairly straightforward. The two most important values are a current *strength* of the pheromone (used to discriminate between two pheromone paths - the stronger is the most likely to be followed) and a *direction*, which indicates the direction of the trail. Another property is a *threshold* value. When the strength falls beneath this threshold, the pheromone is deleted from the system.

While describing the data structure of a pheromone is fairly straightforward, adding support to the system so that the pheromones dynamics (an essential part of the coordination mechanism) are also simulated is another cup of tea. Traditional objectspace technology only provides passive objects, that can be put into the objectspace, and active objects, the agents themselves. There is no support for what we call *dynamic objects*: objects that can be put into an objectspace but that can change over time without agent intervention. This is achieved by allowing dynamic objects to execute some code before and after they are put into an objectspace. So, they can change both themselves and any objectspace before and after they are put in or taken out of an objectspace.

An implementation was done in Java as a meta-layer upon CO^3PS[5] as follows. `DynamicObject` is an abstract base class that defines two methods: `preAction(ObjectSpace os,String operationName)` and `postAction(ObjectSpace os, String operationName)`. When a dynamic object is *put in* an objectspace, the objectspace first calls the preAction method with the target objectspace as an argument. This method executes completely before the dynamic object enters the objectspace. Once this is done, and the object is in, the postAction method is called. When a dynamic object is *taken or read* from the space, *before* the object is returned to the agent, the preAction method is called. Afterwards, thus after the agent is in possession of the object, the postAction method is called. Dynamic objects can distinguish between being put in or taken out by looking at the `operationName` parameter, that can be either "Take", "Read" or "Put".

A pheromone is then a subclass of such a dynamic object. Propagation of the pheromone can be done after it is inserted into an objectspace. For a propagating pheromone, the `postAction` method gets all the objectspaces the target objectspace is connected to, and puts a new version (equal to the original pheromone, with a strength decreased by a propagation factor) of itself in all these connected objectspaces. Thus a local propagation of the pheromone is achieved. Since this can trigger a chain effect, it is crucial that the propagation factor is smaller than one. This ensures that the pheromone's strength will eventually fall below its threshold, thus removing it from the system.

Evaporation is implemented using a preAction: before it is put into an objectspace, the pheromone obtains a time stamp with the current time. Now, every time it is taken out of the space, it reduces its own strength with a factor proportional to the difference between the time it was put in (the timestamp obtained earlier), and the current time. Once it has reached a value below it's threshold, it removes itself from the objectspace and thus is not returned to the agent - as if there is no pheromone. Once again, if the evaporation factor is well chosen a pheromone will eventually disappear from the system.

Notice that dynamic objects are more generic than pheromones - they can for example be used to achieve a multicast (similar to the propagation described above, but without changing the contents of the message). Evaluating some of their other possible uses for coordination purposes will be the subject of future work.

3 Case Study: A P2P System

To validate the synthetic pheromones approach, we applied it to the problem of searching data in a distributed P2P system. To this end, we built a simple simulation of such a network. Each peer in the sumulation is represented by a single objectspace. This objectspace contains a number of passive objects, that point to the logical neighbors of that peer (the known peers). Each objectspace can also contain a number of resources, that can be of various kinds (represented by a Resource object in this simple example). On each objectspace peer, a query generator agent is connected that periodically generates a query for a randomly chosen resource. This generator agent simulates a user of the P2P system.

The query is in fact a small mobile agent, that wanders from objectspace to objectspace, searching for its "food": a Resource object to match its query. Once it has found such a resource, it returns to the peer-objectspace it came from, leaving a pheromone on every objectspace along the path it walked. A query agent that is looking around for a certain resource can check at each peer-objectspace whether there are any pheromones that may be useful for the query it is trying to resolve. If so, it is inclined to follow these.

The idea is then that, when some queries are performed frequently, a path will emerge to a resource matching these queries, thus making the search faster, while still being able to adapt to changing circumstances. The algorithm followed by a query agent is the following:

1. at each node, if a matching resource is not found, read all pheromones from the objectspace that lead to a resource that fulfills the agent's query. To this end, each pheromone has a Query object associated with it, representing the query the dropping agent was looking for. Agents can filter on the available pheromones in a space and only take into account pheromones that match their own query. The strength of the pheromone indicates the agent's preference to go in that direction: all strengths are summed, and the probability an agent takes the direction is equal to the strength for the direction divided by the total pheromone strength. When no pheromones are available, the agent simply picks a direction at random.
2. if the resource is here, report to the originating peer that the resource is found, and walk back along the path followed, putting pheromones on every objectspace along the way.

Tests and results. Tests were done on a small network of 200 nodes, with one kind of resources, and new queries for a random resource were generated periodically at each peer.

We did experiments in two kinds of environments: one where the resource the agents had to find was abundant (resource was available in 1 in 10 nodes), and the other where it was sparse (resource in 1 in 100 nodes). First we used a Gnutella-like search agent as reference experiments. This agent is cloned to all possible outgoing directions at every objectspace until it reaches a hop count limit and then dies. This limit was set to three. This agent returned a successful query result in 79% of the cases for the abundant resource setting. It found a result 13% of the time for the sparse resource setting.

For the ant-like agent, every query is resolved by a single agent, and the maximum number of objectspaces it can visit is set to fifteen (this number does not include the hops on the way back, dropping pheromones). The pheromones the agent dropped evaporate with an evaporation factor of 0.9, and propagate with a propagation factor of 0.9.

In the abundant resources setting 32% of the queries were successfully found, over about 400 generated queries. However, after 700 queries, the hit rate increases to 53%. It is obvious that the Gnutella agent has a much better hit rate than the ant-like agent. This is because the Gnutella agent can search a lot more nodes: by construction, the network has an average degree (outgoing links per node) of 6, so it searches $6^3 = 216$ peers per search. In this simple problem, this amounts to almost the complete network (not taking into account loops and isolated nodes). The ant-like agent searches only 15 peers. In this light, the result of the ant-like agent is fairly good. To verify this statement, we ran some tests where we did allow the ant-like agent to clone itself. We allowed a maximum of two clones per new objectspace (thus less than *all* the outgoing directions the Gnutella agent would clone to), and reduced the maximum number of hops from 15 to 5. As expected, this resulted in an increase from 32% to 41% successes.

In the sparse resources setting, the hit percentages were a lot lower. Only 4% of the queries was returned successfully. Allowing the ant agent to clone itself at most twice, as above, resulted in 10% successes, which is no significant difference from the success rate of the Gnutella agent.

Although in most cases the success percentage of the ant-like agent is lower, it can be seen that the difference can be made smaller or even non-existent if we allow the pheromones to stabilize (thus running the simulation longer), or when we allow some limited cloning of the agent. The advantage of this approach is then that it allows a better usage of bandwidth, at the cost of more storage space and CPU power on the individual peers. We think this is a good trade-off, given the fact that bandwidth is still much more expensive than storage space or CPU cycles.

Discussion. Further tests will be performed to assess the performance of the algorithm, as well as refinements of the algorithm. A main problem we will tackle is the controlled evaporation and propagation of pheromones. Tuning of the strength, propagation and evaporation rate is a manual process, and depends much on the concrete problem.

Choosing a good evaporation factor is difficult since it is dependent on the work load of the peers: if lots of agents gather on one peer, they cannot all be scheduled at the same time. As a result, some agents may miss a pheromone because it is already evaporated before they are scheduled to execute. The proposed extension will make the system more adaptive to these kinds of problems.

Another problem to face is be the problem of scalability. Dropping pheromones at each peer may result in a blowup of the space required at each space. There is a trade off here: one can limit this space by setting a larger evaporation factor (meaning pheromones will evaporate quicker), however it will become more difficult for the agents then to put down a lasting path (i.e. the search will have to be much more popular). Another way to limit space complexity is to collapse specific searches into more general searches (e.g. foo*.jpg into f*.jpg). Again, some information is lost, yet storing too much information may lead to an unmanageable system.

4   Conclusion

This is a progress report on the design of a coordination framework for use in large, open distributed environments. We introduced the notion of synthetic pheromones as an interesting coordination strategy, and proposed the concept of dynamic objects as a useful abstraction of these pheromones. As an evaluation, we presented an algorithm for distributed search in a P2P network, and reported results of the simulations.

References

1. Di Caro, G., Dorigo, M.: AntNet: A mobile agents approach to adaptive routing. Technical Report IRIDIA/97-12, Université Libre de Bruxelles, Belgium (1997)
2. Jennings, N.R., Corera, J.M., Laresgoiti, I.: Developing industrial multi-agent systems. In: Proceedings of the First International Conference on Multi-agent Systems, (ICMAS-95). (1995) 423–430
3. Carriero, N., Gelernter, D., Leichter, J.: Distributed data structures in linda. In: Proc. 13th ACM Symposium on Principles of Programming Languages. (1986)
4. Kielmann, T.: Objective Linda: A Coordination Model for Object-Oriented Parallel Programming. PhD thesis, Dept. of Electrical Engineering and Computer Science, University of Siegen, Germany (1997)
5. Holvoet, T.: An Approach for Open Concurrent Software Development. PhD thesis, Department of Computer Science, KULeuven, Belgium (1997)
6. Cabri, G., Leonardi, L., Zambonelli, F.: Mars: A programmable coordination architecture for mobile agents. IEEE Internet Computing 4 (2000) 26–35
7. Murphy, A., Picco, G.P., Roman, G.C.: Lime: a middleware for physical and logical mobility. In: Proc. of the 21th International Conference on Distributed Computing Systems (ICDCS-21). (2001)
8. Coninx, T., Holvoet, T., Berbers, Y.: Using reprogrammable coordination media as mobile agent execution environments. In: ECOOP - European Conference for Object Oriented Programming - 8th Workshop on Mobile Object Systems. (2002)
9. The Gnutella homepage: http://gnutella.wego.com/ (2002)
10. Brueckner, S.: Return from the Ant - Synthetic Ecosystems for Manufacturing Control. PhD thesis, Humboldt University Berlin (2000)

Incentive Mechanisms for Peer-to-Peer Systems

Bin Yu and Munindar P. Singh

Department of Computer Science
North Carolina State University
Raleigh, NC 27695-7535, USA
{byu, mpsingh}@eos.ncsu.edu

Abstract. Most of the existing research in peer-to-peer systems focuses on protocol design and doesn't consider the rationality of each peer. One phenomenon that
should not be ignored is free riding. Some peers simply consume system resources
but contribute nothing to the system. In this paper we present an agent-based peer-
to-peer system, in which each peer is a software agent and the agents cooperate
to search the whole system through referrals. We present a static and a dynamic
pricing mechanism to motivate each agent to behave rationally while still achieving good overall system performance. We study the behavior of the agents under
two pricing mechanisms and evaluate the impact of free riding using simulations.

1 Introduction

Peer-to-peer (P2P) systems are currently receiving considerable interest in both industry
and academia. P2P systems have emerged as a promising way to share files (Napster,
Gnutella, and FreeNet), computing resource (SETI@home), and other valuable information, e.g., reputation information [16]. P2P systems have also been studied in academia
recently, e.g., CAN [10], Chord [14], and Pastry [11]. These projects study distributed
hashing algorithms. Given an object, the algorithms guarantee to locate a peer that has
that object. However, most of the present research has been focused on protocol design
concerns such as file lookup, data replication, and load balancing. Typically, current
approaches don't consider the rationality of each peer and simply assume that the peers
will follow the given protocols.

One phenomenon that should not be ignored is free riding. Since users do not benefit
directly from sharing files with others, many users choose to decline the requests from
others. Free riding is found in many P2P systems but is not punished [4,9]. For example,
in Gnutella, there is a significant amount of free-riding users. Adar and Huberman found
that 70% of the Gnutella users did not share any content files and 90% did not answer
to any queries from other peers [1]. Uncontrolled or excessive free riding in a P2P
network leads to network congestion at some hotspot peers and the degradation of
system performance. It is thus important to design some mechanisms that encourage
peers to contribute and reduce free riding behavior in the P2P networks.

This paper presents an agent-based peer-to-peer system, e.g., a referral system, in
which each peer is a software agent and the agents cooperate to search the whole system
through referrals. Agents are rational and self-interested, and so they may not always
follow the protocols as the designer expects. Individuals participating in a referral system

can contribute in two ways: The first is simply by answering the queries. The second is by actively giving referrals, thus providing the "glue" that holds the system together. In a querying process, the agents could play one of the following three roles:

- *requesters*, who request and obtain answers from the referral systems.
- *providers*, who answer the queries from requesters.
- *intermediaries*, who provide referrals and facilitate interactions among requesters and providers.

The study of referrals is important for the development of agent-based peer-to-peer systems that lack specialized agents such as brokers or facilitators [2]. MINDS and ReferralWeb are two previous approaches for referral systems. MINDS emphasizes learning heuristics for referral generation [5], whereas ReferralWeb focuses on how to bootstrap the referral system [6]. More recently, we focus on the effects of topology dynamics on information flows and consider how to efficiently search large-scale unstructured P2P systems, e.g., social networks, with the help of agents who act only on the basis of local knowledge [17]. However, the problem of *free riding* remains to be addressed. Many agents simply ignore the requests and may not give any answers.

In order to control free riding, we introduce pricing mechanisms into referral systems. We view the referral systems as a strategic game, in which each agent has a utility function over their possible actions. We assume that a *rational* agent plays a *strategy* to maximize its own expected utility. Free-riding is an example of strategy where rational users free ride and consume a resource but do not produce at the same level as their consumption. We study the behavior of agents under two pricing mechanisms and then evaluate the impact of free riding using experiments. Our goal is to design some incentive mechanisms that motivate each agent to behave rationally while still achieving good overall system performance [8,13].

The rest of this paper is organized as follows. Section 2 provides an overview of peer-to-peer systems and referral systems. Section 3 describes the design of pricing mechanisms and related micropayment protocols. Section 4 presents some experimental results. Section 5 summarizes the relevant literature. Section 6 discusses the main themes and some directions for future research.

2   Agent-Based Peer-to-Peer Systems

The term *peer-to-peer* is a generic label for network architectures where all the nodes offer the same services and follow the same behavior. The topology of peer-to-peer systems could be structured, e.g., CAN [10], Chord [14], and Pastry [11], or unstructured, e.g., Napster, Gnutella, and FreeNet. In this paper we only consider the unstructured P2P systems. There are three main alternatives for the implementation of unstructured P2P systems.

- *Centralized indexes:* The best example is Napster. Napster uses a centralized database to index the files each peer has in the system. To look for a file, a peer first sends a request to the database, and then gets a list of other peers who may have the files.

– *Pure P2P:* The best known examples are Gnutella and FreeNet. Both of them have a pure distributed architecture, where there is no centralized database. All the peers in the systems establish a connection with others through request propagation.
– *Hybrid solutions:* Hybrid solutions have recently emerged, for example, FastTrack. FastTrack has some supernodes, which are used for indexing the contents of part of the system and play a major role in the organization of the systems.

2.1 Peer-to-Peer Systems

In P2P systems, a P2P node broadcasts a request to its peers, who propagate the request to their peers, and so on. Messages that are broadcast are labeled by a unique identifier, which is used by the recipient to detect where the message comes from. To reduce the network congestion, all messages are characterized by a given TTL (Time to Live) that defines the scope of searches. On passing through a node, the TTL of a forwarded message is decreased by one. When the TTL reaches zero, the message is dropped.

However, many P2P systems form in an ad-hoc manner and do not consider the interests of the peers and dynamics of the topology. In this paper we present agent-based P2P systems, in which each peer is a software agent. The agent can learn about which of its peers are more effective than others, and optimize the searching process based on its past experience. Next we introduce a class of agent-based peer-to-peer systems, referral systems, in which each peer is an agent, and the agents cooperate to search the whole systems through referrals.

2.2 Referral Systems

Intuitively, in a referral system, each agent maintains a list of its *acquaintances*. A query in natural language specifies what information is being sought. A query from the agent is sent to agents of the selected contacts. An agent who receives a query can decide if it can answer or not (Each agent is associated with a user, who will eventually answer the query.). If not, the agent *may* respond with referrals to others. In referral systems, the requesting agent does not propagate the request to its peers. All referrals are sent back to the requesting agent, who tracks the search process using a graph and adaptively directs or ends the process.

Each agent maintains models of its *acquaintances*. The closest acquaintances are called *neighbors*. An agent sends its query initially only to some of its neighbors. If an agent receives a referral, it may pursue the referral even if the referred party is not already an acquaintance—this is how acquaintances are added. An agent adapts its models of its acquaintances from its interactions with others, e.g., when they ask or answer a query. Each agent is allowed only a small number of neighbors; however, no hard limit is imposed on the number of acquaintances. Periodically, an agent may promote some of its acquaintances to becoming its neighbors and also demote some existing neighbors to make room for the new ones.

Each agent maintains two kinds of models: a *profile* for itself; and an *acquaintance model* for each of its acquaintances. We capture these models via the vector space model (VSM) [12], a classical information retrieval technique. The vectors in VSM are term vectors indicating a weight for each term. In our formulation, the terms correspond to different areas of expertise. The expertise of each agent is modeled as a term vector. Similarly, the query is modeled as a term vector.

In VSM, the similarity between two term vectors is defined as the cosine of the angle between them. We define the similarity between a query and an expertise vector as the cosine of the angle between them, but scaled by the length of the expertise vector. Intuitively, for two agents with expertise in the same direction, the one with the greater expertise is more desirable, whereas the traditional definition would treat them alike.

Definition 1. Given a query vector $Q = \langle q_1, q_2, \ldots, q_n \rangle$ and an expertise vector $E = \langle e_1, e_2, \ldots, e_n \rangle$, the similarity between Q and E is defined as:

$$Q \diamond E = \frac{\sum_{t=1}^{n} q_t e_t}{\sqrt{n \sum_{t=1}^{n} (q_t)^2}}$$

For example, consider a query vector $Q = \langle 0.1, 0.9 \rangle$ and two expertise vectors $E_1 = \langle 0.5, 0.5 \rangle$ and $E_2 = \langle 1, 1 \rangle$. In VSM, E_1 and E_2 are equally similar with the query vector Q, but in our approach, E_2 is better than E_1, since $Q \diamond E_2 > Q \diamond E_1$.

The sociability of an agent reflects its ability to give good referrals. The intuition is that some agents may not be good experts, but may be well connected and may give good referrals. Therefore, the relevance of a neighbor to a given query depends not only on the similarity of the query to the user's expertise, but also on the weight assigned to sociability versus expertise.

Definition 2. The relevance of a query vector Q to P_j is computed as $Q \triangle P_j = (1 - \eta)(Q \diamond E_j) + \eta S_j$, where E_j is the expertise of P_j, S_j is the sociability of P_j, and η is the weight given to sociability.

Our previous work studied the effects of η on the quality of referral systems [18]. We found that a certain emphasis (during learning and querying) on the agents' referring ability improves the quality of the system, but that an overemphasis on referrals at the cost of expertise is not useful. For simplicity, we only consider the case $\eta = 0.3$ here.

Each agent learns its profile and its acquaintance models based on an evaluation of the answers received as well as the referrals that led to them. A *referral graph* encodes how the computation spreads as a query originates from an agent and referrals or answers are sent back to this agent.

Definition 3. A referral r to A_j returned from A_i is written as $\langle A_i, A_j \rangle$, we say A_i is a *parent* of A_j and A_j is a *child* of A_i.

For convenience, we include the initial query among the referrals. This enables us to write a referral chain of length l for a query originating with A_r as $\langle A_r, A_1, \ldots, A_l \rangle$. Then *ancestor* and *descendant* are easily defined based on parent and child, respectively.

The referral chains for a given query induce a directed graph whose root is the originating agent. The *depth* of a referral is its distance on the shortest path from the root. Our algorithms ensure that the graph remains acyclic.

Definition 4. A referral graph $G(Q)$ for a query Q is a rooted directed graph (A_r, Λ, R), where A_r is the requesting agent (root), $\Lambda = \{A_1, A_2, \ldots, A_n\}$ is a finite set of agents (vertices) that includes A_r, $R \subseteq \Lambda \times \Lambda$ is a set of referrals (edges).

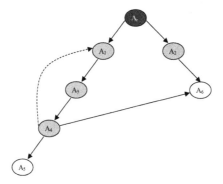

Fig. 1. A referral graph generated from a query. The requesting agent is black; the agents that have been queried are gray; the agent who have not been queried are white.

Definition 5. A referral $r = \langle A_i, A_j \rangle$ is *redundant* for a referral graph (A_r, Λ, R), if and only if $A_i, A_j \in \Lambda$ and A_j is an ancestor of A_i with respect to R.

Clearly, an acyclic referral graph includes no redundant referrals. In the context of Figure 1, a referral $\langle A_4, A_1 \rangle$ would be redundant, since A_1 is an ancestor of A_4. Referral $\langle A_4, A_2 \rangle$ is not redundant, since it introduces no cycles.

3   Mechanism Design

Much of the existing research in P2P systems, including referral systems, assumes that peers or agents will always follow the protocols. However, some agents, representing rational users, may deviate from a designed protocol in order to maximize their outcome. Recently, Shneidman and Parkes advocate mechanism design of P2P systems, in which peers are expected to be rational and self-interested [13]. Feigenbaum and Shenker consider similar problems in distributed algorithmic design. They discuss the challenges of distributed mechanism design in P2P systems and overlay networks with techniques like redundancy and cryptography [3].

We study the mechanism design problem in the context of referral systems. We discuss some micropayment protocols in referral systems, and then study the behavior of agents and the impact of free riding using experiments.

3.1   Types of Agents in Referral Systems

Given a query, some agents may respond unconditionally, and others may respond only if they have some rewards. We categorize the agents in referral systems as one of the following three types.

- **Altruistic:** agents always follow the protocols and give answers or referrals if they can.
- **Rational:** agents play a strategy to maximize their expected outcome.

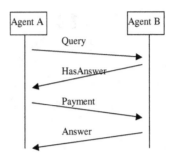

Fig. 2. A referring process involving two agents A and B, where A sends a query to B.

- **Irrational:** agents do not follow a strategy modeled by the mechanism. Antisocial or malicious agents, for instance, prefer strategies that hurt other agents even when these strategies reduce their own utility.

The altruistic and irrational agents are outside of our discussion. In this paper we only focus on rational agents that can strategize about their behavior.

3.2   Micropayment Protocol

A natural approach is to charge agents for every query and to reward them for every referral or answer. [1] In this section we first describe a simple micropayment mechanism, in which the costs for referrals and answers are fixed for all agents. We then present a more complex protocol, where the costs are dynamic. Suppose,

- α is the cost or reward for one or more referrals given for a query.
- β is the cost or reward for an answer to a query.
- T is the initial budget for each agent, e.g., 500 points.

We illustrate the micropayment protocol using two simple examples.

- First, we consider the situation only involving two agents A and B. Agent A sends a query to one of its neighbors B. If agent B finds that it can answer the query, it will answer with a *HasAnswer* message. Agent A will decide if it would like to pay. If A agrees and pays the necessary points, agent B will send the answer to A. In this process,
    - The cost for agent A is β and the balance for agent A becomes $T - \beta$.
    - The reward for agent B is β and the balance for agent B becomes $T + \beta$.
- Second, we consider the situation involving three agents A, B, and C. Agent A sends a query to B, and B finds that it cannot answer the query. However, B has some neighbors who may answer the query from A. B responds with a *HasReferral* message. Agent A will decide if it would like to pay for the referrals. Agent A

---

[1] Another possible payment model is a flat rate membership fee. However, the flat fees are unrelated to agent's strategies, and may not be helpful for the free riding problem.

receives a set of referrals after it pays to B. Suppose one of the referrals leads to agent C and all others lead to dead-ends. C responds with an answer after A pays the points to C.

- The cost for agent A is $\alpha + \beta$ and the balance for agent A becomes $T - \alpha - \beta$.
- The reward for agent B is α and the balance for agent B becomes $T + \alpha$.
- The reward for agent C is β and the balance for agent C becomes $T + \beta$.

Algorithm 1 Constructing a referral graph

1: Suppose agent A_r is the requesting agent, set Λ is the agents being visited.
2: Initially $\Lambda = \{A_r\}$. For any agent $A_i \in \Lambda$, A_r sends a query to A_i.
3: (If $A_i = A_r$, it means that A_r first sends a query to some of its neighbors).
4: **if** (A_i returns a *HasAnswer* message) **then**
5:     A_r pays the points to A_i
6:     A_r receives the answer from A_i
7: **else if** (A_i returns a *HasReferral* message) **then**
8:     A_r pays the points to A_i
9:     A_r receives a set of referrals from A_i
10:    For any referral $r = \langle A_i, A_j \rangle$,
11:    **if** ($A_j \notin \Lambda$) **then**
12:       A_r appends r to the referral graph
13:       A_r adds A_j into Λ
14:    **else if** ($A_j \in \Lambda$) and ($A_j \neq ancestor(A_i)$) **then**
15:       A_r appends r to the referral graph
16:    **else**
17:       Ignore referral r
18:    **end if**
19: **end if**

Algorithm 1 presents the process of constructing a referral graph from a set of referrals. For example, in Figure 1, requesting agent A_r sends a query to its neighbors A_1 and A_2. A_1 refers to A_3, who refers to A_4. A_4 refers to A_1, A_5, and A_6. A_2 refers A_6. Suppose A_5 and A_6 claim they have the answer, and A_r pays to both of them. Eventually A_6 returns an answer, but A_5 doesn't. The costs (rewards) for these agents are,

- The cost for A_r is $4\alpha + 2\beta$.
- The reward for each of A_1, A_2, A_3, and A_4 is α.
- The reward for each of A_5 and A_6 is β.

3.3 Dynamic Pricing

A more complex case is that the costs or rewards are dynamic. Since different agents provide different qualities of services and they may place different prices for their referrals and answers. Also, some agents claim they have the answers or referrals, but they may not respond after the requesting agent pays, e.g., A_5 in Figure 1. The requesting agent needs to decide which service it would like to buy, based on the history of responding agents, and the number of agents who can provide the services.

We assume that each responding agent produces results randomized around a certain quality for referrals and answers. But the quality of referrals and answers from different agents may be different. As mentioned in Section 2, each agent has a profile and a set of acquaintance models. Suppose A_r is the requesting agent, and $\{A_1, A_2, \ldots, A_n\}$ are a set of acquaintances of A_r. A_r has two *selling prices* in its profile: α'_{A_r} for one or more referrals (given for a specific query), and β'_{A_r} for an answer. Similarly, for any agent A_i, $1 \le i \le n$, A_r has two *reserve prices* in A_i's acquaintance model: α_{A_i} for one or more referrals and β_{A_i} for an answer.

The values of α and β are used as the baselines for both selling prices and reserve prices. For example, at time t_0 (which is local to agent A_r), given a requesting agent A_r and any of its acquaintances A_i,

$$\alpha'_{A_r}(t_0) = \alpha_{A_i}(t_0) = \alpha$$
$$\beta'_{A_r}(t_0) = \beta_{A_i}(t_0) = \beta$$

The selling prices are updated as follows

- The two selling prices will decay with a decaying coefficient ρ at every time interval t, where $0 < \rho < 1$. For example, given a agent A_r, its selling price for a referring service at time $t_0 + t$ is updated as $\alpha'_{A_r}(t_0 + t) = \rho * \alpha'_{A_r}(t_0)$.
- The selling prices of a referring service or an answer will increase with a factor σ when any other agents would like to pay the price, where $1 < \sigma < 2$.

The reserve prices are used to estimate if the selling prices from other agents are reasonable. For example, at time t_i, agent A_r receives a set of sell bids of answers from sellers $\{A_1, A_2, \ldots, A_m\}$. For any seller A_j, the reward for agent A_r is

$$\beta_{A_j}(t_i) - \beta'_{A_j}(t_i)$$

where $\beta_{A_j}(t_i)$ is the reserve price of an answer in the acquaintance model for A_j at time t_i and $\beta'_{A_j}(t_i)$ is the selling price of an answer in the profile of agent A_j.

Similarly, for referring services, the requesting agent A_r computes the reward as

$$\alpha_{A_j}(t_i) - \alpha'_{A_j}(t_i)$$

Given a set of referring services or answers, the requesting agent will choose the services from the highest to the lowest rewards. After the requesting agent receives a service, it or its user will evaluate the quality of the service and revise the reserve price for the service. The reserve prices are updated as follows at time t_i if the agent is satisfied with the service from agent A_j,

$$\alpha_{A_j}(t_i) = \alpha_{A_j}(t_i) + \omega_1 \text{ (for referring services)}$$
$$\beta_{A_j}(t_i) = \beta_{A_j}(t_i) + \omega_2 \text{ (for answers)}$$

Otherwise,

$$\alpha_{A_j}(t_i) = \alpha_{A_j}(t_i) - \omega_1 \text{ (for referring services)}$$
$$\beta_{A_j}(t_i) = \beta_{A_j}(t_i) - \omega_2 \text{ (for answers)}$$

where $0 < \omega_1 < \alpha$ and $0 < \omega_2 < \beta$.

4 Experimental Results

Our experiments are based on an extension of a simulation testbed previously developed for information access [18]. The experiments involve between 100 and 500 agents. Each agent is modeled in terms of its *interest* (describing the services it is interested in purchasing) and its *expertise* (describing the services it is able to offer). Both interest and expertise are captured as terms vectors of dimension 5.

The agents are limited in the number of neighbors they may have, here 4. The length of each referral chain is limited to 4. Moreover, we introduce a probability φ between 0 and 1 to model any free riding agents A_i. Agent A_i will generate an answer from its *expertise* vector upon receiving a query with the probability φ even when there is a good match between the query and its expertise vector.

In each simulation cycle, we randomly designate an agent to be the requester. An agent may query some of its neighbors. When an agent receives a query, it may answer the query based on its expertise vector, or may give a referral to some of its neighbors. The originating agent collects all possible referrals, and continues the process by following some of the suggested referrals. Each agent may keep track of certain acquaintances. In our simulation, we allow 12 acquaintances. Periodically, each agent decides which of its acquaintances are dropped and which are promoted to neighbors (a subset of acquaintances).

We initialize the network of agents in the following manner. Following Watts and Strogatz [15], we begin from a ring but, unlike them, we allow for edges to be directed. We use a regular ring with 100 nodes, and 4 out-edges per node (to its neighbors) as a starting point for the experiment.

The initial budget for each agent is 500. The baselines for prices of a referring service and an answer are 1 and 10, respectively. Other parameters for dynamic pricings are defined as follows,

- Decaying coefficient $\rho = 0.9$ for every 100 cycles.
- Factor $\sigma = 1.1$.
- Other factors $\omega_1 = 0.1$, $\omega_2 = 1$ (We choose the values of ω_1 and ω_2 in the same ratio as α and β).

Note that all these parameters are fixed and equal for all agents. An answer is good if and only if the similarity value between the query and the answer is above 0.2.

4.1 Balance of the Free Rider

We suppose, of the total 100 agents, only one agent is a free rider. Its responding probability φ is zero. Figure 3 shows the balance of the free riding agent under fixed and dynamic micropayment protocols. As intuitively expected, the free riding agent cannot survive under either micropayment protocol. The balance of the free riding agent becomes zero after 1200 cycles under fixed pricing mechanism and 900 cycles under dynamic pricing mechanism. The agent who runs out of its budget has to purchase more points with money. In a sense, no one can free ride any more, because they have to pay for the services they receive from others.

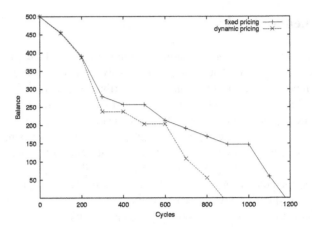

Fig. 3. Balances of the free riding agent under different pricing mechanisms

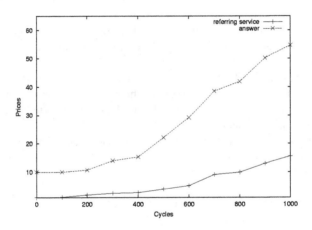

Fig. 4. Selling prices of high-quality services

4.2   Prices for High-Quality Services

Our second experiment studies the selling prices of referrals and answers for an expert agent, where each dimension of its expertise vector is initialized as 1. For example, the selling price of answers (from the expert agent) increases from 10 to about 55 and the selling price of referrals increases from 1 to 15 after 1000 cycles (Figure 4). A consequence of dynamic pricing is that the requesting agents have to pay more for the high-quality services. The prices will help to adjust the traffic at these high-quality service providers. Note that the selling prices for answers and referral from the expert agent may decrease if no agents are willing to pay the prices.

5   Related Work

Golle *et al.* first use a game theoretic approach to analyze the free riding problem in peer-to-peer file sharing systems [4]. They analyze equilibria of user strategies under several micropayment mechanisms. Our micropayment protocol with fixed pricing is similar to theirs. More recently, Ramaswamy and Liu use utility functions to measure the usefulness of peers, e.g., the number of files, the total size of the data, and the popularity of the files, and describe a utility based scheme to control free riding in peer-to-peer systems [9]. Both of the above approaches study the free riding problem in P2P file sharing systems, while we focus on the referral systems, in which the prices of services can be either fixed or dynamic.

Shneidman and Parkes discuss the notions of rationality and self-interest in P2P systems [13]. Similar ideas can also be found in Distributed Algorithmic Mechanism Design (DAMD) [3]. Shneidman and Parkes highlight some open problems in DAMD and specially P2P systems, e.g., computational complexity of mechanisms and effects of mechanism design on network topology formation.

Pricing or micropayment is only one incentive mechanism. Krishnan *et al.* propose other mechanisms to reduce the problem of free riding in P2P systems [7]. They develop some non-priced incentives to encourage efficient behavior in P2P users. Some examples include delay time (e.g., users who share more content with the system have higher priority), network membership (e.g., removing non-sharing members from the systems), or peer ratings of content providers. However, empirical analysis is needed to measure the impact of these mechanisms.

6   Conclusion

This paper examines the problem of free riding in agent-based peer-to-peer systems, especially referral systems. We introduce two classes of micropayment protocols and analyze the strategies of agents under these protocols. Our paper only provides a preliminary study of mechanism design in referral systems. For example, we simply assume that the qualities of services are consistent for each agent. Also, we don't consider the topology of referral graphs and its effects on dynamic pricing. In future work, we plan to focus on these problems and develop more efficient and incentive compatible mechanisms for referral systems.

Acknowledgements. This research was supported by the National Science Foundation under grant ITR-0081742. We are indebted to the anonymous reviewers for their helpful comments.

References

1. E. Adar and B. Huberman. Free riding on Gnutella. *First Monday*, 5(10), 2000.
2. K. Decker, K. Sycara, and M. Williamson. Middle-agents for the Internet. In *Proceedings of the International Joint Conference on Artificial Intelligence (IJCAI)*, pages 578–583, 1997.

3. J. Feigenbaum and S. Shenker. Distributed algorithmic mechanism design: Recent results and future directions. In *Proceedings of the Sixth International Workshop on Discrete Algorithms and Methods for Mobile Computing and Communications*, pages 1–13, 2002.
4. P. Golle, K. Leyton-Brown, I. Mironov, and M. Lillibridge. Incentives for sharing in peer-to-peer networks. In *Proceedings of the Second International Workshop on Electronic Commerce*, pages 75–87, 2001.
5. M. N. Huhns, U. Mukhopadhyay, L. M. Stephens, and R. D. Bonnell. DAI for document retrieval: The MINDS project. In M. N. Huhns, editor, *Distributed Artificial Intelligence*, pages 249–283. Pitman/Morgan Kaufmann, London, 1987.
6. H. Kautz, B. Selman, and M. Shah. The hidden Web. *AI Magazine*, 18(2):27–36, 1997.
7. R. Krishnan, M. D. Smith, and R. Telang. The economics of peer-to-peer networks, 2002. working paper, Carnegie Mellon University.
8. M. J. Osborne and A. Rubinstein. *A Course in Game Theory*. MIT Press, Cambridge, MA, 1994.
9. L. Ramaswamy and L. Liu. Free riding: a new challenge for peer-to-peer file sharing systems. In *Proceedings of Hawaii International Conference on Systems Science 36*, 2003.
10. S. Ratnasamy, P. Francis, M. Handley, R. Karp, and S. Shenker. A scalable content-addressable network. In *Proceedings of ACM SIGCOMM*, pages 161–172, 2001.
11. A. Rowstron and P. Druschel. Pastry: Scalable, distributed object location and routing for large-scale peer-to-peer systems. In *Proceedings of the 18nd IFIP/ACM International Conference on Distributed Systems Platforms*, pages 329–350, 2001.
12. G. Salton and M. McGill. *An Introduction to Modern Information Retrieval*. McGraw-Hill, New York, 1983.
13. J. Shneidman and D. Parkes. Rationality and self-interest in peer-to-peer networks. In *Proceedings of Second International Workshop on Peer-to-Peer Systems*, 2003.
14. I. Stoica, R. Morris, D. Karger, M. F. Kaashoek, and H. Balakrishnan. Chord: A scalable peer-to-peer lookup service for internet applications. In *Proceedings of ACM SIGCOMM*, pages 149–160, 2001.
15. D. J. Watts and S. H. Strogatz. Collective dynamics of 'small-world' networks. *Nature*, 393:440–442, June 1998.
16. B. Yu and M. P. Singh. An evidential model of distributed reputation management. In *Proceedings of First International Joint Conference on Autonomous Agents and Multiagent Systems*, pages 294–301, 2002.
17. B. Yu and M. P. Singh. Searching social networks. In *Proceedings of Second International Joint Conference on Autonomous Agents and Multiagent Systems*, pages 65–72, 2003.
18. B. Yu, M. Venkatraman, and M. P. Singh. An adaptive social network for information access: Theoretical and experimental results. *Applied Artificial Intelligence*, 17(1):21–38, 2003.

A Taxonomy of Incentive Patterns
The Design Space of Incentives for Cooperation*

Philipp Obreiter and Jens Nimis

Institute for Program Structures and Data Organization
Universität Karlsruhe (TH)
D-76128 Karlsruhe, Germany
{obreiter,nimis}@ipd.uni-karlsruhe.de

Abstract. Peer-to-peer systems, multi-agent systems, and ad hoc networks aim at exploiting synergies that result from cooperation. Yet, these systems are composed of autonomous entities that are free to decide whether to cooperate or not. Hence, incentives are indispensable to induce cooperation between autonomous entities. In this paper, we introduce incentive patterns as a means of systematically conceiving incentive schemes with respect to the specifics of the application environment. Based on economics, we derive several incentive patterns and discuss them with respect to a set of general characteristics. Consequently, we propose a taxonomy that classifies the derived incentive patterns.

1 Introduction

Peer-to-peer (P2P) systems and multi-agent systems (MAS) share many of their central concepts and problems, e.g. autonomy and coordination of the participants. One common key concept is the exploitation of synergy, i.e. the combination of capabilities local to individual participants in order to emerge system behaviors that are more powerful than the sum of the individual capabilities. P2P sharing systems like Gnutella, Napster, and others constitute huge distributed databases, while their participants have to provide disk space and bandwidth for only a few data sets. For MAS, consider the numerous supply chain management (SCM) applications. Based on their local knowledge, supplier and recipient agents from different organizations try to optimize the flow of material along a supply chain, possibly rescheduling their local fabrication plans.

The concept of synergy also plays a crucial role for ad hoc networks. There, the compensation for the missing network infrastructure must evolve from the end users' devices. They take over infrastructural tasks in order to ensure the network's effectiveness. Therefore, cooperation among the end users' devices becomes necessary. However, the absence of infrastructure implicates the lack of

---

* The work done for this paper is partially sponsored by the German Research Community (DFG) in the context of the priority program (SPP) no. 1083 and no. 1140. We thank Birgitta König-Ries and Sokshee Goh for their comments on this paper.

G. Moro, C. Sartori, and M.P. Singh (Eds.): AP2PC 2003, LNAI 2872, pp. 89–100, 2004.

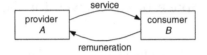

Fig. 1. The terminology of elementary cooperation

any centralized authority that enforces cooperative behavior of the participating devices.

In the context of our work, the common characteristics of P2P systems, MAS, and ad hoc networks are as follows: They all build upon distributed systems of autonomous entities which need cooperation in order to achieve their local and global goals which leads to consumption of their possibly limited resources.

A precise analysis of cooperation among participants reveals the roles that an entity may assume. In [1], it is pointed out that cooperation may be decomposed into a set of elementary cooperations. As the elementary constituent of cooperation, an entity A (*provider*) provides a service that is beneficial for an entity B (*consumer*)[1]. The consumer has to remunerate the provider in order to compensate for its resource consumption. Consequently, this incentive may lead to further provision of services. In the following, cooperative behavior is treated on the elementary provider-consumer level. Figure 1 interrelates the proposed terms.

Incentive schemes play a central role for cooperation in open distributed systems of autonomous entities. Yet, up to now, they are not subject to the system design processes. The choice and further development of incentive schemes is contingent on several system specifics. At the same time, it opens up a new design space. In this paper, we will give a pattern based approach to exploit this new design space.

The history of economics [2] has known several incentive patterns for cooperation, i.e. the provision of goods and services. Therefore, as a guideline for identifying and classifying incentive patterns, it seems to be a promising idea to build a taxonomy based on such economic incentive patterns [3]. This taxonomy should not be based on chronology, but on the characteristics that make a pattern usable or unusable in certain situations.

Outline. The remainder of this paper is organized as follows. Section 2 introduces the notion of incentive patterns and suggests a set of general characteristics. Consequently, we introduce incentive patterns that are trust based (Section 3) and trade based (Section 4). In Section 5, we propose a taxonomy of incentive patterns and compare them to the aforementioned characteristics. We review related approaches in Section 6. Finally, we conclude the paper in Section 7.

An extended version of this paper is available as technical report [4].

---

[1] In our referenced work [1], which has its roots in the area of ad hoc networks, provider and consumer are called *agent entity* and *principal entity*. For sake of clarity this has been changed in this context.

2 Incentives Patterns

Existing incentive schemes apply various patterns of stimulating the provision of services. In this section, we introduce the notion of such incentive patterns and point out the need for a thorough analysis of them. Therefore, we suggest a set of general characteristics that are required for the classification of incentive patterns.

An *incentive pattern* is a pattern of stimulating cooperation. It comprises a set of abstract mechanisms that incentive schemes may apply. If the characteristics of the respective incentive patterns are known, incentive schemes may be conceived more systematically by taking into account the specifics of the application environment and matching them to appropriate incentive patterns. Such systematic design of incentives for cooperation goes beyond the abstract matching of [1], since it considers the specifics of the respective protocols. In this paper, we enlarge the design space of incentive schemes by systematically identifying and classifying further incentive patterns.

General Characteristics. We propose a set of general characteristics that captures the specifics and differences of incentive patterns[2].

- **Roles:** In general, the incentive pattern stimulates an entity to act as provider for a consumer. Then, the roles of the cooperating entities are asymmetric. However, an incentive pattern may impose symmetric roles by stipulating that the consumer has to provide a service in return at the same time.
- **Remuneration:** In most incentive patterns, the consumer remunerates the provider. Depending on the incentive pattern, remuneration assumes a specific form that is called *remuneration type* [1]. Every remunerating incentive pattern introduces its own type. For instance, reputation and checks are both remuneration types. Remuneration types differ with respect to their inherent *granularity*. The remuneration's granularity is implied by the granularity of the respective remuneration type. Hence, coarse remuneration types impose constraints on remuneration assessment. The amount of the remuneration is *assessed* by the consumer and/or the provider. The remuneration is not necessarily obtained and *stored* by the provider. The consumer may also store a remuneration that consists in remembering prior services of the provider. For some remuneration types, remuneration may be *transferred* to third parties. A remunerating incentive pattern should *enforce* the reciprocation of the provider. There are different degrees of incertitude for the provider with regard to the probability of such reciprocation.
- **Trust:** Depending on the incentive pattern, trust either constitutes an incentive for cooperation or it is a prerequisite for remuneration mechanisms.

---

[2] Due to space limitations, we forego discussion of *uncooperative behavior* and *implementability in ad hoc networks*. These characteristics are discussed in [4]. Further characteristics are supposable regarding the Quality-of-Service, e.g., fault-tolerance and performance of the incentive patterns.

Regardless of the incentive pattern, the consumer has to ensure that the provider executes the respective service. Therefore, in this paper, we focus on trust that is necessary for assuring the validity of the remuneration. The provider has to be convinced that its remuneration is valid and worthwhile. Depending on the incentive pattern, the provider must *trust* the consumer or dedicated entities. Trust mechanisms may necessitate to *disclose* the *identity* of the consumer or provider.

- **Scalability:** In this context, scalability refers to the number of entities that apply the incentive pattern. In general, incentive patterns do not scale well with the number of trusted entities.

3   Trust Based Incentive Patterns

At first, we take a closer look on trust which is a straightforward incentive for cooperation. In trust based incentive patterns, the provider executes the demanded service, if it trusts the consumer. Therefore, the consumer does not explicitly remunerate the provider. The provider's trust in the consumer is twofold: The service execution is beneficial for the provider either because it trusts in sharing the same goals with the consumer or because it believes in increasing other entities' cooperativeness.

3.1   The Collective Pattern

Incentive. A collective is a set of entities with mutual trust and unconditional cooperation. The incentive for cooperation in a collective stems from being member of the same collective.

Properties. The provider does not need any remuneration, but it has to ensure that the consumer is part of the same collective. Being a set of entities, a collective is the generalization of an entity. Hence, the remaining incentive patterns may be combined with the collective pattern by applying the notion of provider and consumer to collectives.

3.2   The Community Pattern

Incentive. A community is a group of entities whose incentives for cooperation are based on the trust gained by providing services to other entities of the community. Good reputation is required in order to consume services of other entities.

Properties. The consumer remunerates by increasing its trust in the provider. In this regard, remuneration assessment is performed by the consumer since it consists of re-assessing trust in the provider. Other entities may also increase their trust in the provider if they are able to observe[3] the elementary cooperation. The provider has no guarantees with regard to the effectiveness of the

---

[3] In [1,4], such observation is called sniffing.

reciprocation since it cannot intervene in the trust assessment of the consumer and the observing entities.

An entity's trustworthiness is only known by prior cooperation partners or, in case of observation, by other entities in the proximity. Therefore, good reputation only pays off in communities with stable or localized cooperation patterns [5]. As a result, a community scales badly with respect to the number of its entities. In order to further enforce reciprocation, local trust assessments are generally disseminated throughout the community. Then, entities get known the reputation of an arbitrary entity. However, such disseminations require mechanisms to counter defamations and unjustified praising. In addition, entities that have a poor reputation might still be able to alter their identities and, thus, avert retaliation [6].

In communities, trust is tightly coupled with the remuneration type, i.e., reputation. Other incentive patterns may employ mechanisms of communities for their trust management.

4   Trade Based Incentive Patterns

On contrary to trust based incentive patterns, explicitness of remuneration might be desirable. Such explicit remuneration consists of a service in return. Incentive patterns that are based on this principle are depicted as *trade based incentive patterns*. We differentiate between two types of trade. The consumer might execute the service in return *immediately* during or after the provider's service provision. Alternatively, the consumer might *promise* the service in return.

4.1   Immediate Service in Return – The Barter Trade Pattern

The assumption of mutual trust is too restrictive for highly volatile networks that restrict inter-entity cooperation to one or two elementary cooperations. In such a case, an incentive pattern cannot assume any future cooperation in order to stimulate cooperation. A straightforward solution to this problem consists of abandoning the asymmetry of the provider-consumer pair. This is done by superposing two elementary cooperations so that each entity is provider and consumer at the same time.

Incentive. Barter trade is defined as the exchange of services. Hence, the consumer remunerates the provider by simultaneously providing a service in return.

Properties. The bad scalability of communities ensues from the temporal uncoupling of the initial service and the service in return. Therefore, the barter trade incentive pattern insists on an immediate service in return by the consumer. Hence, reciprocation is effectively enforced. In barter trade, the two participating entities may remain anonymous. Trust is only required if the service in return is not executed simultaneously. Consequently, the barter trade pattern scales better than trust based incentive patterns.

The assessment of the remuneration is bound to the granularity of the service in return which may be too coarse. The negotiation and assessment of the remuneration is complex because two services are assessed at the same time. In any case, an entity only acts as provider if it is interested in a service that the consumer offers.

4.2   Promised Service in Return – Bond Based Incentive Patterns

In general, barter's superposing of two elementary cooperations is infeasible since the provider normally does not need an immediate service in return. Yet, given the fact that the provider is likely to act as consumer in a subsequent elementary cooperation, it might be stimulated by promising a service in return in the future. Bond based incentive patterns stipulate that the consumer hands over a *bond* that promises such a service in return to the provider.

In the following, we introduce key terms the facilitate the discussion of bond based incentive patterns. The *issuer* of a bond is the entity that certifies the bond's promise. The *debtor* of a bond is the entity that, according to the promise, will execute the service in return. Entities that are specialized in the assumption of the debtor's role are called *dedicated debtors*. The consumer is not necessarily the issuer of the bond since it might have acquired the bond in the course of another elementary cooperation. In this regard, promised services in return may be *transferred*. A bond is a *bearer bond* if the services that it promises are arbitrarily transferrable. In the remainder of this section, we propose a generic discussion of bonds and, subsequently, suggest and examine specific bond types.

Incentive. The consumer remunerates the provider by handing over a bond. In this regard, an entity provides a service in order to be promised a service in return.

Properties. On contrary to barter trade, bonds uncouple the initial service and the service in return. Furthermore, the provider is in possession of its remuneration, as opposed to the community pattern.

The bond's promise is not bound to the granularity of the service in return since the promise may specify a fraction of services. This makes sense for entities that accumulate several bonds before honoring them at the debtor. As for the remuneration assessment, the provider demands an extra charge for the deferment and the incertitude regarding the service in return.

The transferability of bearer bonds is desirable since the provider may retransfer the bond for remuneration in subsequent cooperations. However, transferability demands for mechanisms that prevent or detect *double spending* of bonds [7]. Otherwise, the reciprocation of the bond's bearer cannot be enforced.

In general, the debtor of a bond has to disclose its identity in order to prove its trustworthiness. However, the debtor is eager to alter its identity in order to escape from having to provide the service in return.

Table 1. Bond types

Bond	debtor is any party	dedicated debtor		Bearer bond	debtor is any party	dedicated debtor
issuer is debtor	note			issuer is debtor	bearer note	banknote
issuer is not debtor	bill	check		issuer is not debtor	bearer bill	bearer check

Specific Bond Types. In the following, we propose specific bond types and discuss their characteristics. The bond types are illustrated in Figure 1. Each of them defines a bond based incentive pattern[4]. The different types of bonds are discernable with regard to the following five criteria[5]:

1. *Transferability*[6]: May the bond be transferred to another entity?
2. *Issuer vs. debtor:* Does the issuer embody the role of the debtor?
3. *Dedicated entities:* Is the debtor a dedicated debtor?
4. *Delivery*[7]: Is the bond handed over to the provider or to the debtor?
5. *Time of service in return*[8]: When is the service in return provided?

Notes and bearer notes. A *(bearer) note* is a (bearer) bond that is issued by its debtor. This means that the issuer has to disclose its identity in order to prove its trustworthiness. Since every entity may issue a note, this demands for keeping track of the reputation of every entity. Therefore, the (bearer) note pattern does not scale well.

If disseminations are prohibited, the community pattern is similar to the note pattern. Their dissimilarities accrue from the explicitness of remuneration.

Bills and bearer bills. A *(bearer) bill* is a (bearer) bond the issuer and debtor of which differ. Upon receipt of a bill, the provider has to ensure that the debtor exists and is willing to provide the promised service in return on behalf of the bill's issuer.

An entity only accepts a bill if the debtor is trusted to provide the service in return or to retaliate on the issuer. Hence, a bill requires a procuration of the

---

[4] The labelling of bonds based incentive patterns is slightly different than in [4]. There, the bearer check pattern is called banking pattern.

[5] Due to space limitations, we will focus on the first three criteria. A more detailed discussion of the criteria is found in our subsequent work [3].

[6] For clarity reasons, we only consider the two extremes of transferability, i.e., prohibited transferability (bonds) and unrestricted transferability (bearer bonds). In practice, the transferability of bonds is restricted to a specific number of handovers. An important special case are bonds that may only be transferred once.

[7] This criterion is identified in [8]. Delivery to the provider and to the debtor is called direct payment and indirect payment respectively.

[8] The service in return is either provided on presentation of the bond or at a pre-agreed time interval or point of time.

debtor. There are two types of such procuration. On the one hand, an *unlimited procuration* may be appropriate if the debtor is able to retaliate on the issuer if the bill should not have been issued. On the other hand, the scope of a *limited procuration* is bound to a specific bill. A bearer note could represent such limited procuration.

Checks and bearer checks. A *(bearer) check* is a (bearer) bill the debtor of which is a dedicated debtor. Checks are based on the metaphor of banking. Every entity (*account holder*) possesses an account that is managed by a dedicated debtor (the entity's *bank*). The account's balance is a scalar that specifies how many reference services the bank is willing to execute on behalf of the account holder. The consumer remunerates the provider by issuing a check the debtor of which is its bank. The check bearer presents the check to its bank so that its account is credited. If the check bearer's bank differs from the check issuer's one, an inter-bank transaction is required.

In general, each bank is able to retaliate upon an entity for having issued a check without its consent[9]. Therefore, the reciprocation of the provider is enforced more effectively. In addition, only the banks have to disclose their identity and to be trustworthy. Consequently, the (bearer) check pattern scales better than the (bearer) bill pattern. Its scale is only bound to the accessibility of banks and the scale of inter-bank transactions.

Banknotes. A *banknote* is a bearer note[10] that is issued by a dedicated debtor (*bank*). Entities prefer banknotes to bearer notes since such a bank is generally more reachable and trustworthy than common entities. This yields better scalability of the banknote pattern if compared with the (bearer) note pattern. In addition, the bearer of the banknote might not have to disclose its identity[11]. However, the provider has to trust in the banknotes' genuineness. Therefore, either banknotes are unforgeable or, in case of infeasibility of the unforgeability assumption, the consumer has to be trusted, which hinders its anonymity.

5   Taxonomy and Characteristics of Incentive Patterns

In the last sections, we identified several incentive patterns in order to capture and enlarge the design space of incentive schemes. Yet, the ultimate goal of incentive patterns is to systematically conceive incentive schemes by taking into account the specifics of the application environment and matching them to appropriate incentive patterns. Therefore, in this section, we classify the proposed

---

[9] Such consent is not required to be explicit since it may be expressed in a unlimited procuration.

[10] It makes sense to base the definition of banknotes on bearer notes. Otherwise, they can only be used in cooperations with dedicated entities which contradicts the common notion of banknotes in economics.

[11] Nevertheless, most approaches that cope with double spending demand for the disclosure of the bearer's identity.

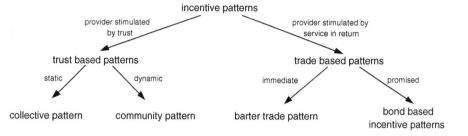

Fig. 2. Taxonomy of incentive patterns

incentive patterns and summarize their characteristics in order to clarify their interrelationship and applicability.

Taxonomy. In Figure 2, a taxonomy of the proposed economic incentive patterns is given. In trust based incentive patterns, the provider is stimulated by the trust it has in the consumer. Trust either accrues from membership *(collective pattern)* or it is subject to entities' behavior and, thus, adapts dynamically *(community pattern)*. On contrary, in trade based incentive patterns, the provider is stimulated by a service in return that is either executed immediately *(barter trade pattern)* or promised *(bond based incentive patterns)*.

Characteristics. The main properties of the proposed incentive patterns are summarized in Table 2. The collective and community pattern seem to be too restrictive with regard to their scalability and fuzzy accounting. However, they are easy to implement and can be combined with other patterns. On the one hand, collectives generalize the notion of entities. On the other hand, communities merge remuneration and trust management. Therefore, their mechanisms provide a sound basis for the assessment of trustworthiness in the other incentive patterns. Barter trade exhibits several characteristics that are desirable, i.e.:

- *Anonymity:* The participating entities do not have to disclose their identity.
- *Enforcement:* Since the service in return is provided immediately, the remuneration is effective even if the participating entities are disconnected immediately after their cooperation.
- *Scalability:* The incentive pattern may be effectively applied by a large number of entities.
- *Localization:* Cooperation and remuneration do not require interaction with dedicated entities. For example, in ad hoc networks, this property is not only desirable, but crucial.

However, in most application domains, it is infeasible to determine an adequate service in return and provide it simultaneously. Therefore, the remaining incentive patterns compensate for these disadvantages by introducing various bonds. However, the desirable characteristics of barter trade then become unsustainable. *Enforcement* calls for a dedicated entity that is often accessible and

Table 2. Characteristics of the incentive patterns

Incentive Patterns / General Characteristics		Trust Based Incentive Patterns		Trade Based Incentive Patterns	Bond Based Incentive Patterns			
		Collective Pattern	Community Pattern	Barter Trade Pattern	(Bearer) Note Pattern	(Bearer) Bill Pattern	(Bearer) Check Pattern	Banknote Pattern
Roles		asymmetric		symmetric	asymmetric			
Remuneration	Type		reputation	service in return	bond[1]			
	Granularity		arbitrary	service	fraction of service			
	Assessment	none	consumer	cons./provider	consumer/provider[2]			
	Storage Site		consumer	none	provider/bearer			
	Transferability	+[3]		0[4]	-/(+)	-/(+)	-/(+)	+
	Enforcement	-		+	0	-	+[5]	+
Trust	Trusted	consumer		none	cons.	cons./debtor	cons./bank	(cons./)bank
	Anonymity	-		+	-	(-)	0	+
Scalability		- -	-	+	-		+	+

[1] The specific bond type of the incentive pattern corresponds with the pattern's label.
[2] In addition, there is an extra charge for the ability to defer consumption and for the risk of validity. This extra charge is determined by the provider.
[3] Requires disseminations.
[4] Demands for re-trading actions.
[5] Requires that banks are able to retaliate upon an entity for having issued a bill without their consent.

provides the promised service in return. Furthermore, trust intensive roles are delegated to such a dedicated entity, in order to maintain *anonymity* of the consumer and provider. By doing so, bearer notes and bills are specialized to banknotes and checks. On the downside, the introduction of a dedicated entity contradicts the *localization* criterion. Conceptually, the transferability of checks and banknotes solves this problem. Yet, the ensuing opportunity for double spending of bonds hampers the enforcement of reciprocation.

6   Related Work and Contribution

Incentives are applied whenever the utility of autonomous entities has to be influenced for effectiveness or efficiency reasons. In economics, incentives assume a predominant role, hence their design has been thoroughly analyzed [9]. However, due to the ubiquity of the banknotes pattern in economics, existing work is not focussed on the choice of appropriate incentive patterns and, thus, abstracts from them. For MAS, there are several approaches that assume the economic perspective in order to apply incentives. All of them presume the availability of a robust payment scheme, which introduces a specific form of remuneration and generally requires a central authority. Thus, the approaches' design of incentive schemes is not contingent upon specific incentive patterns. A generic study of conceiving incentive schemes based on the economic public good theory is found in [10]. For P2P systems, file sharing incentive schemes have been proposed [11, 12]. Incentive Schemes for efficient resource allocation are conceived in agoric computing [13,14]. The transactional exchange of service and remuneration is analyzed in [15] regardless of the respective incentive pattern.

On the other hand, several related approaches restrain to the application and implementation of one specific incentive pattern. For P2P systems, there is ongoing research on distributed reputation systems [16] which are needed for the implementation of the community pattern. Mojo Nation [17] applies the barter trade pattern and the check pattern. The implementation of checks and banknotes is discussed in [7]. According to the classification of incentive schemes in [1], the predominant patterns for ad hoc networks are the collective pattern, the community pattern, and the check pattern.

To our knowledge, incentive patterns have not yet been compiled and discussed with regard to their characteristics and applicability to a specific domain. Therefore, this paper closes the gap between economic approaches that conceive incentives by determining the appropriate amount of remunerations and, on the other hand, approaches that examine how specific incentive patterns may be implemented.

7 Conclusion

P2P systems, MAS, and ad hoc networks are composed of autonomous entities that are free to decide whether to cooperate or not. Hence, incentives are indispensable for cooperation between them. Therefore, we introduced incentive patterns as a means of systematically conceiving incentive schemes with respect to the specifics of the application environment. We suggested a set of general characteristics that are required for the classification of such incentive patterns. At first, we introduced trust based incentive patterns that trust based incentive patterns assume a certain degree of stability. This assumption is not made by the barter trade pattern that enforces an immediate service in return. Since such an immediate service in return is often infeasible, it might be promised in the form of a bond. Consequently, we identified and classified several bond based incentive patterns. We captured the interrelationship of incentive patterns by proposing a taxonomy and summarizing their characteristics.

In the future, we plan to thoroughly analyze the applicability of incentive patterns that are not used in any existing incentive scheme yet. In addition, it seems promising to consider composition of incentives patterns in order to combine their strengths.

References

1. Obreiter, P., König-Ries, B., Klein, M.: Stimulating cooperative behavior of autonomous devices - an analysis of requirements and existing approaches. In: Second International Workshop on Wireless Information Systems (WIS2003). (2003) 71–82
2. Davies, R.: A History of Money from Ancient Times to the Present Day. 3rd edn. University of Wales Press (2002)
3. Anders, R., Obreiter, P.: Economic incentive patterns and their application to ad hoc networks. Technical Report 2003-17, Universität Karlsruhe, Faculty of Informatics (2003) (to appear).
4. Obreiter, P., Nimis, J.: A taxonomy of incentive patterns - the design space of incentives for cooperation. Technical Report 2003-9, Universität Karlsruhe, Faculty of Informatics (2003)
5. Obreiter, P., Klein, M.: Vertical integration of incentives for cooperation - interlayer collaboration as a prerequisite for effectively stimulating cooperation in ad hoc networks. In: Second Mediterranean Workshop on Ad-Hoc Networks (MEDHOC NET 2003), Mahdia, Tunisia (2003)
6. Dellarocas, C.: The digitization of word-of-mouth: Promise and challenges of online feedback mechanisms. Management Science (forthcoming). (2003)
7. Asokan, N., Janson, P.A., Steiner, M., Waidner, M.: The state of the art in electronic payment systems. IEEE Computer 30 (1997) 28–35
8. Asokan, N.: Fairness in Electronic Commerce. PhD thesis, University of Waterloo (1998)
9. Bamberg, G., Spremann, K.: Agency Theory, Information, and Incentives. Springer (1989)
10. Shoham, Y., Tanaka, K.: A dynamic theory of incentives in multi agent systems. In: Proceedings of Fifteenth International Joint Conference on Arti Cial Intelligence (IJCAI) '97, Volume. (1997) 626–631
11. Golle, P., Leyton-Brown, K., Mironov, I., Lillibridge, M.: Incentives for sharing in peer-to-peer networks. Lecture Notes in Computer Science 2232 (2001) 75–86
12. Courcoubetis, C., Antoniadis, P.: Market models for P2P content distribution. In: First International Workshop on Agents and Peer-To-Peer Computing (AP2PC). (2002)
13. Miller, M.S., Drexler, K.E.: Comparative Ecology: A Computational Perspective. In: The Ecology of Computation. B. Huberman (ed.) (1988)
14. Liao, R.F., Wouhaybi, R.H., Campbell, A.: Incentive engineering in wireless LAN based access networks. In: Proc. 10th International Conference on Network Protocols (ICNP), Paris, France (2002)
15. Despotovic, Z., Aberer, K.: Trust-aware delivery of composite goods. In: First International Workshop on Agents and Peer-To-Peer Computing (AP2PC). (2002)
16. Dingledine, R., Freedman, M., Molnar, D.: 16. Accountability. In: Peer-to-Peer: Harnessing The Benefits of a Disruptive Technology. O'Reilly Publishers (2001) 271–340
17. Mojo Nation: http://www.mojonation.net/MojoNation.html (2003)

P2P MetaData Search Layers

Sam Joseph

Strategic Software Division
Graduate School of Information Science and Technnology
University of Tokyo 7-3-1, Hongo, Bunkyo-ku
Tokyo 113-8656 Japan
sam@mtl.t.u-tokyo.ac.jp, sam@neurogrid.com

Abstract. Distributed Hashtables (DHTs) provide a scalable method of associating file-hashes with a particular location in a distributed network environment. Modifying DHTs directly to support meta-data is difficult, and meta-data search systems such as flooding tend to scale poorly. However, a number of more scalable distributed meta-data search systems have recently been developed that could be deployed in tandem with DHTs, and several are discussed here along with some novel simulation results that concern the scalability and resource limitations of a meta-data search layer that employs semantic routing. Semantic routing is a method of pruning a flooding search such that queries are preferentially forwarded to nodes that can answer those queries. Previous simulations [1] showed that under certain circumstances semantic routing leads to a reduction in search path length. This paper presents further simulation results indicating that the scalability of this effect is a function of the query distribution of individual user search activity.

1 Introduction

Given a distributed network environment we can break down the process of obtaining a file or document into three distinct stages:

1. WHAT: Identify which file you want from some meta-data criteria
2. WHERE: Work out where it is (potentially multiple locations/pieces)
3. HOW: Download it (from one or multiple locations)

These stages are merged in some systems, and arguably one could add a stage 0 in which the user specified what kind of meta-data schema they would like to be able to search over [2]. The Freenet system [3] merges the WHERE and HOW stages and relies upon a separate search layer to implement the WHAT stage. Merging stages may be necessary in some cases, however to the extent that they are separable they can be implemented by entirely different systems. For example, one might use FASD [4] to identify a file from keyword meta-data; use Chord [5] to work out the location of the file itself, and then BitTorrent [6] to actually download it. Distributed Hashtables such as Chord and CAN [7], with their bounds on path-length and/or connectivity as network size increases, seem

G. Moro, C. Sartori, and M.P. Singh (Eds.): AP2PC 2003, LNAI 2872, pp. 101–112, 2004.

well suited to providing the functionality of the WHERE stage as opposed to the WHAT stage. Storing file meta-data directly in DHTs, such as by splitting up filenames into n-grams [8], generates routing hotspots where certain nodes end up with heavy routing traffic because they are responsible for a particularly popular meta-data field or n-gram chunk [9].

Among the variety of recent developments in meta-data search layer techniques targeted at the WHAT stage, is "Semantic Routing"; a method of pruning a flooding search such that queries are preferentially forwarded to nodes that can answer those queries. Existing work [1] has shown that under certain circumstances semantic routing leads to a reduction in search path length. This paper describes some new semantic routing simulations and considers results indicating that the scalability of this effect is a function of the query distribution of individual user search activity.

The rest of the paper is structured as follows: in section 2 we review some of the recent developments in scalable meta-data search layers that could be deployed in tandem with DHTs. Section 3 describes a semantic routing meta-data search layer simulation, and includes some analysis of the search query distributions that will be used to make some scalability predictions. In section 4 we look at the simulation results, comparing them with the predictions of section 3 and discuss the scalability implications. Finally in section 5 we discuss the issues arising from trying to develop scalable meta-data search layers, and simulation of p2p systems in general.

2   Related Work

As mentioned in the introduction Freenet [3] merges the WHERE and HOW stages and relies on other systems to implement the WHAT stage. Freenet forwards queries according to beliefs about the contents of other nodes and considers file similarity in terms of closeness in a "key-space" generated by a cryptographic hash. A file's key is used to retrieve/insert files from/into particular locations. Combined with aggressive caching activity the arrangement of files ends up reflecting that of the key-space and the relative demand for different documents. Gnutella [10] relies on individual users sharing files stored locally, using broadcast search to identify file locations from partial search of plain text filenames, and thus merges the WHAT and WHERE stages. The HOW stage is farmed out to HTTP. Other systems have emerged that attempt to deal with the issues of distributed file storage, such as MojoNation [11] (now Mnet), which provides all three stages in one package.

Recently a number of systems have been developed that try to provide sophisticated meta-data search. One possible P2P meta-data approach is to try and use Chord to store keyword-document relations. Kronfol [4] suggests that under this scheme popular query terms would drive excessive traffic to certain nodes. As an alternative Kronfol describes and simulates FASD, which adds keyword searching to the Freenet system by inserting meta-data keys that include the TFIDF (Term Frequency Inverse Document Frequency [12]) rankings of keywords in Freenet documents, as well as the Freenet document key. FASD employs a cosine correlation to determine document-query closeness and Freenet routing techniques such that nodes start to take responsibility for similar meta-data keys, distributing meta-data information throughout the network. Babaoglu et al. [13] propose a not dissimilar scheme, although their routing procedure works on hashes of individual keywords to distribute the load, as opposed to TFIDF vectors. Their scheme, an example application of the Anthill framework combines the WHAT and WHERE stages, and like Gnutella farms out the HOW stage to HTTP.

NeuroGrid [1] maintains routing tables at each node that associate other nodes with query keywords, and routing tables are updated on the basis of user feedback. Each node forwards incoming queries to a subset of the most relevant nodes. This process is called semantic routing and is distinguished from content routing, the process of routing based on n-dimensional hashes rather than meaningful keywords. Semantic routing is a WHAT layer candidate and can be found in other systems, e.g. the LimeWire proposal [14] to add query routing to the Gnutella network, a subset of which was implemented as part of the LimeWire ultra-peers framework. The query-routing proposal involves nodes creating indices that summarise their contents and distributing them to other nodes, such that queries can be routed more effectively. Crespo & Garcia-Molina [15] propose a similar approach called "Routing Indices".

Older work related to semantic routing includes the Whois++ system [16], which provides a mechanism for forwarding queries to distributed servers on the basis of the content of those servers. The Harvest system [17] provided a comparable service along with caching and replication, as did the Content Routing approach of Sheldon et al. [18], which included query refinement and merging of result sets. Q-Pilot [19] is a more recent example of this kind of system that routes queries to different search engines based on their specialization.

3 Simulation

The goal of the simulations presented here is to look at the scalability and efficiency of search in an example meta-data search layer. Previous simulations [1] showed increasing search performance in semantic routing networks relies on two things:

1. connectivity adjustments based on user feedback
2. a relation between node meta-data and the searches they generate

The current simulations take a look at how the final stable network connectivity varies as a function of the search query distribution, under the following assumptions:

1. document meta-data consists of keywords
2. each node contains some documents (or location pointers)
3. nodes maintain connections to a subset of other nodes

4. nodes have some knowledge about other nodes content

The various simulation parameters can be seen in the following table:

K	Set of Keywords	$\{k_1, k_2, ...\}$
D	Set of Documents	$\{d_1, d_2, ...\}$
N	Set of Nodes	$\{n_1, n_2, ...\}$
M	Document Meta-Data	Subset of KxD
P	Node Contents	Subset of DxN
C	Node Connectivity	Subset of NxN
B	Node Knowledge Base	Subset of NxKxN
nkd	Number of keywords describing a document	
ndn	Number of documents contained in each node	
noc	Number of initial outgoing connections for each node	
moc	Maximum number of outgoing connections for each node	
mka	Maximum number of knowledge associations for each node	
$|D|$	Overall number of documents	
$|K|$	Overall number of keywords	
$|N|$	Overall number of nodes	
mpl	Maximum path length - number of hops before a query is discarded	
fd	Forwarding degree - #connections along which a query is forwarded	
KD	Distribution from which keywords are taken to create documents	
DD	Distribution from which documents are taken to create contents	
ND	Distribution from which nodes are taken to create connections	
TD	Distribution from which a target document d' will be taken	
SD	Distribution from which the search origin node s' will be taken	
SP	Search Policy that determines which nodes to forward to	

The objective is to identify the target locations $T(d) = \{n|(d, n) \in P\}$, where $T(d)$ is the set of target locations that contain a target document d. Ideally we would start the search process by selecting some subset of keywords from some kind of keyword search distribution, however in order to avoid searches with no targets an alternative approach is to specify a document to search for, d, and then select a search origin node, s. Others have also taken this simplifying approach in p2p simulation studies [20] and we hope to improve upon it in future simulations. The document can be selected from D according to some distribution TD, or selected according to other criteria that relate it to the contents of the origin node. This latter approach is important in semantic routing as it means that adjustments in connectivity following successful searches cause nodes to become specialists in the location of a documents described by a limited subset of keywords. The general search procedure can be specified in set theoretic terms as follows:

1. Choose d such that: $d \in SD \wedge \exists n[(d, n) \in P]$
2. Select $K'(d)$ such that: $K'(d) = \{k | (k, d) \in M\}$
3. Choose s such that: $s \in N \wedge (d, s) \notin P$
4. Set $n' = s$
5. Select $N'(k, n')$ such that: $N'(k, n') = \{n | (n', k, n) \in B \wedge k \in K'(d)\}$
6. if $|N'(k, n')| = fd$ then set $N'' = N'(k, n')$
7. else if $|N'(k, n')| < fd$ then set $N'' = N'(k, n')$ and set $N'' = N'' \cup \{n | n \in N\}$ until $|N''| = fd$
8. else if $|N'(k, n')| > fd$ then make $N'' \subset N'(k, n')$ where $|N''| = fd$
9. For each $n'' \in N''$
   a. if $\forall k[k \in K' \wedge (k, d) \in M \wedge (d, n'') \in P]$ then set $T' = T' \cup \{n''\}$ and set $C = C \cup \{(n'', s)\}$
   b. else set $s = n''$ goto 5

The procedure in plain English

1. Select a target document that exists somewhere in the network
2. Construct a search query based on the target documents keywords
3. Find a start node that does not already contain the target document
4. Make a record of the start node
5. Use the start node's knowledge base to determine a set of nodes to query
6. If the #nodes is equal to the forwarding degree select those nodes
7. If the #nodes are less than the forwarding degree select additional nodes
8. If the #nodes are more than the forwarding degree then select a subset
9. For each selected node
   a. If the node contains the target document update connectivity
   b. If it does not, continue the search using this node as the start

For clarity the above pseudo-code leaves out a couple of other constraints, i.e. that no node can process a given search request more than once, and all search requests cease once they have been passed along mpl times. An alternative to step 1 is:

1. Choose d such that: $\exists n[(d, n) \in P] \wedge (d', s) \in P \wedge (k, d) \in M \wedge (k, d') \in M \wedge (d, s) \notin P$

Or more simply, "Select a target document that is present in the network and has at least one keyword in common with the documents in the search start node, but is not actually in the start node". This alternative allows semantic routing to support improved search efficiency and we shall look at this more closely in Section 4. For the moment let us focus on other aspects of the simulation, e.g. that for an fd value of 2 or above the search proceeds in parallel (see fig 1), allowing more than one match to be found. Also important is that whenever matches are found the origin node becomes connected to the node that contains the matching document; removing its eldest connection if the moc has been exceeded.

In a real network this connectivity adjustment would depend on user feedback indicating whether a search was really successful. This simulation assumes

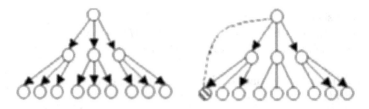

Fig. 1. A Gnutella-like flooding scheme (left) compared with a semantic routing scheme (right). In the semantic routing scheme, each node consults its knowledge base to determine which nodes to forward the query to. A match triggers a new connection to the start node, and the addition of that node and search keywords to the start nodes knowledge base.

ideal users who are always happy with the search results; an assumption that naturally we are working to remove. Node knowledge is updated in a similar fashion to the node connectivity, i.e. the node conducting the search adds data to its knowledge base associating the keywords of the target document with the node that contained the matching document.

Previous simulations [1] of this kind have shown us that the alternative target selection approach that links search targets to a nodes local meta-data contribute to improving search performance. Given knowledge of the sets K, D and N, the parameters nkd and ndn and assuming KD, ND and DD are all uniform distributions; we can infer the expected number of search targets for each node under the alternate target selection scheme. First we calculate the expected number of unique keywords of all the documents in a single node, $E[k]$, given $|K|$, nkd and ndn is:

$$E[k] = |K| \cdot \left[1 - \left(\prod_{i=1}^{i=nkd} \frac{|K| - i}{|K| - i + 1} \right)^{ndn} \right] \tag{1}$$

i.e. the number of keywords times the probability a single keyword will be selected for inclusion in some set of ndn documents each with nkd, where keywords are selected without replacement for each document. Further, the expected number of documents that will share a given keyword, $E[d]$, can be expressed as:

$$E[d] = |D| \cdot \left[1 - \left(\prod_{i=1}^{i=nkd} \frac{|K| - i}{|K| - i + 1} \right) \right] \tag{2}$$

i.e. the number of keywords times the probability a single keyword will be selected for inclusion in some set of ndn documents each with nkd keywords are selected without replacement for each document. Multiplying $E[k]$ and $E[d]$ we get roughly the expected number of documents that will become search targets for the alternative target selection scheme, where a target document is selected on the basis that it shares a keyword in common with the contents of the search origin node. In the next section we shall see how this value relates to the stable state of a converged network that has employed semantic routing.

4   Results

Previous simulation studies [1] demonstrated that network simulations using semantic routing and the alternative target selection scheme would find their path
lengths converging, whereas equivalent networks using random routing would
fail to show any significant reduction in search path length. It was also shown
that adjusting the keyword-document distribution (KD) had a significant effect
on this convergence process, with a Zipf distribution slowing the convergence.
Joseph [1] suggested that this effect might be due to fact that the Zipf distribution caused more documents to share keywords and thus increase the range
of search targets being selected for each node. Analysis of the simulation model
along with some the simulations presented in this paper back up this explanation.

Simulations were performed for values of $|D| = 2000$, $|K| = 1000$, $nkd = 3$ and
for a few different values of ndn. [Other parameters were $|N| = 1000$, $moc = 100$,
$mka = 300$, $mpl = 9$, $fd = 2$, $noc = 3$] The average connectivity of the simulated
networks after 100000 search iterations is shown in fig 2, along with the predicted
number of target documents for the alternative target selection scheme. Under
the right conditions, simulations of networks using semantic routing converge to
a stable state with low search path length (somewhere between 1 and 2 hops),
and increased connectivity levels i.e. an increased average number of connections
per node. What figure 2 is showing us is that the number of connections per node
in a converged network appears to mirror the expected number of search targets.
This supports the idea that the connectivity level of the converged network is a

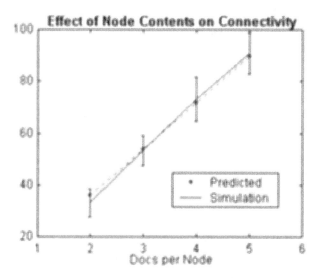

Fig. 2. Average connectivity levels (no of connections per node) of the converged network on the y-axis, with predicated (red dotted line) and simulated values (blue solid
line - error bars are standard deviation) for different values of the number of documents
in each node (ndn).

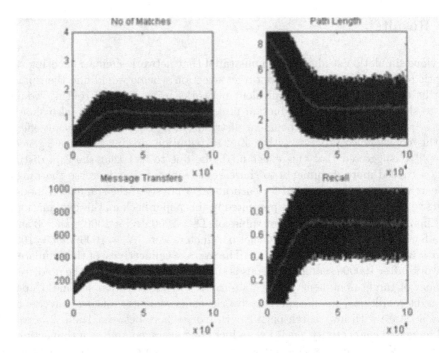

Fig. 3. Evolution of no of matches (actual number of documents retrieved), recall (proportion of possible matches retrieved), message transfers and path length of first match, for increasing search iterations.

function of the range of documents being searched for by each individual node. The results in fig 2 are for a simulation with only a loose constraint (i.e. max 100) upon the number of allowed connections. To the extent that one places tighter restrictions on the connectivity level, the converged network path length increases. For example, if we restrict the connectivity to a maximum number of 20 in a network with an *ndn* of 3, i.e. below what it would normally stabilise at, we get results like those in fig 3.

In this case the path length converges to a value around 3, with a much higher standard deviation than the equivalent case where the connectivity level is allowed to rise unconstrained [1]. This indicates that the operation of semantic routing, in combination with connection/knowledge updates and an appropriate target selection scheme, causes nodes to stabilize their connectivity levels when they are connected to enough other nodes that can directly service their search needs. So if the target selection scheme is such that each node will likely generate searches for 40 different documents, then a connectivity of around 40 will allow the node to meet all its search needs in a single hop, albeit by having connected itself to the nodes that contain all the documents it will ever need. If the node is restricted to connect to 20 nodes, the search path length will still stabilise but at a higher value, as now some documents will be a few more hops away. Simulations performed on larger networks found that convergence may take many more search iterations, but that convergence can be achieved given that a large enough number of searches originate from each individual node. So for example 100,000 search iterations on a 1000 node network gives an average of 100 searches starting at each node, enough searches to allow a good proportion of the possible targets to be the basis for an actual search. Thus, to achieve the same number of searches originating from each node in a 10,000-node network we need to perform a million searches. Simulations of a million search iterations on a 10,000-node network showed that the network converged to a path length of around 2, but that its connectivity level is comparable with that of a 1000 node network.

5   Conclusion

So what are these rather preliminary simulations telling us about the scalability of this path length reduction effect? Firstly that it can be attributed to adjustments in the network connectivity, and that secondly the connectivity required by the network is not, at least superficially, a function of the number of nodes in the network. This suggests that the effect should be scalable to larger networks, but on the other hand it is not quite clear if semantic routing is actually necessary - perhaps connectivity adjustment alone would suffice? Actually, assessing scalability now switches to understanding the query distribution of the individual users. In networks that adjust their connectivity to meet search needs, users that search for similar documents within a consistent section of the meta-data space will have their needs met swiftly, but more unpredictable users will not be served so well. What this indicates is a need to examine not just the average path length, but also the path length of searches for different users characterised by their query distributions, as well as for different searches generated by the same user. Another area of ambiguity is time to converge to a stable network, which could become prohibitively large. The dynamic nature of real p2p networks may mean that the network can never reach this stable state, so we would need to study performance away from equilibrium. One hopes that semantic routing might give a reduction in network traffic over flooding, but what needs to be checked is whether flooding in combination with connectivity changes would lead to swifter convergence.

One way forward is more realistic simulations using parameters and distributions that reflect real network environments. In addition the nature of the convergence of the variables (e.g. path-length and connectivity) needs to be statistically assessed in a more rigorous fashion. Ideally we would move towards some standardised approach to p2p simulations as advocated in [20]. The simulations presented in this paper were all run on the open source NeuroGrid p2p simulator, which can be found at http://www.neurogrid.net. The NeuroGrid p2p simulator is designed to be an extensible system that supports many different types of simulation, and provides access to shared requirements such as providing test distributions for simulation parameters.

6   Discussion

So semantic routing allows each node to become a specialist in a particular meta-data area. One can argue about whether the search query distribution SD in a real P2P network would be similar to the alternative target selection scheme that supports this result, but it seems plausible that users will search for things that are related (if tangentially) to files they possess. Studies of the Gnutella network [21] suggest that the search queries follow a Zipf distribution, but it is difficult to determine (due to the mechanics of Gnutella) what the search distributions of individual users are, and how they relate to the files in the users local node. This kind of data might also be obtained from Search Engine companies [22], but it has proved difficult to obtain this data, since these companies are understandably cautious about giving away potentially valuable marketing data. Meta-data search layers face additional issues as follows:

Q1: P2P systems exhibit high churn - nodes coming and going rapidly. How does this affect the ongoing adjustment of node knowledge?

A1: A semantic routing layer that is updating local node state clearly relies on some degree of regularity in the environment in order to route queries effectively. To the extent that the environment changes faster than the system can update, the system will not forward queries effectively. However proper integration with user feedback will allow the system to isolate those stable aspects of the environment that can be relied upon.

Q2: There is also high churn of content - how will a semantic routing search layer deal with short-lived content, or unpopular content on short-lived nodes?

A2: If content is not available for any length of time then nodes' knowledge will not be updated fast enough to direct queries against this data. To the extent that the short-lived content is related to the existing content of the node making it (or the reference to it) available, then the semantic routing will be effective. The only alternative for short-lived content would be some kind of advertising system that would be susceptible to adversarial nodes broadcasting inaccurate meta-data. More realistically short-lived content should be cached automatically. Unpopular content is a different matter. Given that at least some nodes become specialists in a particular type of content, then as soon as one accesses those nodes, the unpopular content can be easily found. The difficulty of finding the right nodes will depend on how broad a range of data can be stored by the largest nodes in the system, and on whether the network connectivity does form a small world [23]. This relates to how knowledge base storage limits should be enforced (see Q5).

Q3: How much state must each node keep? What other network parameters will this be related to?

A3: The nature of semantic routing systems would seem to operate well in tandem with giving a user freedom to store as much or as little data on "their" node as they like. Different users have different bandwidth, CPU and storage resources available to them. The simulations presented above suggest that the number of connections that each node must store in order to support low search path lengths is a function of the query search distribution of that node. One would imagine that in a real system that would have a different query search distribution for each node/user, that connectivity would form a small world network. The simulations above suggest that limiting connectivity to below the level required by the search query distribution does not cripple the network, but simply places lower bounds on the average search path length. Also in a small world, not having enough resources to support a large connectivity or knowledge base do not mean terrible performance as long as you can connect to users/nodes that do.

Q4: What are the trade-offs in choosing which nodes to maintain knowledge on, and which to ignore? What policies will be employed to limit the size of knowledge bases?

A4: Clearly any node will only be able to devote a certain amount of resources to its knowledge base. Naturally one would try to optimize the use of that resource by tracking the more reliable nodes; reliable that is in terms of being able to respond to queries and being able to supply things the user is interested in. Ideally more storage resources are devoted to things that interest the user, i.e. the keywords being frequently used in queries. The simulations above enforced their limits on connectivity and knowledge by removing the oldest entries when limits were exceeded. There are other options including least recently used caches, and ideally nodes and beliefs about their contents will be tracked to the extent that they participate in searches that lead to positive user feedback. This line of reasoning suggests that one might employ a scheme similar to backpropagation in neural networks, where each node in the neural network is strengthened or weakened to the extent that it participates in the correct identification of incoming stimuli. Such an approach in a p2p network would require additional messaging to provide feedback data after the user at the search origin node has assessed the results. Realistically this kind of scheme would only seem practical in a network of co-operating non-adversarial nodes.

Q5: How will the system deal with adversarial nodes that provide inaccurate responses to meta-data queries, and forward queries inappropriately?

A5: Adversarial nodes are a problem in many p2p systems and the semantic routing approach, in combination with user feedback, attempts to deal with this by effectively storing reputation information about other nodes in the knowledge of each node. As the number of adversarial nodes increases finding reliable trustworthy nodes becomes more and more difficult. Still, to the extent that one can identify these reliable nodes, valid search results can still be extracted from the network. Some authors have started to address this issue [20], and the NeuroGrid simulator is being modified to incorporate adversarial or dishonest nodes, along with attempts to make all aspects of the simulations more realistic with regards to ranges of parameters, distributions and operational reliable (i.e. node, connection, and content churn). Being able to cope with adversarial nodes, churn and other hazards of p2p networks is the main objective of this research, and there is still a long way to go.

References

1. Joseph, S.: Neurogrid: Semantically routing queries in peer-topeer. In: International Workshop on Peer-to-Peer Computing. (2002)
2. Nejdl, W., Wolf, B., Qu, C., Decker, S., Sintek, M., Naeve, A., Nilsson, M., Palmer, M., Risch, T.: Edutella: A p2p networking infrastructure based on rdf (2001)
3. Clarke, I., Sandberg, O., Wiley, B., Hong, T.W.: Freenet: A distributed anonymous information storage and retrieval system. LNCS **2009** (2001) 46+
4. Kronfol, A.Z.: Fasd: A fault-tolerant, adaptive scalable, distributed search engine. Technical report, Princeton University (2002)
5. Stoica, I., Morris, R., Karger, D., Kaashoek, M.F., Balakrishnan, H.: Chord: A scalable peer-to-peer lookup service for internet applications. In: SIGCOMM, ACM Press (2001) 149–160
6. Cohen, B.: Incentives build robustness in bittorrent. In: Workshop on Economics of Peer-to-Peer Systems. (2003)
7. Ratnasamy, S., Francis, P., Handley, M., Karp, R., Shenker, S.: A scalable content addressable network. In: ACM SIGCOMM. (2001)
8. Harren, M., Hellerstein, J.M., Huebsch, R., Loo, B.T., Shenker, S., Stoica, I.: Complex queries in dht-based peer-to-peer networks. In: 1st IPTPS. (2002)
9. Ratnasamy, S., Shenker, S., Stoica, I.: Routing algorithms for dhts: Some open questions. In: 1st IPTPS. (2002)
10. Kan, G.: 8. In: Peer-to-Peer: Harnessing the Benefits of Disruptive Technologies. O'Reilly & Associates (2001) 94–122
11. Wilcox-O'Hearn, B.: Experiences deploying a large-scale emergent network. In: 1st IPTPS. (2002)
12. Salton, G., Yang, C.: On the specification of term values in automatic indexing. Journal of Documentation **29** (1973) 351–372
13. Babaoglu, O., Meling, H., Montresor, A.: Anthill: A framework for the development of agent-based peer-to-peer systems. In: 22nd ICDCS. (2002)
14. Rohrs, C.: Query routing for the gnutella network (2002)
15. Crespo, A., Garcia-Molina, H.: Routing indices for peer-to-peer systems. In: 22nd ICDCS. (2002)
16. Deutsch, P., Schoultz, R., Faltstrom, P., Weider, C.: Architecture of the whois++ service (1995)
17. Bowman, C.M., Danzig, P.B., Hardy, D.R., Manber, U., Schwartz, M.F.: The Harvest information discovery and access system. Computer Networks and ISDN Systems **28** (1995) 119–126
18. Sheldon, M.A., Duda, A., Weiss, R., Gifford, D.K.: Discover: a resource discovery system based on content routing. Computer Networks and ISDN Systems **27** (1995) 953–972
19. Sugiura, A., Etzioni, O.: Query routing for web search engines: Architecture and experiments. In: 9th WWW. (2000)
20. Kamvar, S., Schlosser, M., Garcia-Molina, H.: Eigenrep: Reputation management in p2p networks. In: 12th WWW. (2003)
21. Sripanidkulchai, K.: The popularity of gnutella queries and its implications on scalability (2001)
22. Xie, Y., O'Hallaron, D.: Locality in search engine queries and its implications for caching. In: Infocom. (2002)
23. DJ, W., SH, S.: Collective dynamics of small-world networks. Nature **393** (1998) 440–442

A Peer-to-Peer Information System for the Semantic Web

Sonia Bergamaschi[1,2], Francesco Guerra[1], and Maurizio Vincini[1]

[1] Dipartimento di Ingegneria dell'Informazione
University of Modena and Reggio Emilia
Via Vignolese 905, 41100 Modena, Italy
{bergamaschi.sonia,guerra.francesco,vincini.maurizio}@unimo.it
[2] IEIIT-BO-CNR, Viale Risorgimento 2,
I-40136 Bologna, Italy

Abstract. Data integration, in the context of the web, faces new problems, due in particular to the heterogeneity of sources, to the fragmentation of the information and to the absence of a unique way to structure and view information. In such areas, the traditional paradigms, on which database foundations are based (i.e. client server architecture, few sources containing large information), have to be overcome by new architectures. The peer-to-peer (P2P) architecture seems to be the best way to fulfill these new kinds of data sources, offering an alternative to traditional client/server architecture.
In this paper we present the SEWASIE system that aims at providing access to heterogeneous web information sources. An enhancement of the system architecture in the direction of P2P architecture, where connections among SEWASIE peers rely on exchange of XML metadata, is described.

1 Introduction

Data integration has been extensively studied in the past, in the domain of company infrastructures. Data integration, in the context of the web, faces new problems, due in particular to the heterogeneity of sources, to the fragmentation of the information and to the absence of a unique way to structure and view information. In such areas, the traditional paradigms, on which database foundations are based (i.e. client server architecture, few sources containing large information), have to be overcome by new architectures. The peer-to-peer (P2P) architecture seems to be the best way to fulfill of these new kinds of data sources, offering an alternative to traditional client/server architecture. The most relevant advantages of the approach are related to the improved scalability (increased storage, increased bandwidth) and flexibility of the systems.

New problems, related to the definition of specific ways to describe the contents of a source, i.e. its metadata w.r.t this architecture, and to allow sources to exchange data with each other, have to be faced. These issues are being recently addressed, and partially resolved by (proposed) standard like XML (that

G. Moro, C. Sartori, and M.P. Singh (Eds.): AP2PC 2003, LNAI 2872, pp. 113–122, 2004.
© Springer-Verlag Berlin Heidelberg 2004

allows systems to exchange data across different platform), RDF (that provides a uniform manner to describe sources), OWL (that is a proposal of a standard ontology definition language) and WSLD (that is the language to define web services). In this paper, we focus on research problems associated with knowledge management and search in data-sharing P2P systems. Starting from a previous work [1], we present the SEWASIE system that aims at providing access to heterogeneous web information sources. An enhancement of the system architecture in the direction of P2P architecture, where connections among SEWASIE peers rely on exchange of XML metadata, is described.

2   Peer-to-Peer Approach

Though data-sharing P2P systems are capable of sharing enormous amounts of data (e.g., 0.36 petabytes on the Morpheus network as of October 2001), such a collection is useless without mechanisms allowing users to quickly understand and search for desired pieces of data. Designing such a mechanism is difficult in P2P systems for several reasons: scale of the system, unreliability of individual peers, different semantics associated to similar peers, etc. In particular it has to define the behavior of peers in three areas:

Topology: Defines how peers are connected to each other. In some systems (e.g. Gnutella, www.gnutella.com), peers may connect to whomever they wish. In other systems, peers are organized into a rigid structure, in which the number and nature of connections is dictated by the protocol. Defining a rigid topology may increase efficiency, but will restrict autonomy.

Data placement: Defines how data or metadata is distributed across the network of peers. For example, in Gnutella, each node stores only its own collection of data. In Chord[2], data or metadata is carefully placed across nodes in a deterministic fashion. In super-peer networks [3], metadata for a small group of peers is centralized onto a single super-peer.

Message routing: Defines how messages are propagated through the network. When a peer submits a query, the query message is sent to a number of the peer's "neighbors" (that is, nodes to whom the peer is connected), who may in turn forward the message sequentially or in parallel to some of their neighbors, and so on. When, and to whom, messages are sent is dictated by the routing protocol. Often, the routing protocol can take advantage of known patterns in topology and data placement, in order to reduce the number of messages sent.

The distributed, heterogeneous and unstructured nature of the Web poses a new challenge to query-answering over multiple data sources. In particular, it is no longer realistic to assume that the involved data sources act as if they were a single (virtual) source, modeled as a global schema, as is done in classical data integration approaches. In this paper, we propose an alternative approach where we replace the role of a single virtual data source schema with a peer-to-peer approach relying on limited shared (or overlapping) vocabularies between peers. Since overlaps between vocabularies of peers will be limited, query processing will have to be approximate. We provide a formal model for such approximate

query processing based on limited shared vocabularies between peers, and we
show how the quality of the approximation can be adjusted in a gradual manner. The result is a flexible architecture for query-processing in large, distributed
and heterogeneous environments, based on a formal foundation. This architecture is suitable for knowledge-sharing in the peer-to-peer-style networks that are
expected to be typical of the Semantic Web.

3   Core Topics

3.1   Global Architecture

The idea underlying our proposal is that *at a local level things may be done more
richly than at a wider level.* Each peer contains specific information about the
involved domains but only an high layer of this knowledge should be exported to
other peers by using a standard language and a standard model to represent the
structure of the source. We should therefore envision a multi-level architecture,
with local nodes and communities with strong ties helping them develop a strong
integration of their knowledge and information, with a semantic context which
is well defined and offers a globally integrated ontology to represent everything,
while at a wider level the relationships among distinct nodes are established by
means of weaker mappings. The definition of the architecture is guided by the
following reference scenarios:

- **Building and maintaining a new information node:** We think each
  web site is a peer of this P2P network. Updates on the web sites will involve
  a change in the exported information.
- **Establishing and maintaining mapping relationships among distinct information nodes**, that directly derives of the previous point: a
  change of the peer information will generate a change of the mappings among
  different peers.
- **Querying the system by a user**, in order to obtain the required information

A satisfying the aforementioned principles, goals, and desiderata system architecture is shown in Figure 1.

The **information nodes (SINodes)** group together modules which work
to define and maintain a single administrative, or logical node of information
presented to the whole network. A single information node may comprise several
different systems.

The **user interface** contains modules which work together to offer an integrated user interaction with the semantic search system. Typically each user in
the network will install and configure its own instance of the user interface. This
interface has to be personalised and configured with the specific user profile and
the reference to the ontologies which are commonly used by this user.

The **brokering agents** are the peers responsible for maintaining a view of
the knowledge handled by the network, as well as the information on the specific

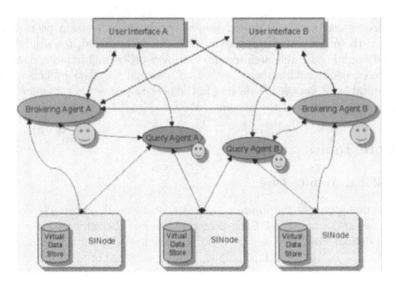

Fig. 1. General Overview of the peer-to-peer SEWASIE architecture

content of some information nodes which are under direct control. These agents have direct control over a number of information nodes, and provide the means to publish a manifesto within the network of the locally held information.

The **query agents** are the carriers of the user query from the user interface to the information nodes, and have the task of solving a query, interacting with the brokering agent network. Starting from a user- or task- specified brokering agent, they may access other BAs, connect with several information nodes, collect partial answers, and integrate them.

3.2   Information Nodes

Information Nodes (**SINodes**) are mediator-based systems, each including a Virtual Data Store, an Ontology Builder, and a Query Manager. In [4,5] we proposed the mediator-based system *MOMIS* (Mediator envirOnment for Multiple Information Sources) as a pool of tools to provide an integrated access to heterogeneous information. More to face the issues related to scalability in the large-scale, in [6,7] we propose the exploitation of *mobile agents* in the information integration area, and, in particular, their integration in the *MOMIS* infrastructure.

Virtual Data Store (VDS): It represents a virtual view of the overall information managed within any SINode and consists of the managed information sources, wrappers, and a metadata repository. The managed Information Sources are heterogeneous collections of structured, semi-structured, or unstructured data, e.g. relational databases, XML or HTML documents.

Wrappers are the "docking stations" of the heterogeneous data sources. They are software modules in charge of the mediation between the internal representation of each data source and the functionalities of the SINode. Different wrappers have to be defined to cover structurally diverse sources. The wrapper interface will be uniform and independent of the underlying source type. Two major functions need to be performed by the wrappers: to support the translation of the structure of the information managed by local sources into the SINode description language and the translation of the queries from the SINode query language into the specific query language of the underlying source.

The architecture of the VDS module is inherently distributed (i.e. in most cases its functionality will be distributed among several host machines of different types). As a consequence, these components will all need to have inter-process communication functionalities to support the interaction.

Ontology Builder (OB): It is the collective name of a set of functionalities which will support the creation and maintenance of a *global virtual view* (GVV) of the managed sources and the mapping description between the GVV itself and the integrated sources. The ontology building process is a cooperative one, involving the designers; it begins with the creation of a common thesaurus of the information provided by wrappers, that is terminological intensional and extensional relationships describing intra-schema knowledge about classes and attributes of each source schemas.

Based on such information and on designer supplied relationships capturing specific domain knowledge, the OB performs semiautomatic intra and inter-schema analysis by exploiting lexicon derived relationships, which are based on processes like synonyms identification or generalisation-specialisation relations, and inferring new relationships.

All these relationships are considered in the subsequent phase of construction of the ontology. Such an activity is based on hierarchical clustering techniques and supports the emergence of a number of global classes (GVV) representative of all the classes coming from the sources and of a mapping description between the GVV and the local sources.

Query Manager (QM): It is the coordinated set of functions which take an incoming query, define a decomposition of the query w.r.t. the mapping of the GVV of the SINode onto the data sources relevant for the query, send the queries to the wrappers in charge of the data sources, collect their answers, perform any residual filtering as necessary, and finally deliver to the requesting query agent.

3.3   Brokering Agents

In a distributed information system it is necessary to maintain and share the information about the knowledge made available by the system. In order to facilitate the interoperability and reusability of knowledge resources, we need to provide a flexible infrastructure to taking into account the change of data and metadata and not to provide a specific application useful only to a target domain. The proposed approach builds on the W3C XML standard and uses an object oriented data and query model [4] throughout the SEWASIE Network. In the proposed architecture this task is performed by the brokering agents (BAs), which are peers of the network that share knowledge and metadata. The knowledge within a brokering agent is represented as an ontology, i.e. a network of interrelated concepts. Relationships between concepts are defined as mappings expressed by a formal language. The language, called ODL_{I^3} (see [4] for a detailed description) is based on ODMG object model and OLCD Description Logic [8] and is represented by XML language. The ODL_{I^3} language [4] may be used to describe heterogeneous schemata of data sources in a common way. In the context of the global ontology of an information node ODL_{I^3} introduces new constructors useful in the integration process and in the global integrated view representation. In particular, there are intensional relationships expressing inter-schema knowledge for the source schemas defined between classes and attributes names (terms): SYN (Synonyms), BT (Broader Terms), NT (Narrower Terms) and RT (Related Terms). Intensional relationships SYN, BT and NT between two classes may be "strengthened" by establishing that they are also extensional relationships. Moreover, mappings between the global integrated view and schemata of data sources can be defined.

A brokering agent knows exactly all the ontologies which are present in the underlying information nodes, and has general information about related (to its own) ontologies in other nodes.

The depth of the information of the BA becomes more and more shallow with the distance (with respect to some metrics) between the ontologies for which it is "expert" (those of its underlying information nodes) and other ontologies covered within the system. Its information on other (non local) ontologies is incomplete.

Different brokering agent roles may be envisioned, depending on the business model of the organisation which deploys the brokering agent. A company (or a group of companies) may establish a brokering agent to manage a common access to its information sources. On the other end, a specialised information brokering enterprise may establish a brokering agent that combines ontologies provided by several other brokering agents and clustering around a specific domain. Thus, we can identify the following classes of brokering agents:

- local service BAs are servicing a single information node or a group of nodes and are usually close to the nodes
- pure informant BAs are collectors of references to several brokering agents and may specialise in a certain domain, and may be positioned anywhere in the network

At an abstract level, the operation of the brokering agent can be divided into two phases:

1. Design Phase (mapping time)
    - The brokering agent receives a local ontology describing data available from a information node and has to map it into its own map of ontologies.
    - The brokering agent receives information about other ontologies from other brokering agents. This information also has to be mapped into the existing ontology of the brokering agent.

2. Runtime Phase (query time)
   – A query agent wants to know where it can find the information for a query. The terms of the query are then matched with the concepts known by the brokering agent. The brokering agent looks up its internal meta information and returns pointers to the information nodes or other brokering agents which have the requested information (or parts thereof).
   – A component of the system (e.g., the query interface) extracts the complete ontology which is managed by the brokering agent.

The design and runtime phases are not strictly separated. Ontologies need to be mapped and updated during the whole life cycle of a brokering agent.

The crucial role of the brokering agent is the creation and maintenance of the map of semantic relationships among concepts from different information nodes in the system. In particular, the correlation among the concepts coming from different sources (ontologies of information nodes and other brokering agents) relies on terminological relationships. They are created by the brokering agent which, in a (semi-) automatic way, analyses the meaning of the concepts in different ontologies and tries to discover terminological relationships among them by exploiting lexical ontologies such as Wordnet. Once the repository of these mappings has been created, the brokering agent is in charge of its maintenance: changes in the network have to be integrated to make the repository consistent with the new scenario.

At runtime, when a request from a query agent is received, the quality of the answer of the BA (and of the query agent) depends to a large degree on the quality of the semantic relationships that have been created. Incorrect relationships will lead to incorrect answers of the query agent, e.g. data that should not be included in an answer to a query will be delivered as result. Incomplete (or missing) relationships will lead to incomplete results, e.g. data that should be included in the answer is not delivered as a result (although it is somewhere available in the network). Thus, special attendance has to be given to the creation of the semantic relationships. Automatic creation of the semantic relationships is possible, but the creation of relationships based only on the lexical similarity between terms will lead to incorrect and incomplete results. On the other hand, manual control of the creation is not possible in every case as a brokering agent might handle a large number of information nodes. Thus, updates to the semantic relationships might happen quite frequently and manual control would significantly slow down the process of establishing semantic relationships.

BA's Architecture

The basic architectural schema of the BA is described in figure 2. The map keeper is the maintainer of the mapping information concerning the local information nodes and the other BAs and supported ontologies. It builds is a partial description of the information available within the system, with varying degrees of precision and richness; higher detail will be available for the local information nodes, less detail will be available for other ontologies.

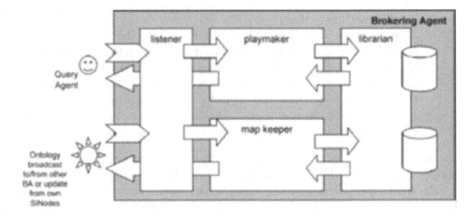

Fig. 2. Basic Architectural Schema of the BA

The playmaker receives a request from the listener on behalf of a query agent, and identifies the information nodes or other BAs which may offer an answer (or parts thereof). It connects with the waiting query agent and provides the corresponding directions, consisting of addresses of SINodes and/or other BAs, plus ontology information so that the Query Agent can perform the necessary query rewriting before submitting the queries to the SINodes.

The listener process is in charge of receiving requests from other entities in the system; in fact, it embeds much of the transport layer and communication support, including the enforcement of security and policy features. The listener is in charge of authentication (identification of the user, identification of the server), establishing the parameters for a secure connection, logging, and verifying the user profile vs the requested service. After receiving a request it dispatches it to an instance of the playmaker or the map keeper for further processing. In this phase the listener may also act as a load balancer when the playmaking and map keeping functionalities are deployed on a distributed architecture.

The librarian is a service component, being the provider of repository services to the other components of the BA. It is made of a listening module and one or more repository modules. Wrappers may be used to encapsulate different long term storage devices (like DBMSs, file systems, XML files, or whatever else).

3.4   Query Agents

The query agent is the actual carrier of a query from a user to the system. The term "query" has to be interpreted as a general statement in a known intermediate query language which is interpreted by SINode components (SINode query managers) within the system. This query includes information on the context of the user at the time of the establishment of the query. This means that information about the specific activity of the user, his/her preferences, feedback on appreciation of the results of similar queries in the past under similar circumstances, and so on, are embedded in the query.

The query agent is the network query manager and "motion item" of the system, and it should be the only carrier of information among the users and the system. Therefore it should be able to do several jobs:

– carrying a query and the relevant pieces of the user ontology/profile which may help the brokering agents to qualify the semantics of the query (this includes both the case of a user–defined query and the case of system–defined query, like a query issued by the monitoring agent)
– defining the query plan, doing the query rewriting for a specific SINode, and merging the results from several SINodes
– processing the information given by the BA and identifying the SINodes to be accessed for answering the query, and on which further BA peers to contact to possible get more answer to the query
– carrying back the results (both data and metadata)

Query agents are instantiated by the users for each request to the system, or also by the system itself for a load balancing criteria. In a such a way, the user performs a global search in a virtual environment and ignores where the information has been actually maintained and managed.

4   Concluding Remarks

Within highly decentralized, dynamic and mobile information system, the traditional client/server architecture seems not to be sufficient. Searching in the web by using a client/server paradigm, i.e. search engines, cover only a subset of available information and often the information is not up to date due to large amount of time for the crawling operation.

In contrast, querying information sources in a P2P network performs the retrieval of up to date information stored only in the relevant data stores. In this context Napster and Gnutella are examples of application in which every peer shares information with all other peers of the community.

In this paper, we present the SEWASIE system that aims at providing access to heterogeneous information sources. Our approach, like above systems, supposes each peer shares information and each data source (i.e. customers of SEWASIE network) decides directly what data and information they want to make available over the network, without the need for publishing and maintaining them in a specific server. So that, each peer (i.e. the BA) is responsible for the subset of information it makes available on the network and no centralized global information system is required. In fact, by choosing a peer-to-peer platform for our application, we have overcome the need for building a centralized (virtual or materialized) repository for a large amount of semi-structured information, with the related problems of synchronizing multiple accesses to the data and the scalability problems of each centralized architecture.

Acknowledgements. This work is supported in part by the 5th Framework IST programme of the European Community through project SEWASIE within the

Semantic Web Action Line. The SEWASIE consortium comprises in addition to the author' organization (Sonia Bergamaschi is the coordinator of the project), the Universities of Aachen RWTH (M. Jarke), Roma La Sapienza (M. Lenzerini, T. Catarci), Bolzano (E. Franconi), as well as IBM Italia (G. Vetere), Thinking Networks AG (C. Engels) and CNA (A. Tavernari) as user organisation.

References

1. Bergamaschi, S., Guerra, F.: Peer to peer paradigm for a semantic search engine. In: Workshop on Agents and Peer-to-Peer Computing. (2002) LNCS 2530, Springer.
2. Stoica, I., Morris, R., Liben-Nowell, D., Karger, D., Kaashoek, M.F., Dabek, F., Balakrishnan, H.: Chord: a scalable peer-to-peer lookup protocol for internet applications. IEEE/ACM Transactions on Networking 11 (2003) 17–32
3. Daswani, N., Garcia-Molina, H., Yang, B.: Open problems in data-sharing peerto-peer systems. In: Proceedings of the 9th International Conference on Database Theory. (2003)
4. Bergamaschi, S., Castano, S., Beneventano, D., Vincini, M.: Semantic integration of heterogenous information sources. Journal of Data and Knowledge Engineering 36 (2001) 215–249
5. Beneventano, D., Bergamaschi, S., Castano, S., Corni, A., Guidetti, R., Malvezzi, G., Melchiori, M., Vincini, M.: Information integration: The momis project demonstration. In: VLDB 2000, Proceedings of 26th International Conference on Very Large Data Bases, September, 2000, Cairo, Egypt, Morgan Kaufmann (2000) 611–614
6. Bergamaschi, S., Cabri, G., Guerra, F., Leonardi, L., Vincini, M., Zambonelli, F.: Exploiting agents to support information integration. International Journal on Cooperative Information Systems 11 (2002)
7. Beneventano, D., Bergamaschi, S., Gelati, G., Guerra, F., Vincini, M.: Miks: an agent framework supporting information access and integration. In Bergamaschi, S., Klusch, M., Edwards, P., Petta, P., eds.: Intelligent Information Agents - The AgentLink Perspective Lecture Notes in Computer Science N. 2586, Heidelberg, Germany, Springer-Verlag (2003) 22–49
8. Beneventano, D., Bergamaschi, S., Sartori, C.: Description logics for semantic query optimization in object-oriented database systems. ACM Transactions on Database Systems 28 (2003) 1–50

G-Grid: A Class of Scalable and Self-Organizing Data Structures for Multi-dimensional Querying and Content Routing in P2P Networks

Aris M. Ouksel[1,*] and Gianluca Moro[2]

[1] Department of Information and Decision Sciences, University of Illinois at Chicago
2402 University Hall, 601 South Morgan Street
M/C 294 Chicago, IL 60607-7124, USA
aris@uic.edu
[2] Department of Electronics, Computer Science and Systems, University of Bologna
Via Venezia, 52, I-47023 Cesena (FC), Italy
gmoro@deis.unibo.it

Abstract. Peer-to-Peer (P2P) technologies promise to provide efficient distribution, sharing and management of resources, such as storage, processing, routing and other sundry service capabilities, over autonomous and heterogeneous peers. Yet, most current P2P systems only support rudimentary query and content routing over a single data attribute, such as the file-sharing applications popularized in Napster, Gnutella and so forth. Full-fledged applications in distributed data management and grid computing demand more complex functionality, including querying and content routing over multiple attributes. In this paper we present a class of scalable and self-organizing multi-dimensional distributed data structures able to efficiently perform range queries in totally decentralized dynamic P2P environments. These structures are not imposed a priori over the network of peers. Rather, they emerge from the independent interactions of autonomous peers. They are also adaptive to unanticipated changes in the network topology. This robustness property expands their range of usefulness to many application areas such as mobile ad-hoc networks.

1 Introduction

Peer-to-Peer (P2P) networks are emerging as a new computing paradigm for locating and managing contents distributed over a large number of autonomous peers. Autonomy implies that peers are not subject to central coordination. Each peer plays at least three roles, either as (i) a server of data and services, (ii) a client of data and services; and/or (iii) a router for network messages. P2P systems offer the prospect of realizing several desirable properties of emergent systems, including self-organization, which provides the ability to self-administer, scalability, which enables support large number of users and resources without

---

* Research partially supported by NSF grant IIS-0326284

G. Moro, C. Sartori, and M.P. Singh (Eds.): AP2PC 2003, LNAI 2872, pp. 123–137, 2004.
© Springer-Verlag Berlin Heidelberg 2004

performance degradation, and robustness, which makes the system fault-tolerant in the event of peer failure or a peer leaving the distributed system [1].

Content in P2P systems can be conceptually represented as a single relational table, with multiple data attributes, horizontally partitioned among peers. Just as in distributed databases, the location of data partitions is transparent to users. Many popular and currently-deployed P2P systems actually follow this model in organizing shared files on the web. Some of the most well-known are Gnutella [2,3] and its descendants such as Kazaa, Morpheous, WinMX, Emule. This first generation of P2P systems provided a valued service for many users, but they suffered from several drawbacks including, the inefficiency of the routing mechanism and the poor query expressibility. Routing is based on message flooding, with a likely implication of increasing network congestion in data-intensive applications. Queries are limited to single-attribute lookup operations, restricting thus the range of possible of applications in a P2P environment. These problems along with the demands of web users spurred research for alternative structures. Building on previous work in uni-dimensional distributed data structures, such as RP*, LH* [4,5], DRT [6], [7], several new approaches were proposed. Among the most noteworthy are Chord [8], tapestry [9], Pastry [10], P-Grid [11], PeerDB [12]. These new systems did indeed improve performance and extended the flexibility of search by allowing querying by content. However, their limitation to single-attribute queries have continue to stymie efforts to expand the range of applications within acceptable performance results.

Many P2P applications demand richer query semantics over several attributes, comparable to those available in centralized relational DBMSs. Consider for example distributed data mining in a health application. In several practical scenarios, the data is likely to be distributed across a large number of hospitals, where each hospital can be viewed as an autonomous peer. The discovery of patient clusters with similar characteristics, such as gravity of disease, age, residence, sex and so on, requires executing partial range queries on multiple-attribute data distributed across several hospitals. Processing such queries would involve running a combination of individual single attribute queries, followed by an intersection step to filters out unqualified patients. Clearly, this operation will be cost-prohibitive in a distributed environment. This is only one example. Many similar applications will require efficient solutions to complex distributed range queries.

Multi-dimensional structures have been extensively investigated over the last 20 years where the main goal is to support efficiently complex range queries over multiple attributes. A literature survey in this area as well as two specific structures, IBGF and NIBGF, can be found in [14,15]. These structures have been designed for environments where both control and data are centralized, and significant performance improvements have been achieved for both partial and complete range queries. Yet, their adoption in commercial relational DBMSs has remained very limited. We believe distributed environments may actually provide more compelling justifications for their acceptance. While, in centralized systems, range queries over a set of attributes may be processed using single-attribute structures with acceptable performance, despite the large number of local accesses to disk, the same queries in P2P systems will be singularly cost-prohibitive without a multi-dimensional structure, as each local data access will now give rise to several network messages. Dynamic pure P2P networks will naturally amplify the severity of the costs because of continuous changes in the content, its distribution, and the underlying network topology.

Because of autonomy of peers, P2P networks are analogous to complex dynamic organisms in their behavior. For example, local changes in the molecular structure of a chemical compound may aggregate to yield altogether a new compound. A global property emerges generally from a series of simple local interactions. The same phenomenon may also occur in the distribution of content as autonomous peers interact independently with each other in a P2P system. Thus, in addition to scalability, our goal is to seek structures for P2P systems which exhibit emergence and self-organization properties characteristic of complex systems, where local interactions and self-organization of peers lead to a global organizational structure with excellent performance characteristics.

This paper is organized as follows: section 2 introduces the G-Grid structure and its principal features; section 3 illustrates G-Grid at work in P2P environments; section 4 discusses briefly performance issues; section 5 highlights synthetically the robustness, and finally, section 6 summarizes the main ideas presented in this paper.

2   G-Grid Definition

The G-Grid is a distributed multidimensional data structure, which organizes a set of objects across any number of peers in a network. It is a novel structure we developed and studied [13] from preceding works on multidimensional data structures for centralized systems [14,15,16,17]. Each dimension represents one attribute of the objects. For example, location of an object may be one possible attribute. The G-Grid partitions the space of objects, based on the attribute values, into regions and structures these regions into a tree as follows (see the example of Figure 1): a node of the tree represents a region in the multidimensional data space and an edge links two regions, where one, called the child region, is properly nested in the other, called the father region. The root node represents the whole object space. One or more regions are assigned to one peer, and as result one or more nodes of the G-Grid tree structure are associated with a peer.

Formally, consider a relation table $\mathbf{T}$ with attributes $A_0, A_1, \ldots, A_{(d-1)}$, also called *keys*, taking their values from domains $D_0, D_1, \ldots, D_{(d-1)}$, respectively. In G-Grid a relation is viewed as a bounded d-dimensional hypercube
$$[\min D_0, \max D_0)x...x[\min D_{d-1}, \max D_{d-1})$$
where each attribute is represented by one dimension of the space. For the sake of generality, let us assume for now that this hypercube is normalized to the unit cube. In other words, each attribute value is mapped to a rational number in the half-open interval $\mathbf{U}=[0,1)$ by simple interpolation, assuming the attribute domains are bounded but not necessarily finite. In practice, this is not necessary.

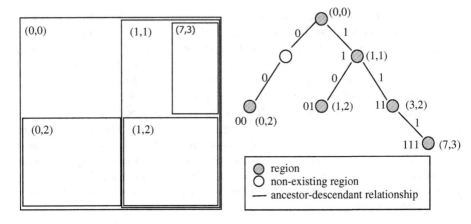

Fig. 1. An example of a partitioned 2-dimensional space and its counterpart tree

The entire data space is U^d, where each tuple of the relation is attached to a point in U^d, which is precisely the point whose coordinates along each dimension represent the scaled values obtained by interpolation from the tuple. Given a record $k = (k_0, k_1, \ldots, k_{(d-1)})$ of a relation R, each record k is represented by a point $k^0 = (k_0^0, k_1^0, \ldots, k_{(d-1)}^0)$ in U^d.

The data space U^d is decomposed into subspaces called regions, as in the example of Figure 1. A *region* R is a d-dimensional hyper-rectangular subspace of U^d delineated by the pair $I = (x^{\min}, x^{\max})$, where $x^{\min}$ and $x^{\max}$ are d-dimensional vectors representing the coordinates of the minimum and the maximum points in the subspace, respectively. Let x be a point in U^d. Then a region R can be defined formally as: R= $\{x/x^{\min} \leq x < x^{\max}\}$. We refer to I as the identifier of region R. Initially, the data space consists only of one region R=U^d whose identifier is $I = \{x^{\min} = (0,0), x^{\max} = (1,1)\}$. Any point in U^d can be viewed as the identifier of a region with a measure 0. The records that fall within a region R are stored in a bucket of fixed size B. R is split when the number of records in it exceeds B. The decomposition of R is carried out by carving out a region R' from the overflowing region. In the ideal case, R and R' will split the records in B in half. This split mechanism has been first introduced in [15] and subsequently reutilized in another novel structure, the Generalized Grid File (GGF), designed for cluster P2P computing [18]. Other researchers have also adopted it, but for the single dimensional case, as for example in [11]. In [15], it is shown that this split mechanism guarantees a storage utilization of no less than one-third of the total size of a bucket. As a result, degenerate space partitioning is avoided with positive consequence on the information retrieval capability.

Every region, and therefore any records, can also be identified by a pair of integer number (π, l), where l means the number of times that the starting region (labelled $(0,0)$) has been split, while the binary conversion of π represents precisely the path from the root to the node representing the region (see Figure 1). Value l represents also the size of the region, i.e., $1/2^l$.

It is important to note that the splitting of any region is totally a local operation, and thus does not require any global information of the space. Looking at the Figure 1 it is easy to understand that l also represents the length of the binary conversion of π. When a new region is generated through a split we will take the π of the direct parent region, calculate the value $bin(\pi)$, adding in case some "0" on the left to reach the length l, attach a "0" in the beginning of the string for the left child or a "1" for the right one and then convert it again into decimal value. For instance, the left child region of $(1,2)$ will be $\pi = $ "0" $+ bin(1) = $ "001" $= 1$ and the right one $\pi = $ "1" $+ bin(1) = $ "101" $= 5$.

This splitting approach leads to regions that are either disjoint or properly contain each other. The binary representing these regions differ in at least one bit, in the case, or one is the prefix of the other in the second. Figure 1 illustrates this relationship between regions. All regions at the same level cover disjoint subspaces of the space, we refer to this as the *spatial property*; whereas regions on the same are contained in each other, we refer to this as the *cover property*. As a consequence, the identifier of the deepest region where a record might be located can be computed prior to starting the search using the current maximum number of splits. If the target region does not exist, then the record will be located in one of its parent along the same path in the binary tree. As a result of the balanced load achieved by the split mechanism, and the fact that search is done along on the same path of the tree, the record search cost is logarithmic in the number of messages between regions. Next Section shows that thanks to a full *learning capability*, which is another fundamental feature we have introduced in G-Grid, search costs are less than logarithmic and can also be constant in some realistic scenarios independently on the number of peers in the overlay network.

3   G-Grid in P2P Environments

The G-Grid tree structure is embedded in the network of peers. Not all peers in a network are necessarily part of the G-Grid. Thus an edge in the tree structure may actually correspond to a path in the network.

The network consists of two kinds of peers: (i) s-peers, or structure-peers, are those that do manage at least one region of the G-Grid; (ii) c-peers, or client-peers, are those that do not manage any region. Both s-peers and c-peers may issue operations (object search requests, insertions, and possibly deletions) to other s-peers, and in addition s-peers provide routing tables to the operations. Initially the G-Grid may consist of only one s-peer. In the process of performing search operations, peers learn their routing table by learning new edges as shown in Figure 2. Progressively, they build an internal map of the whole object space across all s-peers in the G-Grid. This information is eventually exploited during subsequent operations to find more efficient routes to the desired objects. The goal is to minimize the number of hops in dynamic P2P networks where the structure grows and the interaction between peers increases. In addition the

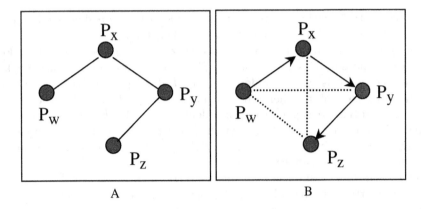

Fig. 2. A) Peers involved by an operation issued by Peer P_w routed towards P_z; B) Learning of new (dot line) links among them after completing the operation.

learning mechanism contributes to distribute the workload among peers, even if they are hierarchical structured according to a tree. We report in the next section some experiments and theoretical analyses that explain the crucial variables governing the complex behaviours of the system.

Two interacting peers may decide to distribute control of their objects through a partitioning of their respective object spaces. What does trigger the distribution of control ? When the set of objects in an s-peer grows in a way that the s-peer becomes a bottleneck, an s-peer may spawn new nested regions, which are then handed over to other interacting peers (s-peers or c-peers, which then evolve to become s-peers) for control. Alternatively, the hand over may occur through direct solicitation of other available peers.

Spawning may also be triggered by application-specific considerations. For example, let us assume that objects represented in the G-Grid structure are mobile, and one of the attribute is location. If the distance between the location of a peer and the location of its objects goes over a pre-specified threshold, a new region may be spawned into an appropriate available c-peer or merged into an available s-peer in a way which reduces the distance between peers and the objects in the region. Thus, the objects in peers migrate from one peer to another to bring them closer to the actual objects they represent. The *proximity concept* applies also in the case of mobile s-peers. As an s-peer moves away from the location of objects it manages, these objects are handed over to an s-peer that is closer to the objects. While the notion of proximity is used here in the context of geographic distance, it can be readily extended to other types of attributes.

In summary the main features of the G-Grid are the following:

- distributed: The objects in the G-Grid are distributed across autonomous peers.
- emerging: The structure is not imposed a-priori on the set objects in the distributed environment. Rather, the structure is built incrementally and

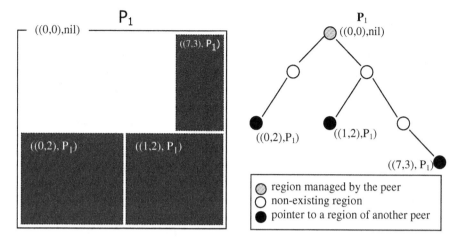

Fig. 3. A partitioned 2-dim space locally at Peer P_1 and its counterpart tree

emerges dynamically as peers interact with each other and learn each other's content.

- self-organizing: The decision for two peers to participate in the G-Grid structure and to distribute control among them is not imposed externally.
- scalable: The G-Grid is scalable in that its performance does not deteriorate as the number of peer increases.

3.1 G-Grid Split Rules

Peers are autonomous, and each peer views itself initially in control of its own whole object space $(0,0)$, but at any one time it contains data located in only one region of the partitioned space. The remainder of the space is represented by index entries to other data regions contained in other peers. Initially, the data region in a peer coincides exactly with space $(0,0)$. Each peer maintains a portion of the overall index, i.e., routing table, learned through its direct interactions with other peers.

As two peers interact and voluntarily decide to participate in the G-Grid, their spaces are partitioned into two nested regions with each peer taking control of one of the regions and keeping a pointer to the other peer and the region it holds. In general one of the two nested region may be collapsed in its father region. For instance, Figure 3 depicts a structure partitioned in three regions distributed across three peers. In particular the Figure depicts the physical partitioning at Peer 1, which stores locally the region $(0,0)$ and three pointers to Peers managing the black-colored regions. The interacting peers will also keep track of the region descriptor describing each other's assigned region. These latter descriptors become part of a local content-based routing table. The partitioning policy is flexible and may be driven by application and performance considerations.

Here we formally introduce the split rules giving also an example.
Let us introduce the following notations:

- Let (r, λ) denote the identifier of the region assigned to a peer P, denoted also $P(r, \lambda)$ in case of ambiguity with peers managing a region with the same identifier; region (r, λ) contains both data elements and index entries and, when there is no ambiguity, it will also represent its content.
- Let $+$, $*$, and $-$ represent the set union, intersection, and difference operators.
- Let $\overline{(r, \lambda)}$ denote the complement of (r, λ), namely $(r, \lambda) + \overline{(r, \lambda)} = (0, 0)$, that is the whole space, and $(r, \lambda) * \overline{(r, \lambda)} = \emptyset$. Note that $\overline{(r, \lambda)}$ is a concave space and therefore does not satisfy the definition of a region, moreover it contains only pointers to regions, which may enclose (r, λ) or be disjoint with it. Pointers are learnt through interactions with other peers.
- Let $((r', \lambda'), P')$ denote an index entry in P indicating that (r', λ') is located in peer P'; in case of ambiguity it is denoted $P((r', \lambda'), P')$. Note that when P'=nil, then the content of the region is local.
- Let $(r', \lambda')_H$ denote a special pointer in P, which represents a placeholder for region (r', λ') whose elements are those not in $P(r, \lambda)$. At some step during the lifecycle of the structure, (r', λ') was the region contained in P and then was later reduced to region (r, λ). The contents in $(r', \lambda') - (r, \lambda)$ were transferred to P' from P during the split operation.

The placeholder has no impact on the logical organization of the structure, the search procedure, except perhaps to increase the number of elements in a peer. It acts simply as a routing element necessary during transient states of the structure. This indirection in the search is necessary for those peers interacting with P and requesting elements in $(r', \lambda') - (r, \lambda)$. After the first interaction, these peers will have learned the new path and therefore it is no longer necessary to go through P, and instead go directly to P'. In other words, the organization will adapt naturally and incrementally to the new structure.

The split is always local to the two peers being split. There is no propagation to other peers and the completeness defined in [18] is preserved in G-Grid by construction.

Let us assume that two peers P_1 and P_2 meet and that they manage (r_1, λ_1) and (r_2, λ_2) respectively. There are two cases:

A. $(r_1, \lambda_1) * (r_2, \lambda_2) = \emptyset$, namely they manage two disjoint regions
B. $(r_1, \lambda_1) \subseteq (r_2, \lambda_2)$ or vice versa

which correspond to the two following rules:

A. $(r_1, \lambda_1) * (r_2, \lambda_2) = \emptyset$
- $(r_1', \lambda_1') = (r_1, \lambda_1) + \overline{(r_2, \lambda_2)} / (r_1, \lambda_1);$
  $(r_2', \lambda_2') = (r_2, \lambda_2) + \overline{(r_1, \lambda_1)} / (r_2, \lambda_2);$
- $\overline{(r_1', \lambda_1')} = \overline{(r_1, \lambda_1)} - \overline{(r_1, \lambda_1)} / (r_2, \lambda_2) + ((r_2, \lambda_2), P_2);$
- $\overline{(r_2', \lambda_2')} = \overline{(r_2, \lambda_2)} - \overline{(r_2, \lambda_2)} / (r_1, \lambda_1) + ((r_1, \lambda_1), P_1);$

B. $(r_2, \lambda_2) * (r_1, \lambda_1) \neq \emptyset$.

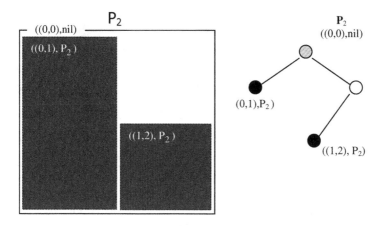

Fig. 4. A partitioned 2-dim space locally at Peer P_2 and its counterpart tree

- Let $(r_1, \lambda_1) = (r_1, \lambda_1) + (r_2, \lambda_2)$;
- Split (r_1, λ_1) into (r_1, λ_1) and (r_2', λ_2')
- $(r_1', \lambda_1') \quad = \quad \overline{(r_1, \lambda_1)} - \quad ((r_2, \lambda_2), P_2) - ((r_1, \lambda_1), nil) + (r_1', \lambda_1'), nil))$
  $+((r_2', \lambda_2'), P_2)$;
- $(r_2', \lambda_2') \quad = \quad \overline{(r_2, \lambda_2)} - \quad ((r_1, \lambda_1), P_1) - ((r_2, \lambda_2), nil) + ((r_2', \lambda_2'), nil) +$
  $((r_1', \lambda_1'), P_1)$;
- If $r_2 \subset r_2$ **Then** $\overline{(r_2, \lambda_2)} = \overline{(r_2, \lambda_2)} + ((r_2, \lambda_2), P_1)_H$
  Else if $r_2 \subset r_2'$ Then
  * $\overline{(r_2', \lambda_2')} = \overline{(r_2', \lambda_2')} - \overline{(r_2, \lambda_2)} / ((r_2', \lambda_2') - (r_2, \lambda_2))$ and
  * $(r_2, \lambda_2) = (r_2, \lambda_2) + \overline{(r_2, \lambda_2)} / ((r_2', \lambda_2') - (r_2, \lambda_2))$.

For space reasons we limit the description of the rules by giving a single example related to the meeting of Peer 1 and 2 represented in Figure 3 and Figure 4 respectively. In each Figure is depicted both the spatial structure and its correspondent tree. The two peers manage the same region (0,0), therefore must be applied the rule B. First of all the two structures of Figure 3 and Figure 4 are conceptually merged by simply superimposing the two trees (see Figure 5A); a region identifier may be associated with a list of peers containing data located in the same spatial region.

Then, as illustrated in Figure 5B the rule performs a buddy split of the region (0,0) generating two regions: (0,1) and (1,1). Finally, the merged structure is divided between the two peers as depicted in Figure 6. We highlight that the region (0,1) has been collapsed in (0,0) of Peer 1, while Peer 2 has introduced a placeholder towards Peer 1.

4   Performance Analyses

For space reasons we present here only some of the empirical results, which we have conducted by implementing a simulation of G-Grid, and some theoreti-

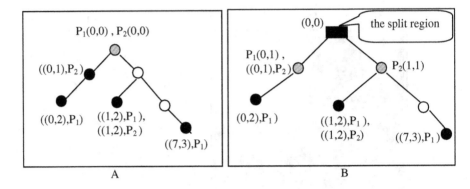

Fig. 5. A) Merged tree by superimposing the one of Fig. 3 and Fig. 4; B) Merged tree after the split of the region (0,0) in (0,1) and (1,1)

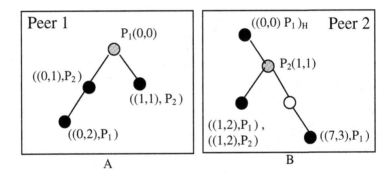

Fig. 6. Physical configurations A) at Peer 1 by collapsing (0,1) in (0,0), and B) at Peer 2 with a placeholder to (0,0) of Peer 1

cal results confirming these experiments. The simulation manages exact match queries and record insertions and incorporates both the region splitting mechanism and the learning capability. Moreover it can be configured with some parameters, such as the region bucket size b and the rate of insertions with respect to queries $\frac{insertions}{queries}$. In the experiments the structure evolves and grows in a dynamic fashion starting from one peers and by generating operations randomly. On this basis G-Grid is a stochastic system with complex behaviours where each state of the system depends on the preceding one, but the set itself of the states evolves dynamically over the time growing very quickly and making hard any analysis based on Markov chains.

However we have found the split probability, which predicts the growth of the system and it is useful to find important theoretical results related to the *average path length* (APL) to deliver any message in the system.

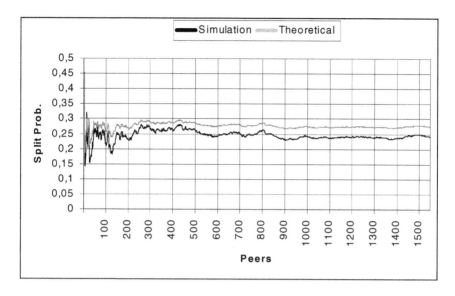

Fig. 7. The approximated theoretical split prob. compared with a simulation

For space reasons we limit to present here the simplest version which well approximates the mentioned above probability for very low values of the bucket size.

Split Probability Definition: Let t be any instant in the life of a G-Grid structure G and let us denote the following variables:

- N_t = records at the instant t randomly distributed in G
- M_t = regions/peers in G at the instant t
- b = the region bucket size

then the split probability is the probability that a record insertion at the instant t ends in a region already full with b records, namely:

$$P_s(N_t, M_t, b) = \frac{1}{k - j + 1} \cdot \sum_{i=j}^{k} \frac{i}{M_t} \tag{1}$$

where j and k, which are the minimum and maximum number of full regions respectively, are the following:

$$j = max(N_t - M_t \cdot (b - 1), 0) \qquad k = floor\left(\frac{N_t - \frac{b}{3} \cdot M_t}{\frac{2}{3} \cdot b}\right) \tag{2}$$

Figure 7 illustrates a numeric comparison between the formula 1 and an experiment conducted with $b = 6$ where the system grows up to more than 1500 peers. The two split probabilities oscillate until there are less than 50 peers,

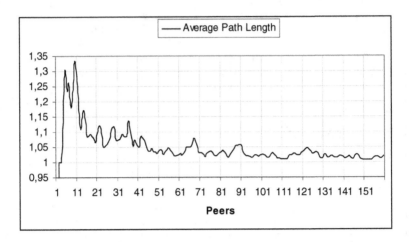

Fig. 8. When $\frac{insertions}{queries} \approx \frac{1}{M_t^2}$ the average path length to deliver messages tends to 1

then both of them stabilize with a difference around 2.5%; in all experiments the stabilization occurs always independently on the rate $\frac{insertions}{queries}$. Experiments have also confirmed an average *storage utilization* per region equals to $\frac{2b}{3}$, that is the number of records stored on average by regions.

The rate $\frac{insertions}{queries}$ instead is determining for the APL in the system, in fact if the rate remains constant the APL tends to grow, but less than logarithmically with respect to the number of peers. This effect is due to the learning capability which reduces the distances in the system by creating new links. Finally, we verified both theoretically and experimentally that if the rate $\frac{insertions}{queries}$ changes like $\Theta(\frac{1}{M_t^2})$ then the APL in the system tends quickly to 1 (see Figure 8). Intuitively this can explained by the fact that both queries and insertions creates new links in the system, but in addition insertions cause splits introducing new regions and new peers which increase the APL. In several realistic scenarios the number of queries is more than quadratic with respect to the number of users/machines, for instance in the World Wide Web each user access may originate in cascade many messages and queries. Also the execution of more traditional queries, such as joins and range queries, can generate that number of requests.

5 Robustness

The G-Grid allows peers to connect and disconnect autonomously from the structure. C-peers can connect and disconnect without an impact on the overall G-Grid structure, except perhaps that responses to their already initiated requests will not have a return address. On the other hand, an non-anticipated disconnection of an s-peers may make the s-peer's objects and local routing table inaccessible. Thus, it is important that s-peer return local information to the system in non-catastrophic disconnection. An **orderly disconnection** is one where an s-peer hands over its content to another peer to preserve data accessibility and routing information. It can: either (i) merge its local information (both objects and routing table) to its father s-peer or a child s-peer., or, (ii) solicit a c-peer as a replacement. The choice is determined based on policies which will enhance the overall performance of the system.

A **disorderly disconnection** of a s-peer occurs in catastrophic situations such as computer crashes or physical network problems. Objects in the s-peer become inaccessible and routing through the s-peer is no longer possible. Depending on the network topology, a disorderly disconnection could cause the G-Grid partitioning into two disjoint component. To enhance robustness of the system, one approach is through duplication of information in s-peers. Besides the associated information integrity problems, duplication does not eliminate the problem of G-Grid partitioning, it only reduces the likelihood of its occurrence. Our approach is to avoid altogether duplication and rely on the learning mechanism of the system, which establishes incrementally links between the various s-peers as the level of interaction increases, and thus provides multiple routes to get to s-peers. To what extent does the learning mechanism reduce the likelihood of G-Grid partitioning? Our preliminary experimental results show that the likelihood of partitioning is practically nil. What will be the effect on performance and availibility of data in combining both duplication and the learning mechanism? Answers to these questions require an extensive robustness analysis, which we intend to do in the future.

After a disorderly disconnection, an s-peer may rejoin the G-GRID either as a c-peer or as an s-peer. If it chooses the former approach, it will have to issue direct insertion requests for all its objects to the G-Grid system. In the latter, it will have to wait for an interaction with another s-peer and then integrate its content through the normal partitioning process.

As indicated earlier, an important concept in the G-Grid is the peers' ability to learn other peers' local routing tables during search operations. As a peer interacts with other peers, its local routing table grows and improves its capability to find the most efficient route to its target objects. Clearly, learning content-based routing tables is an emergent property in that the minimum path to a target peer is discovered without having to encode into the system a minimum path algorithm.

6   Conclusions

In this paper, a class of scalable self-organizing data structures for P2P networks, called the G-Grid, is introduced. These structures enable efficient multidimensional search based on partial range queries. We have also illustrated how peers can exploit the properties of these structures to learn dynamically both the distribution of content and the network topology, and thereby, provide algorithms for efficient processing of range queries. In the worst case, search costs for a single object, measured as the number of hops over peers, are logarithmic in the number of peers. But, for many realistic workloads of insertions of new objects and retrievals, such as those currently taking place on the web, the average is equal or less than 2 hops, independently on the wideness of the P2P network. We have also sketched out an aspect which is seldom treated in P2P literature, namely the possibility of merging independently constructed data structures. This is particularly important for two autonomous organization, which make the decision to share data between them for commercial or scientific reasons.

This work is a summary of ongoing work towards the idea of achieving virtual DBMSs from P2P systems as a set of emergent services, but which abide by the same desirable properties of centralized DBMSs, namely, data integrity and consistence, transaction processing and a complete SQL expressiveness.

References

1. Moro, G., Ouksel, A.M., Sartori, C.: Agents and peer-to-peer computing: a promising combination of paradigms. In: Proceedings of the First International Workshop on Agents and Peer-to-Peer Computing, Bologna, Italy, July 2002. Volume 2530., Springer (2003) 1–14
2. Jovanovic, M.A., Annexstein, F.S., Berman, K.A.: Scalability issues in large peer-to-peer networks - a case study of gnutella. Technical Report Technical Report, University of Cincinnati (2001)
3. Kan, G.: 8. In: Peer-to-Peer: Harnessing the Benefits of Disruptive Technologies. O'Reilly & Associates (2001) 94–122
4. W. Litwin, M. A. Neitmat, D.A.S.: RP*–A Family of Ordered–Preserving Scalable Distributed Data Structures. In: In Proceedings of the 20th International Conference on Very Large Data Bases (VLDB'94), Santiago, Chile. (1994) 342–353
5. W. Litwin, M. A. Neitmat, D.A.S.: LH*–Linear Hashing for Distributed Files. ACM Transactions on Database Systems 4 (1996) 480–525
6. B. Kröll, P.W.: Distributing a search tree among a growing number of processors. In: In Proceedings of the ACM International Conference on Management of Data (SIGMOD'94), Minneapolis, MN, USA, ACM Press (1994) 265–276
7. Pasquale, A.D., Nardelli, E.: Adst: An order preserving scalable distributed data structure with constant access costs. In Carey, M.J., Schneider, D.A., eds.: Proceedings of the 28th Conference on Current Trends in Theory and Practice of Informatics (SOFSEM'01), Piestany, Slovak Republic. Volume 2234., Springer-Verlag (2001) 211–222
8. Stoica, I., Morris, R., Karger, D., Kaashoek, M.F., Balakrishnan, H.: Chord: A scalable peer-to-peer lookup service for internet applications. In: SIGCOMM, ACM Press (2001) 149–160
9. Zhao, B.Y., Kubiatowicz, J., Joseph, A.: Tapestry: An Infrastructure for Fault-tolerant Wide-area Location and Routing. In: Technical report, UCB/CSD-01-1141, University of California, Berkeley. (2001)
10. Rowstron, A., Druschel, P.: Pastry: Scalable, decentralized object location, and routing for large-scale peer-to-peer systems. Lecture Notes in Computer Science 2218 (2001) 329–340
11. Aberer, K., Cudré-Mauroux, P., Datta, A., Despotovic, Z., Hauswirth, M., Punceva, M., Schmidt, R.: P-Grid: A Self-organizing Structured P2P System. SIGMOD Record 2 (2003)

12. Ng, W.S., Ooi, B.C., Tan, K.L., Zhou, A.Y.: Peerdb: A P2P-based System for Distributed Data Sharing. In: International Conference on Data Engineering (ICDE). (2003) 633–644
13. Ouksel, A.M., Moro, G.: G-Grid: A Class of Scalable and Self-Organizing Data Structures for Multi-dimensional Querying and Content Routing in P2P Networks. Technical Report DEIS-LIA-002-04, February, DEIS University of Bologna (2004)
14. Ouksel, A.M.: The interpolation-based grid file. In: Proceedings of the ACM SICACT-SIGMOD Symposium on Principles Of Data Base Systems, ACM (1985) 20–27
15. Ouksel, A.M., Mayer, O.: A robust and efficient spatial data structure: The nested interpolation-based grid file. Acta Informatica **29** (1992) 335–373
16. Ouksel, A.M., Kumar, V., Majumdar, C.: Management of concurrency in interpolation-based grid file organization and its performance. Information Sciences Journal **2** (1994) 129–158
17. Ouksel, A.M., Kammermeier, F.: The interpolation-based grid file revisited. Technical Report Progress Report, PhD dissertation, Computer Science Department, Kaiserslautern University (2002)
18. Ouksel, A.M., Moro, G., Litwin, W.: GGF: A Generalized Grid File for Distributed Environments. Technical Report UIC-IDS-CRIM/TECH-REPORT No.2002-05, University of Illinois at Chicago, DEIS University of Bologna (2002)

Fuzzy Cost Modeling for Peer-to-Peer Systems

Bo Ling[1], Wee Siong Ng[2], YanFeng Shu[3], and AoYing Zhou[1]

[1] Department of Computer Science and Engineering,
Fudan University, Shanghai, P.R. China
{lingbo, aoying}@fudan.edu.cn
[2] Singapore-MIT Alliance,
[3] Department of Computer Science,
National University of Singapore, Singapore
smangws@nus.edu.sg, shuyanfe@comp.nus.edu.sg

Abstract. Exiting cost estimation models suffer from several limitations. First, static cost model is not capable of reflecting real-time situations. Second, dynamic cost model is not scalable due to its extensive probe queries. Third, these models are not designed for ad-hoc systems such as P2P, since dynamism of peers is not taken into consideration. In this paper, first, we propose a progressive "push-based" remote cost monitoring approach. We derive a generic static cost model from conventional static approach. Agents will be sent to remote hosts with a generic cost model and epsilons (ε) indicating the acceptable magnitude of cost change, i.e., percentage of coefficient changed. An update will be sent (pushed) to original host once the magnitude of the cost changes exceeds . Second, we introduce a fuzzy cost evaluation metric in additional to traditional evaluation criteria for handling the dynamism of P2P systems. This metric gives a confident measurement of a peer's reliability.

1 Introduction

Peer-to-Peer (P2P) has opened up a new area of research in networking and distributed computing. Such systems are inexpensive, easy to use, highly scaleable and do not require centralized administration. Despite the advantages offered by P2P technology, it poses many novel challenges for the research community. Querying remote cost information for producing an effective query plan is among one of the crucial challenges, especially in supporting complex P2P query systems, such as OLAP caching [1] and P2P DBMS [2] applications.

Many approaches have been suggested for estimating query cost in distributed information sources. Generally, it can be categorized into static cost model and dynamic cost model. Static cost model derives a generic model based on calibration [3][4], sampling [4] or statistical approach [5]. These models are seldom changed (i.e., the coefficient) once they have been derived and all parameters used for the cost estimation are known a priori before execution of the plans. It is assumed to work in a static environment where the workload of remote hosts may not change dynamically. However in the context of heterogeneous and dynamic environment such as Internet and P2P, it is unrealistic to assume

G. Moro, C. Sartori, and M.P. Singh (Eds.): AP2PC 2003, LNAI 2872, pp. 138–143, 2004.
© Springer-Verlag Berlin Heidelberg 2004

that every site has the same query execution capabilities. Moreover, workload of a host might be increased dynamically when concurrency tasks are being supported. As a result, executing cost will be significantly increased. Hence, cost estimation deployed in a static environment cannot be migrated directly into dynamic environments without major modification. Adali et. al. [4] have proposed a *semi-dynamic* approach, a cost estimation strategy based on statistics. The statistics are cached for each actual call to remote sources. Consequently, cost of the possible plans can be estimated based on the available statistics cached previously. A dynamic cost model with a probe-based optimization strategy is proposed in [6]. This approach is capable of reflecting more accurately real-time cost statistic of remote hosts. However, it is not scalable due to extensive increase in the number of probe queries.

Furthermore, existing cost models employ discrete functions as their cost measurement metric, which we claim are not appropriate for ad-hoc P2P systems. For an example, assuming there are two peers in the system namely *Peer1* and *Peer2* with both offering similar resources. Let *PeerQ* be the peer who initiated a query. Assume the cost of executing a query *q* at *Peer1* and *Peer2* is 5 and 6 units respectively. Based on these discrete cost values, *PeerQ* expects the query is executed cheaper in *Peer1* than in *Peer2* for execution. However, in reality, *Peer1* might not be reliable, e.g., the frequency of its disconnection from the network might be higher than *Peer2*, which is not reflected in the discrete cost model. Upon *PeerQ* notices *Peer1* is disconnected from the network, it has to resubmit the query to *Peer2* for processing. As a result, *PeerQ* may end up paying higher cost than the plan of originally submitting to *Peer2* due to the disconnection of *Peer1*.

Based on the above observations, we propose the following solutions. First, we follow a different approach focusing on a "push-based" mechanism. The approach relies on agents that monitor cost on the remote data sources with progressive cost updating. We first derive a generic static cost model from a conventional approach [3][4]. Each agent will be sent to remote hosts with a generic cost model and epsilons (ε) indicating the acceptable magnitude of cost changes, i.e., percentage of coefficient change. An update will be sent (push) to the original host once the magnitude of the cost changes is greater than ε. Consequently, a query optimizer can have near-real-time cost information (i.e., estimation based on the coefficients and ε) of remote peers without heavily probing for the answer. Second, we propose a fuzzy cost evaluation metric in addition to traditional evaluation criteria such as CPU, I/O and communication costs. Unlike the conventional discrete cost model, fuzzy cost model is described in terms of possibilities of occurrences of events. Since it is possible to estimate a maximum processing time for a query based on history statistic records or sampling technique, a query optimizer needs to ensure choosing only peers with certain degree of reliability, i.e., peer which is accessible during the period of query processing. In this regard, we propose a fuzzy *Reliability* metric to describe the reliable cost of remote peers. Therefore, the objective for a query optimizer is to find a good plan that minimizes the processing cost and maximizes the reliability for a query.

As a result, it can minimize performance degradation due to remote peer failure which would cause query resubmission.

2 Cost Model

In this section, we start by defining the problem of query optimization in a P2P environment. Subsequently, we describe a mechanism for progressive remote cost monitoring. Finally, we propose our Reliability fuzzy metric for handling dynamism of peers.

2.1 Problem Statement

Suppose there is a peer P who has n identifiers in its contact list . These n peers are dynamic, i.e., they are allowed to leave and then join the network at any time. Consider a query, q, requires a resource R for processing. Assume there are k peers who have the sharable resource R, where $k \leq n$. The objective is to select one peer from the k, which provides a minimum query response time, and with highest confidence that it will be the least likely offline during the period of query processing.

The solution for the problem is two-fold. First, we would like to perform a quick filtering on k peers; select the top-i ($i \ll k$) peers who have offered the cheapest cost to process the query. The optimum situation is to have all the "near-accurate" remote cost information stored in the local cache. Therefore, decisions can be made instantly. Second, for each of the i peers, a simple query will be sent to verify its reliability. Let's assume a query requires maximum t time to process. Peers with highest reliability which will be accessible for at least a continues period of $now + t$, is considered as the candidate to process the query.

2.2 Progressive Cost Monitoring

There are several criteria that greatly influence the cost needed for processing a remote query, such as communication cost, load, remote invocation etc. For simplicity, we outline the cost model at a very high level. Our purpose is not to present the model details per se but to demonstrate an effective alternative approach for remote cost monitoring with progressive updating. Typically, the cost model estimates the cost in terms of time. We present a generic cost model as $Cost = \alpha_1 \cdot T_{cpu} + \alpha_2(T_{i/o} \cdot \#I/Os) + \alpha_3 \cdot T_{com} + \alpha_4(T_{trm} \cdot \#size)$, where the x is the coefficient with respect to each evaluation criterion. T_{cpu} is the time for CPU instructions and $T_{i/o}$ is the time for a disk I/O. Together T_{cpu} and $T_{i/o}$ are the components that measure the remote processing cost. T_{com} is the time required for initiating remote communication during network establishment. It is a fixed cost in most situations. Finally, T_{trm} is the time it takes to transmit a data unit (i.e., the size might be in terms of bytes for a packet or could be in a different unit) from one peer to another. Previous studies on static query optimization assume all the mentioned costs (i.e., T_{cpu}, $T_{i/o}$, T_{com} and T_{trm}) remain constant. While total transmission cost (i.e., $T_{trm} \cdot \#size$) is proportional to the size of data transferred. This may not be true for Internet-based environment as pointed out in literature [6].

Our proposed solution is as follows. For each peer in the contact list, an agent carrying the generic cost model will be sent to the remote peer. The objective is to figure out the coefficients of the cost formulation. Local peer maintains a cache to store the coefficients of remote peers. Query optimizer reads the local cache when processing cost estimation for plan selection. However, when coefficients are not found in local cache, e.g., a new peer has just been added into the contact list, a new agent will be constructed and sent to the remote peer for collecting the cost coefficient. Subsequently, that agent will be hosted there for continual cost monitoring. Each evaluation criterion is associated with an epsilon which indicates the range of an acceptable changes without notifying the original peers. The purpose is to reduce the number of communication between the agents and home peer. If a peer is removed from the contact list, its corresponding cost monitoring agent at the remote site will be dropped.

2.3 Peer Reliability

In this section, we introduce the Time-Hierarchical (TM-H) structure and formulation of *Reliability* fuzzy set to estimate the costs associated with dynamism of peers.

Time-Hierarchical (TM-H) structure. Most of the computer users exhibit certain patterns of usage behavior when they join and leave the network. This behavior is strongly correlated to the Time-Of-Day or Day-of-Week, e.g., office users may connect to the network during office hours (9am to 6pm), from Monday to Friday. Therefore, in order to predict the reliability of a peer, the timing is important. For example, office users may have high reliability during 9am to 11am as compared to 9pm to 11pm. Based on this observation, we proposed a Time-Hierarchical (TM-H) model to capture the behavior and formulate a *Reliability* fuzzy characteristic to evaluate it

Fig 1 (left) illustrates the TM-H model. It is a tree-like structure where each peer in the network maintains its own TM-H structure. In addition, it is also an append-only structure which supports "add" and "update" operation. The leaf (H-Level) provides the basic cost information. This cost information is

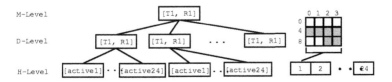

Fig. 1. The TM-H Architecture And The Basic *active* Component

measured in terms of *active*. Each active corresponds to five minutes network connection time, i.e., time that it is accessible by other peers. Intuitively, we can visualize the basic component at the H-Level as an array of 24 discrete boxes representing 24 hours of the day. Each box is further subdivided into 12 *active*. Fig 1 (right) shows a graphical representation of *active* component with the gray shaded boxes indicating the total number of *active* at time 1am. The six gray shaded boxes indicate that at 1am, there has been about 30 minutes of continuous online activity. The parent of H-Level has an average *Reliability* of a peer at that particular day (denotes as D-Level). Depending on the necessity of applications, numbers of level supports can easily be extended, e.g., month (denotes as M-Level in Figure 1) or year. Each node of the TM-H structure except nodes at H-level stores a pair value [*Time_Tag, Reliability*] where the *Time_Tag* is time object that indicates the time/date where the *Reliability* is valid. For example, a node with pair value [1, 0.7] at D-Level indicates that the peer has 0.7 reliability on Monday (assuming *Time_Tag* = 1 is corresponding to Monday). All levels other than leaves can be computed from their immediately lower level. Based on this TM-H model and *active*, we present how to formulate the *Reliability* of a peer.

2.4   Reliability Formulation

We denote $\bigcup$ as an universe of discourse where it denotes the total possible *active* gained for a peer p in an hour, $\bigcup = \{1,...,12\}$, which is a real number between 1 to 12. Each peer has a minimum 1 *active* once it has been connected to the network and maximum 12 *active*. We define the *Reliable* characteristic functions as in equation (1).

$$\mu(x) = \begin{cases} 0 & for\ 1 \le x \le 4; \\ \left\{1 + [(x-4)/2]^{-2}\right\}^{-1} & for\ 4 < x \le 12; \end{cases} \tag{1}$$

$$\Re_p(t_m, t_n) = \left[\sum_{i=m}^{n} \hat{S}(t_i)\right] \Big/ (n-m) + 1 \tag{2}$$

As denoted in equation (1), a peer is considered reliable when its total number of *active* is greater than 4 and the equation $\left\{1 + [(x-4)/2]^{-2}\right\}^{-1}$ is defined to measure its characteristic. Let us denote $\hat{S}_p(x) = \{\mu(x)|x \in U\}$ as degree of *Reliability* of peer p. Hence, when peer is highly reliable, i.e., $\hat{S}_p(x)$ is approaching 1 if and only if the total *active* is closing to 12. For illustration of the idea, Table 1 shows an example of peer's *Reliability* from time T1 to T5. Based on the active, we can compute the degree of peer's *Reliability* at each time. For example, at time T1, the *active* is 6, hence $\mu(6) = \hat{S}_p(6) = 0.5$.

We have shown the formulation of peer's *reliability* at any single time t previously. Here we extend it to support multiple time units, we define *Reliability*, $\Re_p(t_m, t_n)$ (equation (2)), of a peer p during time t_m to t_n as an average possibility that peer remains active and accessible without any interruption between time t_m to time t_n where $t_m \ne t_n$. Clearly, if $t_m = t_n$, $\Re_p(t_m, t_n) = \Re_p(t)$. Let's

Table 1. Example of the Reliability values set

Time(Hour)	T1	T2	T3	T4	T5
$active$	6	5	3	7	10
$\hat{S}(x)$	0.5	0.2	0.0	0.7	0.9

consider Table 1 as an example again. The *Reliability* of peer p during time $T1$ to time $T5$ is computed as $\Re_p(T1,T5) = (0.5+0.2+0.0+0.7+0.9)/5 = 0.46$. Based on the formulation of $\Re_p(t_m,t_n)$, we can easily compute the reliability at the parent level. A node in D-Level has the *reliability* of $\Re_p(T1,T24)$ for all of it child nodes. Higher levels will take an average of their child $\Re_p(t)$s.

3 Conclusion

In this paper we have dealt with the problem of remote cost estimation in ad-hoc P2P network. Cost estimation is crucial for producing an execution strategy for a query. While most existing approaches are limited to static cost model or probe-based approach, we proposed a progressive "push-based" remote cost monitoring approach by using agents. Each agent will be sent to remote hosts with a generic cost model and epsilons (ε) indicating the acceptable magnitude of cost changes, i.e., percentage of coefficient changed. An update will be sent (pushed) to the original host once the magnitude of the cost changes is greater than ε. Consequently, a query optimizer can have near real-time cost information (i.e., cost $\pm\varepsilon$) of remote peers without heavily probing for the answer. In addition, we introduce Time-Hierarchical (TM-H) model to capture the behavior of users usage pattern and formulate a *Reliability* fuzzy characteristic as an evaluation criterion to measure the dynamism of peers.

References

1. Kalnis, P., Ng, W., Ooi, B., Papadias, D., Tan, K.: An adaptive peer-to-peer network for distributed caching of OLAP results. In: ACM SIGMOD. (2002)
2. Ng, W., Ooi, B., Tan, K., Zhou, A.: Peerdb: A p2p based system for distributed data sharing. In: ICDE. (2003) 633–644
3. Zhu, Q., Larson, P.: Solving local cost estimation problem for global query optimization in multidatabase-systems. In: Distributed and Parallel Databases, vol.(6). (1998) 373–420
4. Adali, S., Candan, K., Papakonstantinou, Y., Subrahmanian, V.: Query caching and optimization in distributed mediator systems. In: ACM SIGMOD. (1996) 137–148
5. Du, W., Krishnamurthy, R., Shan, M.: Query optimization in heterogeneous dbms. In: VLDB. (1992) 277–291
6. Shahabi, C., Khan, L., McLeod, D.: An adaptive probe-based technique to optimize join queries in distributed internet databases. In: Knowledge and Information Systems 2(3). (2001) 373–385

A P2P Approach to ClassLoading in Java

Daryl Parker and David Cleary

Applied Research Laboratories, Ericsson System Expertise, Cornamaddy Road,
Athlone, Ireland {Daryl.Parker, David.Cleary}@ericsson.com

Abstract. The Classloader has long been one of the key extensibility
points of the Java Virtual Machine architecture. In this paper we propose
a new architecture for remote loading of classes based on the Peer-to-Peer
paradigm. This solution incorporates some novel approaches, addressing
many of the problems inherent in current solutions. We also discuss our
reference implementation of this approach over both traditional TCP/IP
and JXTA based networks.

1 Introduction

Internet file sharing, and similar high profile applications have ushered in a new
era of distributed systems technologies. As business models turn more towards
service driven architectures, the focus is aimed at migrating functionality towards
the edge of the network. The plethora of new high-end Java based terminals
necessitates the need for a new breed of service, capable of displaying the same
characteristics that have made Peer-to-Peer technologies such a success.

A number of questions have been raised regarding the use of today's distributed technologies within such a domain. High among these are; static configuration, terminal limitations, service provisioning, scalability, redundancy and
the abolition of a centralized architecture.

This paper presents an overview of the various distributed systems technologies supported by the Java platform, and investigates perceived limitations of
these technologies when applied within a Peer-to-Peer context. We derive a set of
formal requirements for a new distributed class loading mechanism, and with the
aid of UML models a proposed architecture is presented, and various technical
challenges are discussed.

2 Current Class Loading Techniques

The Java language classloading mechanisms can be easily partitioned into two
basic categories; classloading within a single VM, and exchange of classes between multiple VM's. The Java platform provides implementations in both categories, however to understand the motivation behind the work detailed in this
paper, it is important to dissect these mechanisms and their various limitations.

G. Moro, C. Sartori, and M.P. Singh (Eds.): AP2PC 2003, LNAI 2872, pp. 144–149, 2004.
© Springer-Verlag Berlin Heidelberg 2004

2.1 Past and Present Loading Mechanisms

The Java language has matured through two generations of language [1] and virtual machine specifications [2], having undergone radical changes. Classloading is no exception. Two variants exist; pre and post 1.2 versions. The Java 1.1 model allowed loading of Java classes from virtually any source, but this flexibility carried the price of complexity. The abstract class *java.lang.ClassLoader* exposed a single method; *loadClass()*. The functionality of the loadClass() method is quite involved, requiring :

- Checking if the class has been loaded by this or the system loader
- Loading the class from the repository
- Defining and resolving the class
- Returning the new class definition to the caller

The advantage of this mechanism was that the custom classloader always maintained complete control over the classloading process, but this model forced the custom classloader to do all the work for loading a class. Further issues regarding security and access permissions also exist and are detailed in [3].

Java 1.2 introduced the delegation model for [4], which automatically delegates class loading to the parent. In the event of the parent ClassLoader being unable to load the class, a new method, *findClass()*, is called on the ClassLoader subclass. Thus the custom ClassLoader is responsible for loading only the classes not accessible by the parent.

While there are advantages to the delegation model, in complete contrast to the Java 1.1 mechanism the system classloader is given the first attempt to load the class, only falling back to the custom loader on failure to load the class. This restricts the usage of the custom classloader, to loading classes only from sources unknown to the system classloader.

2.2 Remote/Inter-VM Classloading

Java provides numerous mechanisms for loading classes over a network. Java's distributed classloading mechanisms, Applets, RMI [5], Jini [6],[7] all rely on the same basic mechanism, *the codebase*. A codebase is similar to the classpath; a list of URL's pointing to the location of necessary classes. Applets embed the codebase within the initiating html file, while RMI and Jini use a system property *java.rmi.server.codebase*. Details on how the codebase is used by the *RMIClassLoader* can be found at [8]. When attempting to apply these mechanisms within a Peer-to-Peer domain, a number of considerations must be taken into account:

- Supporting services Rmid, Rmiregistry (RMI) and LookupServer (Jini)
- One or more HttpServers must be running to serve class files
- Explicit packaging of client side code into individual jars
- Static configuration of codebases, security policies, redundancy
- Program towards an explicit set of technology API's

3   P2P Classloading

Our new P2P classloading mechanism aims to remove static configuration, and explicit code packaging, while providing network transport independence and inherently addressing both scalability and redundancy. Fig 2 shows the main interfaces of our P2P classloader. The main application interface is provided via the *DistributedClassLoader*. It overrides a number of methods to provide the necessary logic for our distributed classloader; *findClass()*, *getResourceAsStream()*, *findResource()* and *findResources()*.

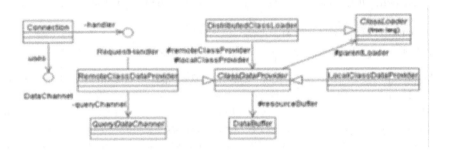

Fig. 1. Peer-to-Peer Classloader architecture class diagram

LocalClassDataProviders load classes from local code sources; files, jars, while *RemoteClassDataLoaders* provide mechanisms for loading classes from remote sources. The *RemoteClassDataProvider* encapsulates all of the control logic for remote connection, operating on generic *QueryChannel* and *DataChannel* interfaces. To provide a new network binding, implementations for the *QueryChannel* and *DataChannel* interfaces must be provided, and the two classes, *DistributedClassLoader* and *RemoteClassDataProvider* must be extended.

The P2P classloader first attempts to load the class data using the *LocalClassDataProviders*. If successful the class is defined/loaded and the VM resumes, if not found, control is passed to the *RemoteClassDataProviders* which will propagate a request for the specified class data. The details of the propagation mechanism are encapsulated by the *QueryChannel* implementation provided. A neighboring *RemoteClassDataProvider* receiving a request, will attempt to load the class using its own *LocalClassDataProviders*, however will not re-propagate the request, thus reducing requests in the network removing the need for loop detection, TTL mechanisms.

Due to the spatial locality of code, the full jar/zip will be sent to the requesting *RemoteClassDataProvider* and buffered, allowing future requests for classes to be resolved by the *LocalClassDataProviders*, from the buffer. The system is inherently fault tolerant, with redundant instances of buffered data residing on each peer, and displays basic load balancing characteristics, with a larger number of peers available to serve requests, reducing performance bottlenecks typically experienced in centralized systems.

4   Technical Challenges

One of our design goals required any class files specified on the classpath, a well-understood mechanism, to be available to our *LocalClassDataProviders*. If a new remote class is needed, it will likely be referred to from one of our application classes, loaded via the classpath by the system classloader. An attempt to load the remote class will result in the *loadClass()* method of the system classloader being called, due to the delegation model, as its the application classes initiating loader. The system classloader will fail to load the class, never deferring control to our custom classloader.

Many solutions [3],[4],[9], trim the classpath, or statically configure alternative sources for use by the custom loader. Others exist [10] that filter the system classes, based on explicit package names, e.g. *java.**, *javax.**, explicity configured during construction of the classloader. Due to the increasing number of previously optional APIs that are being bundled in the rt.jar and similar bootstrap packages, we felt this approach would not be adequate

Our solution uses the *sun.boot.class.path* system property to acquire the bootstrap classpath used by the VM for system classes, to construct a list of package names that can be used for the filtering process within our custom classloader. To ensure the system classloader does not load any application classes, the custom classloader must override the *loadClass()* method instead of the usual *findClass()* method, to prevent automatic delegation to the parent/system classloader. Alternatively a two-stage approach can be used by placing an intermediate classloader between the system and custom classloader. The intermediate classloader can do the filtering and delegate to the system or custom classloader as necessary.

ResourceBundles pose a real problem if required from a remote source. ResourceBundles created from a properties file e.g. *example.configfiles.config* result in the VM trying a number of combinations. Even if the *conifg.properties* file is found, the VM will attempt to find the `config_en` and `config_en_GB` files. Were each attempt made via a remote request an application would endure five request timeout intervals before continuing.

The ResourceBundle solution is somewhat involved. From the classloader perspective there is no way to identify that this request is coming from a *ResourceBundle.getBundle()* call. A naive approach could use a strict naming convention for bundle classes and properties, placing the onus on the developer to adhere to such a convention. Alternatively a new *Throwable* could be created and its stacktrace analyzed to determine if the *findClass()* is the result of a *getBundle()* call, placing prohibitive overhead on the class loader mechanism.

A preferred approach is to take advantage of the overhead involved in performing a remote request in the first place. If the locale information is included as part of the initial remote request, the remote client can check for all the ResourceBundle combinations. The computational overhead of resolving the permutations on the remote machine is proportionally insignificant to the overhead of the request. The returned results can be buffered ensuring that subsequent *findClass()* and *getResourceAsStream()* methods invoked as part of the *getBundle()* don't require further remote requests.

5   Reference Implementations

This section details our two reference implementations. A new *DistributedClass-Loader* must tell the base class which *LocalClassDataProviders*, and *Remote-ClassDataProviders* will be used for the binding. Likewise the *RemoteClass-DataProvider* must be informed of the class providing the *QueryChannel* implementation. All are achieved via the properties: *loader.provider.localprovider*, *loader.provider.remoteprovider* and *loader.channel.querychannel*. The Tcp/Ip *DataChannel* interface is implemented via standard Java sockets. The *QueryChannel* uses a *java.net.MulticastSocket* to broadcast requests, and a *java.net.ServerSocket* to accept connections from peers. Requests use *java.net.DatagramPacket* objects for transport via the *MulticastSocket.*

The second reference implementation was based on the JXTA initiative led by Sun Microsystems [11]. JXTA provides an XML based middleware encapsulating all the basic mechanisms required in a Peer-to-Peer system. It introduces the concept of *Pipes*; unidirectional virtual communication channels that can span multiple peers. Resource discovery is provided by a core JXTA service, the *ResolverService*, a providing generic query/response mechanism.

The *QueryChannel* for the JXTA binding uses the *ResolverService* to broadcast its class requests which are enveloped within the generic *ResolverQuery* and *ResolverResponse* messages. The *QueryChannel* makes use of the *BidirectionalPipe* class provided by the *net.jxta.utils* package, to handle the setup of the pipes in both directions.

The *DataChannel* implementation requires methods for accessing the *InputStream* and *OutputStream* of the *DataChannel*, neither of which are supported by JXTA pipes. We decided to implement *InputStream* and *OutputStream* adapters for JXTA pipes, enabling us to extend the capabilities of the *Pipe* mechanism, allowing standard Java streams (*ObjectStreams, BufferedStreams*) to be stacked on top of JXTA pipes. Fig 5, details the architecture of the adapters and our read/write byte buffer implementation.

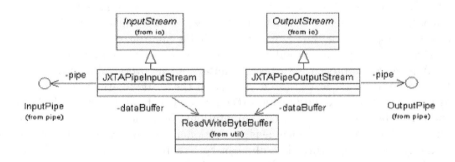

Fig. 2. JXTA Pipe/Stream Adapter

6 Conclusions

This paper presented an overview of various Java distributed systems technologies and highlighted some of the inherent limitations when used within a Peer-to-Peer domain. Having decomposed these technologies, formal requirements for a new distributed class loading mechanism were presented and with the aid of UML diagrams, a proposed architecture was outlined. We further presented some of the technical challenges faced while implementing the proposed design, and detailed the solutions employed. In conclusion, the two Reference Implementations of our proposed architecture are described, illustrating the flexibility afforded by our design, proving the Peer-to-Peer paradigm to be a valid approach to solving many of the technology limitations intrinsic to the current generation of distributed systems architectures

References

1. James Gosling, Bill Joy, Guy Steele, Gilad Bracha: The Java Language Specification 2nd Edition Addison Wesley, ISBN 0-201-31008-2, 2000
2. Tim Lindholm, Frank Yellin: The Java Virtual Machine Specification 2nd Edition Addison Wesley, ISBN 0-201-43294-3, 2002
3. Chuck McManis: The Basics of Java Class Loaders. JavaWorld, October 1996. http://www.javaworld.com/javaworld/jw-10-1996/jw-10-indepth.html
4. Ken McCrary: Create a custom Java 1.2-style ClassLoader. JavaWorld, March 2000. http://www.javaworld.com/javaworld/jw-03-2000/jw-03-classload.html
5. The java remote method invocation (RMI) specification. Technical report, Sun Microsystems Incorporated. 1998. http://www.javasoft.com/products/jdk/1.2/docs/guide/rmi/spec/rmiTOC.doc.html
6. K. Arnold, B. O'Sullivan, R. W. Scheifler, J. Waldo, and A. Wollrath: The Jini Specification, Addison Wesley, 1999.
7. Suns Jini whitepaper http://www.sun.com/jini/whitepapers/jini-datasheet0601.pdf
8. Ann Wollrath, Jim Waldo: The Java Tutorial - RMI http://java.sun.com/docs/books/tutorial/rmi/TOC.html
9. Philip W. L. Fong and Robert D. Cameron: Java proof linking with multiple classloaders.Technical Report SFU CMPT TR 2000-04, Simon Fraser University, 2000 http://citeseer.nj.nec.com/fong00java.html
10. BCEL, The Byte Code Engineering Library http://jakarta.apache.org/bcel/manual.html
11. "JXTA v1.0 Protocol Specification", June 2001 http://spec.jxta.org/v1.0/docbook/JXTAProtocols.html

Multi-agent Interaction Technology for Peer-to-Peer Computing in Electronic Trading Environments

Martin Purvis, Mariusz Nowostawski, Stephen Cranefield, and Marcos Oliveira

Department of Information Science, University of Otago, Dunedin, New Zealand
{mpurvis, mnowostawski, scranefield, moliveira}@infoscience.otago.ac.nz

Abstract. Open trading environments involve a type of peer-to-peer computing characterised by well-defined interaction protocols that are used by the traders and sometimes updated dynamically. New traders can arrive at any time and acquire the protocols that are current. Multi-agent system technology is appropriate for these circumstances, and in this paper we present an approach that can be used to support multiple trader agents on multiple computing platforms. The approach involves the use of FIPA-compliant trader agents which (a) incorporate micro-agents for specific local tasks and (b) use coloured Petri nets in order to keep track of the local context of agent conversations. In order to enhance efficiency and employ standard transport services, the trader agents interact with peers on other platforms by means of JXTA technology. We illustrate the working of our approach by examining the operation of an example multi-agent system in a commodities trading scenario.

1 Introduction

Peer-to-peer computing applications in open economic trading spheres must be able to interoperate effectively in distributed, heterogeneous, and sometimes unreliable environments. Multi-agent system technology, wherein agents communicate by exchanging declarative statements, has the potential to provide a robust and scalable infrastructure to support such systems [1]. With agent architectures, individual agent participants can be replaced or supplemented by improved agents, which can enable the overall system to introduce improvements, adapt to changing conditions, and extend the scope of operations to new domains.

In the international e-business climate, autonomous agents or groups of such agents from distinct organizations may come together in a competitive environment and exchange information and services. In order for multi-agent systems to operate effectively under these circumstances, they must be able to coordinate their activities with other agents in a satisfactory manner, and this coordination is accomplished by having suitable interaction protocols between agents. In addition, the deployed agents must be able to respond rapidly in competitive trading environments, and so should be developed to employ standard infrastructural

G. Moro, C. Sartori, and M.P. Singh (Eds.): AP2PC 2003, LNAI 2872, pp. 150–161, 2004.
© Springer-Verlag Berlin Heidelberg 2004

P2P services wherever possible. In this paper we describe our approach to the representation and use of agent interaction protocols and discuss our implementation that combines the use of standard agent [2] and P2P [3] technology. The implementation of our approach is demonstrated in the context of a commodities trading scenario.

2 Multi-agent Systems

Agents must share an understanding of the possible message types and the terms that are used in their communication. A common approach that has been used to deal with the potential complexity of these messages is to have messages represented in a declarative format, with the basic message types limited to a few standard types and the individual terms used in the message content represented by an ontology that has been developed for the application domain of interest [4].

2.1 FIPA Agents

The Foundation for Intelligent Physical Agents Agent Communication Language (FIPA ACL) has a relatively small set of message types (the Communicative Act Library [2]) based on speech acts [5]. Examples of FIPA communicative acts are quite general (such as *inform, request, propose,* etc.), and the content to which the general communicative acts refer (*e.g.* what is being 'requested' or 'proposed') is contained in the bodies of the messages. The task of understanding the message body containing terms that refer to an ontology can require a considerable amount of reasoning, but this task can be assisted by employing conversation policies, or interaction protocols [6], which can reduce the number of options that need to be considered for appropriate response to an incoming message. An interaction protocol specifies a limited range of responses that are appropriate to specific message types when a particular protocol is in operation, and this is a way of situating a sequence of exchanged messages in a context. FIPA has produced a short list of specifications [2] for several standard interaction protocols, but these are somewhat limited and may not offer sufficient assistance for many of the potential interactions in which agents are likely to engage.

Interaction protocols represented in the FIPA specifications focus on the explicit exchange of information that takes place between the agents, but there is no concern or representation to assist in the understanding of what is contained in the body of the message. That kind of task is left to an agent's own devices and is not treated by the FIPA interaction protocols. Instead of leaving all of the rest of what transpires in connection with the interaction outside of the specification and up to the individual agents, however, we consider it to be advantageous to consider within the protocol what the other agent is doing with the information.

2.2   Interaction Protocols

Although FIPA uses AUML [7] to represent its standard interaction protocols, we use coloured Petri nets (CPNs) [8,9], because their formal properties facilitate the modelling of concurrent conversations in an integrated fashion. The availability of net analysis tools[1] means that it is possible to check the designed protocols and role interactions for undesired loops and deadlock conditions, and this can then help eliminate human errors introduced in the design process.

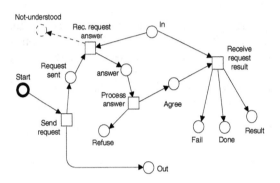

Fig. 1. The *Request* IP: the Initiator role

Figures 1 and 2 show our representation of the FIPA *request* interaction protocol. Each interaction protocol is modelled in terms of the individual agent roles in the interaction: for each individual role there is a separate Petri net. The collection of individual Petri nets associated with all the relevant roles represents the entire interaction protocol.

For every conversation, there are always at least two roles: that of the initiator of the conversation and the roles of the other participants in the conversation.

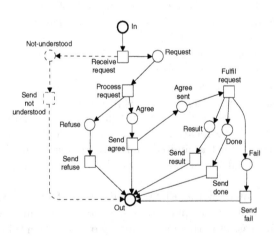

Fig. 2. The *Request* IP: the Participant role

Figure 1 depicts the initiator of the FIPA *request* interaction and Figure 2 shows the Participant interaction. For diagrammatic simplicity, we omit the inscriptions from the diagram, but we will describe some of them below. The *In* place (in this and the following Petri net diagrams) will have tokens placed there when the agent receives messages from other agents. The *In* place is a *fusion node* (a place common to two or more nets): the very same *In* place may exist on other Petri nets that also represent conversations in which the agent may be engaged. When the agent receives a message from another agent, a token with information associated with the message is placed in the *In* place, which may

---

[1] See, for example, http://www.daimi.au.dk/PetriNets/tools/db.html.

be shared by several Petri nets. The transitions connected to the *In* place have guards on them such that the transitions are only enabled by a token in the *In* place with the appropriate qualification. The Initiator of the request interaction will have a token placed in the *Start* place, and this will trigger the *Send request* transition to place a token in the *Out* place. We assume that the communication transport machinery causes tokens to disappear from a Petri net's *Out* place and (usually) a corresponding token to appear in the *In* place of another agent. The transfer may not be instantaneous, or even guaranteed to occur; it is possible for a token to disappear from one role's *Out* place without a corresponding token appearing in another agent's *In* place.

Note that the Initiator could be involved in several concurrent request interaction conversations, and the placement of specific tokens in the *Agree* place enables this agent to keep track of which responses correspond to which conversations. This shows how the coloured Petri net representation facilitates the management of concurrent interactions involving the same protocol.

3   Electronic Trading Scenario

We consider here a simplified business example that covers some essential issues but avoids extraneous matters, that is based on the card game Pit^2, which is modelled after commodity trading. In the standard *Pit* card game, three to seven players may play and a dealer distributes nine cards to each player from a shuffled deck of cards. The game comes equipped with a deck of cards, each of which has a 'suit' that represents one of a few commodity types, such as corn, barley, wheat and rice, and there are nine cards of each commodity type in the deck. When the game is played, the deck is prepared so that the number of commodity types in the deck matches the number of players for the given game. When play begins, the players independently and asynchronously exchange cards with each other, attempting to "corner" the market by getting all nine cards of any one type. On any single exchange, they can only trade up to four cards from their own hands, and all the cards traded must belong to a single commodity type. Thus if a player has six barley cards, two 'wheat' cards and one 'rice' card, he will typically initially attempt to trade away his two 'wheat' cards, hoping to acquire one or two 'barley' cards. Trading is carried out by a player (the "bidder") announcing, for example, that he has some cards to trade. If another player (a "trader") also wishes to trade the same number of cards, the two players may make an exchange. Whenever a player manages to get a 'corner', he announces that fact to the dealer, and the given "hand" is finished (the protocol shown here is for a single hand). Players who get a corner in 'wheat' (by getting all nine 'wheat' cards) get 100 points, a corner in 'corn' gets 75 points, in 'oats' gets 60 points, etc. The winner of the game is the first player to collect 500 points.

In our implementation of the basic (non-extended) game, trading bids are sent to the dealer, which, in turn, broadcasts the bids to all the players. Figure 3

---

^{2} http://www.hasbro.com/common/instruct/pit.pdf

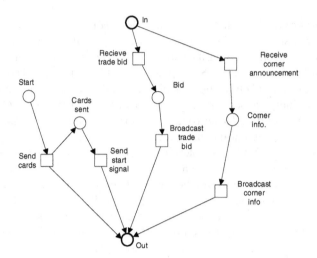

Fig. 3. The Pit Game interaction protocol for the Dealer role

shows the interaction protocol for the Dealer role. The Dealer deals out the cards and then sends the "start" signal to all the players (a broadcast message).

The player role is shown in Figure 4. Whenever a player has a hand of cards, it always checks to see if it has a corner. If so, it announces this to the Dealer, which, in turn, announces this to the rest of the players, thus signalling the end of the hand. After players receive the start signal, and assuming that they don't have a corner, they can choose to make a bid. They do this by sending their bid to the Dealer, which in turn broadcasts the bid to all other players. At this point in the protocol, a token is deposited in the "cards offered" place, identifying the cards being offered for trade. Whenever an external bid is received, the player can choose to accept the bid by comparing the bid with its own hand. If the player accepts the bid, a message is sent to the player (not the Dealer) and a token is stored in the "cards offered" place. If the trader player subsequently receives a message from the bidder that its acceptance was rejected (the "Rec rejec. of trade offer" transition), then it will give up on this potential deal and restore its offered cards back to the "cards" place.

A trade of cards can take place if a bid has been made and another player has offered to make a trade matching the bid. Thus if player A has made a trade offer in response to player B's bid, and has received an acceptance message from B that this trade offer has been accepted, then A will send its cards to B (and expect to receive a corresponding number of cards from B). When a player receives a trade offer message from another player indicating that its bid has been accepted, it is stored in the "Accpt." place. The "Make trade" transition checks (by means of a guard) to make sure that the accepted bid matches information in the token located in the "cards offered" place. If so, the cards are sent to the other player. If the player receives a trade offer that is not applicable (such as a second trade offer that has come in after it has already decided to trade

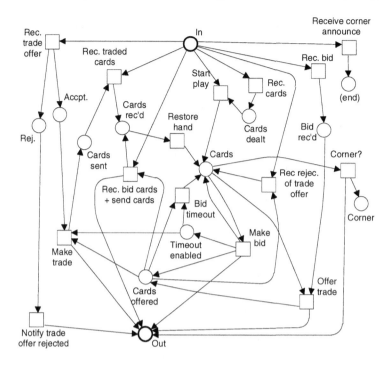

Fig. 4. The Pit game interaction protocol for the Player role

cards with another player that has sent in an earlier trade offer), then the other player is sent a rejection notice ("Notify trade offer rejected" transition). When a 'trader' receives cards ("Rec. traded cards" transition) the incoming trades are checked against the token in the "Cards sent" place (the number of cards should match) and the received cards are placed in the "Cards rec'd" place. When a 'bidder' receives cards, it makes a similar check with the token in the "cards offered" place, sends those offered cards to the other player, clears the token in the "Timeout enabled" place (see next sentence), and places the incoming cards in the "Cards rec'd" place. The "Bid timeout" transition is enabled if there have been no takers of a bid before a certain timeout period has elapsed. When this transition is fired, the cards are returned to the hand, and the player may chose to make another bid. Whenever there are cards in the "Cards rec'd" place, the "Restore hand" transition is enabled and this causes the received cards to be deposited back in the "Cards" place.

In e-commerce applications, new agents can come and go, so it is necessary that new participants be informed of the governing interaction protocols in the trading arena. This can be accomplished if the entire interaction protocol can be sent to the new player and that new player can then begin to interact according to that prescribed protocol. In the next section we discuss our implementation of the interaction protocol scheme and how the dynamic inclusion of new agent participants is handled.

4   Peer-to-Peer Implementation for Electronic Trading

For our multi-agent implementation, we use Opal [10], a platform for agent-based development in Java that provides support for the FIPA agent specifications. Included with Opal is JFern[3], a Java-based tool for the enactment and simulation of coloured Petri nets. When new agents appear and are to be incorporated into the network of available agents, they are sent a FIPA *Propose* message by the group manager with a message content containing an XML encoding of the interaction protocol that is used. The interaction protocol comprises a coloured Petri net and the associated ontology, represented in UML, for the terms used in the interaction protocol. Both the Petri net and the UML-encoded ontology information are encoded in XML and sent to the newcomer agent when it joins a group.

4.1   The P2P Pit Game

We have adapted the Pit game to make it more characteristic of a peer-to-peer environment of autonomous components. The modified game has the same goal as in the standard game: each player is playing for itself, and is trying to corner a single commodity. However, there is now no centralized dealer. In addition, players can leave and join during the game at any time, and new commodities are generated automatically depending on the current number of players. All commodities are ordered according to their value, *e.g.* the first commodity, com1, has a corner value of 10pts, com2 = 20pts, and so on, in an ascending order.

The maximum number of players that can participate in a game is set to some high value, N_max. In any single game, there are N players playing at the same time, with $N < N\_max$. Each player has N_cards, where $N\_cards > N\_max$. Thus, there are always N commodities in the game, and each commodity has N_cards that are in circulation.[4] Since there is no dealer, each player takes on part of dealer's responsibilities. That includes keeping track of who is playing the game, keeping track of all current commodities in the game, and keeping track of the scores of other players. All that information is synchronized between players by means of public announcements.

Some cards in the game can be marked *inactive*, and in such a case they cannot be used to count towards a corner in the given hand. A player who has inactive cards must exchange them with cards from another player. Once an inactive card has been traded, it becomes *active*. When a new player joins a game, it must ask another player what commodities are being currently used in the game. The new player will then create a new commodity and a new hand for itself of N_cards inactive cards representing the new commodity. These inactive cards must all be traded away by the new player, and by so doing so, the inactive cards become

---

[3] http://sourceforge.net/projects/jfern/
[4] These rules followed the original Pit Game rules; however, we have noticed that when a large number (dozens or more) of players are in the game, it can be difficult for any player to get a corner, and we are investigating a future scoring modification that would offer proportional rewards to players who have a near corner of the market.

active and can be collected as any other cards by any of the players. The cards are exchanged at random and in an asynchronous manner between individual players. The maximum number of cards exchanged during a single transaction is *(N_cards /2) - 1*. All exchanged cards must be of the same commodity type.

To facilitate the mixing of inactive cards from a new player's hand, a new rule has been added to the game ('inactive card demand'): any player can be requested to provide one or more cards in exchange for another player's inactive cards. The requested player may decide how many cards it wants to exchange, but it cannot refuse the inactive card demand. Apart from this one-round inactive card demand, all inactive cards are exchanged as normal commodities.

A new game starts when a single player creates a group, advertises it, and creates for itself *N_cards* cards of the lowest priced commodity. All the cards in its hand are marked inactive. This player sets the group players count, N, to 1, and records the value of the current highest commodity and lowest commodity. When a second player joins the group, it is informed of the current number of players in the group and what is the next commodity price (the second lowest). The newly joined player creates a hand of this commodity, and marks all its cards inactive. When a third player joins in, again, the player counter is incremented and a new commodity set is created. All players are aware of the number of players in the group, and all know the current highest priced commodity. This is kept up to date by making public announcements within the group. After the third player joins the group, cards may be traded, and players can make bids and announcements.

New players can join a playing group at any time during the play. They simply join the group, ask about the number of players and the highest priced commodity, create a hand of inactive cards of a new commodity, and start exchanging cards with others. Once the player gets a corner, it adds an appropriate amount of points to its account, marks all the cards in its hand to be inactive, and continues to play. The player can leave the play just after getting a corner. This is the only time the player can "retire".

There are two types of announcements: public announcements, and individual agent-to-agent messages. The former are done through the underlying network infrastructure to all the agents in the game. The latter are done between only two interested parties. This is discussed in more detail in Section 5.

4.2 P2P Pit Game User Interface

A screen shot from the implementation of the P2P Pit game is shown in Figure 5. Card collections and hands are represented schematically by an ordered list of commodities with the number of cards in each commodity. So, for example, for a deck of cards with three commodities and ten cards per hand, a hand that has four cards of the first commodity, five cards of the second and one card of the third commodity would be represented by the following list: [04] [05] [01]. A hand with all ten cards of the third commodity would be [00] [00] [10].

The top window on the left-hand side of the figure represents all the micro-agents (see below) and micro-agent roles instantiated in the system. Graphical user interface (GUI) elements which are recognisable by the MainWindow agent

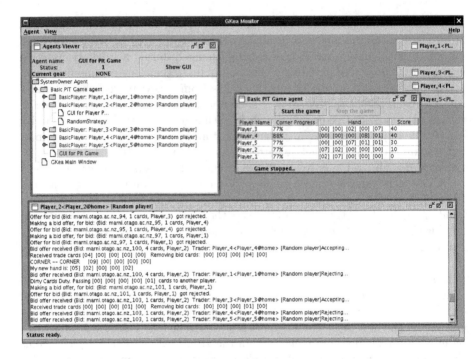

Fig. 5. Software implementation of the P2P Pit game

can be dynamically displayed on the desktop. The top window on the right-hand side is the GUI for the actual Pit Game agent. It shows all the agents, with their current progress toward cornering the market, the current hand and the cumulative score obtained so far. The bottom window represents an individual player. It shows different decision the agents is making, and the current announcements: bids and trade offers.

5   Implementation Infrastructure

The implementation using the Opal FIPA Platform also includes the KEA[5] micro-agent framework [11]. The interaction architecture is shown in Figure 6. The use of micro-agents allows us to maintain agent-oriented software modelling and implementation on all levels of abstraction. GUI components and internal processing units, such as the *Strategy* micro-agent are represented and implemented as agents and/or roles. At a higher level all players are treated as individual FIPA agents, which communicate between themselves using FIPA ACL messages. The player agents delegate particular tasks to appropriate micro-agents. This approach offers the advantage of reusing components, together with late dynamic binding between particular roles.

---

[5] http://sourceforge.net/projects/javaprs

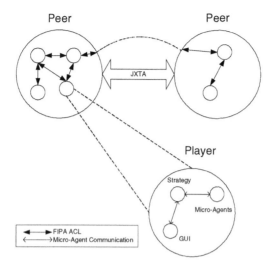

Fig. 6. Agent, micro-agent, and JXTA interaction

5.1   JXTA

To facilitate the dynamic discovery of peers on the network and peer-to-peer messaging, we have used the JXTA infrastructure [3], which is a set of open protocols that allow any connected device on the network to communicate and collaborate in a P2P manner. In this paper we show how JXTA peers and JXTA announcements can co-exist with the notion of agent-to-agent messaging and FIPA ACL.

The fundamental notion in JXTA is a peer, which represents any networked device that implements one or more of the JXTA protocols. To send messages to one another, JXTA peers use pipes, which represent an asynchronous and unidirectional message transfer mechanism used for service communication. Another important JXTA mode of communication is *advertisements*, which are language-neutral metadata structures represented as XML documents and are used to describe and publish the existence of a peer's resources. Peers discover resources by searching for their corresponding advertisements and may cache any discovered advertisements locally. Each advertisement is published along with a *lifetime* that specifies the time availability of its associated resource. Lifetimes enable the deletion of obsolete resources without requiring any centralized control (an advertisement can be republished before the original advertisement expires in order to extend the lifetime of a resource). In particular, a *content advertisement* describes content that can be shared in a peer group, and we use content advertisements to provide the notion of "public announcements" within a given agent group. All Pit game bids are announced for a specific time publicly, and trade offers are delivered to individual agents over traditional ACL channels.

5.2   Messaging

Messaging at the lowest micro-agent level (for example between the micro-agent Player and its Strategy sub-agent) is implemented using method calls, and its semantics is expressed simply by method call signatures. At a higher level micro-agents employ a limited model of communication, based on the notion of goals, declarations, and commitments, with the semantics expressed by UML models of goals and their relationships. At the highest level agents use standard FIPA ACL augmented with the notion of object-oriented ontologies represented in UML [12].

We observe, however, that FIPA ACL does not have a notion of an agent group, and there is no notion of a public announcement to the group. This is where JXTA plays an important role. We have introduced a special "wrapper" agent, called a *Peer* agent. Currently, there is a single Peer Agent for each JXTA peer (*i.e.* a single Peer Agent per machine). All the communication between individual Players and a Peer Agent is done by standard FIPA ACL; but the communication between Peer Agents, themselves, is performed by means of JXTA announcements and pipes (*i.e.* outside normal FIPA ACL messaging). All public announcements are done via JXTA announcements, and all peer-to-peer communication, *i.e.* all the individual agent conversations, are performed using standard FIPA messaging mechanisms transmitted via the JXTA Pipe infrastructure. Thus in the P2P Pit game each agent sends bids over FIPA ACL to the Peer Agent, which in turn performs multicast messaging on behalf of the agents (for public announcements like bids). All the public announcements are done in an asynchronous manner over the standard JXTA content advertisements. Since the Peer Agent also has a standard pipe for FIPA text-based ACL messaging, all communication can be considered to be performed over JXTA.

6   Discussion

In the current P2P implementation we have introduced an extra transport layer between the FIPA agent and the (FIPA-compliant) Transport System. This layer is provided by the specialist Peer Agent, which intercepts all Pit-related messages from individual Player agents, and propagates them appropriately for the P2P environment.

For messages addressed to a single individual agent registered on the local peer, the Peer Agent simply forwards the message directly to the recipient. If the receiver is registered on a remote peer, the local Peer Agent passes the message to that recipient's Peer Agent, which in turn passes the message down to the individual recipient. If, however, the original message is a public announcement (such as a bid), then the local Peer Agent passes the announcement to all locally registered agents and also passes it to all other Peer Agents, which in turn pass it down to all their local players. In the current implementation, the Peer Agent is implemented on a level below the FIPA ACL level, so all its communications are not based on the FIPA ACL itself, but rather on a proprietary protocol implemented on our Opal platform.

Opal has been built to conform to the FIPA Abstract Architecture (FIPA AA). The transport protocols in Opal (IIOP and HTTP) have now been extended to include JXTA. The Transport Service, as specified in FIPA AA, only provides a communication protocol for ACL messages between two end-points and consequently does not cover some aspects of communication, such as discovery, multicasts or broadcasts. Since these were needed for our application, we implemented them using our own proprietary interfaces and protocols. From this work, we have come to believe that there would be advantages in extending the basic FIPA AA infrastructure to cover discovery and broadcasts. This would provide a bootstrapping infrastructure for agent directory data exchange and dynamic caching of remote agent directory services. We have not yet implemented broadcasts in our JXTA-based Transport Service for Opal, because FIPA currently lacks this notion. But it would be straightforward to do so if a standard were established. With such an addition, the Pit game public announcement messaging would be simpler at the agent level, without the necessity of using proprietary Peer Agents or JXTA wrappers. We believe such an addition to the FIPA AA would facilitate agent use in P2P applications.

References

1. Jennings, N.R.: Agent-oriented software engineering. In: Proceedings of the 12th International Conference on Industrial and Engineering Applications of AI. (1999) 4–10
2. Foundation for Intelligent Physical Agents: FIPA specification repository. http://www.fipa.org/repository/ (2003)
3. Project JXTA Web site. http://www.jxta.org/ (2003)
4. Ontology.org Web site. http://www.ontology.org/ (2003)
5. Searle, J.: Speech Acts: An Essay in the Philosophy of Language. Cambridge University Press (1970)
6. Dignum., F., Greaves, M., eds.: Issues in Agent Communication. Lecture Notes in Computer Science, Vol. 1916. Springer (2000)
7. Odell, J., Parunak, H.V.D., Bauer, B.: Representing agent interaction protocols in UML. In Ciancarini, P., Wooldridge, M., eds.: Agent-Oriented Software Engineering. Lecture Notes in Computer Science, Vol. 1957. Springer (2001) 121–140
8. Cost, R., Chen, Y., Finin, T., Labrou, Y., Peng, Y.: Using colored Petri nets for conversation modeling. In [6], 178–192
9. Jensen, K.: Coloured Petri Nets: Basic Concepts, Analysis Methods and Practical Use, Volume 1: Basic Concepts. Monographs in Theoretical Computer Science. Springer (1992)
10. Purvis, M., Cranefield, S., Nowostawski, M., Carter, D.: Opal: A multi-level infrastructure for agent-oriented software development. Discussion Paper 2002/01, Department of Information Science, University of Otago (2002)
11. Nowostawski, M., Purvis, M., Cranefield, S.: KEA: Multi-level agent infrastructure. In: Proceedings of the 2nd International Workshop of Central and Eastern Europe on Multi-Agent Systems (CEEMAS 2001), University of Mining and Metallurgy, Krakow, Poland (2001) 355–362
12. Cranefield, S., Purvis, M.: A UML profile and mapping for the generation of ontology-specific content languages. Knowledge Engineering Review **17** (2002) 21–39

Location-Based and Content-Based Information Access in Mobile Peer-to-Peer Computing: The TOTA Approach

Marco Mamei and Franco Zambonelli

Dipartimento di Scienze e Metodi dell'Ingegneria,
University of Modena and Reggio Emilia
Via Allegri 13, 42100 Reggio Emilia, Italy
{mamei.marco, franco.zambonelli}@unimo.it

Abstract. Mobile peer-to-peer computing calls for suitable middleware and programming models to provide dynamic access to information and resources in dynamic network environments. In particular, location-based access and content-based access to information appear two very useful mechanisms. Here we present how both these two kinds of information access can be realized via TOTA ("Tuples On The Air"), a novel middleware that relies on spatially distributed tuples for supporting uncoupled and adaptive interactions between application agents. The TOTA middleware takes care of both propagating tuples across a network on the basis of application-specific rules and of adaptively re-shaping the resulting distributed structures accordingly to changes in the network structures. In particular, the effectiveness of our model will be tested in providing means for both location-based and content-based access to information.

1 Introduction

Far from being only a mean to share music over the Internet, Peer-to-Peer (P2P) computing is likely to be the reference model for next generation distributed computing. In several information technology scenarios in fact, there appears to be a drift from the idea of applications accessing a central service provider to applications creating a web of shared services. One of the most striking example is Internet-scale data sharing and teamwork, where rather than accessing a central data repository or a central workflow management system, users create a community and share their resource or coordinate directly. These kind of application have always been regarded as the killer applications for P2P systems and while several systems for file sharing have already been widely used [6],[14],[10], other systems trying to extend P2P methodology to teamwork and computer supported cooperative work (CSCW) are currently being studied and developed [13],[15]. More than that, there are new emerging scenarios, like mobile or pervasive computing, in which P2P seems to be the only option. In mobile computing for example, devices with wireless networking capabilities can create dynamically

G. Moro, C. Sartori, and M.P. Singh (Eds.): AP2PC 2003, LNAI 2872, pp. 162–173, 2004.

mobile ad hoc networks (MANET) and then interact directly. This possibility opens new scenarios where a device by moving in an environment continuously connects to the other devices or resources that are in its wireless network range, thus creating an ever changing network of peers with whom to interact. In such a situation it is rather clear that only approaches that respect the inherent symmetry in the network of wireless devices will be successful and the P2P approach naturally matches this situation. A central issue, in the development of P2P applications, it to provide peers (i.e. agents) with suitable mechanisms to access distributed information. In its broader meaning, information access is at the basis of data sharing, context-awareness (i.e. access to context related information), but also interactions (i.e. access to communication partners) whatever, the application scenario. In particular, it appears like two different methods may be both useful to retrieve information in dynamic and P2P scenarios:

- *Location-based access*, where an agent takes advantage of location information to access resources within suitable locality constraints (e.g. find all the printers on this floor, or find the closest gas station);
- *Content-based access*, where data - are searched and accessed on the basis of their content rather than on the basis of nodes' network addresses or location. For example, in a P2P sensor network, an agent may be interested to the occurrence of the data named "truck sightings". The network must provide means to effectively access these data wherever they happened.

Although, both these access method have been studied, see [20] for location-based access and [19] for content based access, to the best of our knowledge, a model addressing both these access methods with common abstractions has not been proposed before. In this paper we present how to realize both location-based and content-based access to information, using the abstractions promoted by a novel interaction middleware called TOTA ("Tuples On The Air"). In TOTA, all interactions between application agents take place in a fully uncoupled way via tuple exchanges. However, there is not any notion like a centralized shared tuple space. Rather, tuples can be "injected" into the network from any node and can propagate and diffuse accordingly to tuple-specific propagation patterns. The middleware takes care of tuple propagation by automatically re-adapting propagation patterns accordingly to the dynamic changes that can occur in the network (as due by, e.g., mobile or ephemeral nodes). Agents can exploit a simple API to define and inject new tuples in the network and to locally sense both tuples and events associated with changes in the tuples' distributed structures (e.g., arrival and dismissing of tuples). As we will show in the paper, these abstractions enable a straightforward implementations of both location-based and content-based access to information in P2P networks. To realize location-based access, tuples can take advantage of the fact that their shape is preserved, by the middleware, despite peers' movements. In this way a tuple issued to collect information 10m away from the current location, will correctly perform its task even if, after injecting the tuple, the peer moves in another location. To realize a content-based access, tuples' propagation will be guided by the content of the information being searched, with the goal of connecting the issuing peer with all the other peers having relevant information. Using the tuples as trials, information can be then routed back to the issuing peer. The following of this paper is organized as follows. Section 2 overviews the key characteristics of TOTA and report current implementation status. Section 3 introduces the problem of determining location in a P2P network. Section 4 describes how to manage location-based information access in TOTA. Section 5 describes how to manage content-based information access in TOTA. Section 6 discusses related works. Section 7 concludes and outlines future works.

2   The Tuples on the Air Approach

The definition of TOTA is mainly driven by the above considerations. It gathers concepts from both tuple space approaches [4] and event-based ones [5] - thus preserving uncoupling in interactions - and extends them to provide agents with abstract - simple yet effective - representations of the context. The goal is to enable specific coordination activities to be implicitly and with minimal effort realized by application agents, and to be automatically adapted to the dynamics of the execution scenarios

2.1   Overview

The driving objective of our approach is to exploit a unified and flexible mechanism to deal with both context representation and agents' interaction, and thus leading to simpler, and lighter to be supported, applications. In TOTA, we propose relying on distributed tuples for both representing contextual information and enabling uncoupled interaction among distributed application agents. Unlike traditional shared data space models, tuples are not associated to a specific node (or to a specific data space) of the network. Instead, tuples are injected in the network and can autonomously propagate and diffuse in the network accordingly to a specified pattern. Thus, TOTA tuples form a sort of spatially distributed data structure able to express not only messages to be transmitted between application agents but, more generally, some contextual information on the distributed environment. To support this idea, TOTA is composed by a peer-to-peer network of possibly mobile nodes, each running a local version of the TOTA middleware. Each TOTA node holds references to a limited set of neighboring nodes. The structure of the network, as determined by the neighborhood relations, is automatically maintained and updated by the nodes to support dynamic changes, whether due to nodes' mobility or to nodes' failures. The specific nature of the network scenario determines how each node can found its neighbors: e.g., in a MANET scenario, TOTA nodes are found within the range of their wireless connection; in the Internet they can be found via an expanding ring search (the same used in most Internet peer-to-peer systems). Upon the distributed space identified by the dynamic network of TOTA nodes, each agent is capable of locally storing tuples and letting them diffuse through the network.

Tuples are injected in the system from a particular node, and spread hop-by-hop accordingly to their propagation rule. In fact, a TOTA tuple is defined in terms of a "content", and a "propagation rule". $T=(C,P)$. The content C is an ordered set of typed fields representing the information carried on by the tuple. The propagation rule P determines how the tuple should be distributed and propagated in the network. This includes determining the "scope" of the tuple (i.e. the distance at which such tuple should be propagated and possibly the spatial direction of propagation) and how such propagation can be affected by the presence or the absence of other tuples in the system. In addition, the propagation rules can determine how tuple's content should change while it is propagated. Tuples are not necessarily distributed replicas: by assuming different values in different nodes, tuples can be effectively used to build a distributed overlay data structure expressing some kind of contextual and spatial information. Propagation of tuples is not driven by a publish-subscribe schema, as in traditional event based models, but it is directly encoded in tuples' propagation rule and, unlike an event, a tuple can change its content during propagation. The spatial structures induced by tuples propagation must be maintained coherent despite network dynamism. To this end, the TOTA middleware supports tuples propagation actively and adaptively: by constantly monitoring the network local topology and the income of new tuples, the middleware automatically re-propagates tuples as soon as appropriate conditions occur. For instance, when new nodes get in touch with a network, TOTA automatically checks the propagation rules of the already stored tuples and eventually propagates the tuples to the new nodes. Similarly, when the topology changes due to nodes' movements, the distributed tuple structure automatically changes to reflect the new topology. For instance, Figures 1 shows how the structure of a distributed tuple can be kept coherent by TOTA in a MANET scenario, despite dynamic network reconfigurations. From the application agents' point of view, executing and interacting basically reduces to inject tuples, perceive local tuples and local events, and act accordingly to some application-specific policy. Software agents on a TOTA node can inject new tuples in the network, defining their content and their propagation rule. They have full access to the local content of the middleware (i.e., of the local tuple space), and can query the local tuple space - via a pattern-matching mechanism - to check for the local presence of specific tuples. In addition, agents can be notified of locally occurring events (i.e., changes in tuple space content and in the structure of the network neighborhood). In TOTA there is not any primitive notion of distributed query. Still, it is possible for a node to inject a tuple in the network and have such distributed tuple be interpreted as a query at the application-level, by having other agents in the network react to the income of such tuple, i.e., by injecting a reply tuple propagating towards the enquiring node. The overall resulting scenario - making it sharp the analogy with the physical world anticipated in the introduction - is that of applications whose agents: *(i)* can influence the TOTA space by propagating application-specific tuples; *(ii)* execute by being influenced in both their internal and coordination activities by the locally sensed tuples; and *(iii)* implicitly tune their activities to

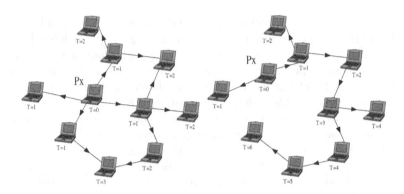

Fig. 1. (left) Px propagates a tuple that increases its value by one at every hop. (right) when the tuple source Px moves, all tuples are updated to take into account the new topology.

reflect network dynamics, as enabled by the automatic re-shaping of tuples' distributions of the TOTA middleware. Further details on the TOTA architecture can be found in [11], the TOTA API and programming model are described in more detail in [12].

2.2   Implementation

From an implementation point of view, we developed a first prototype of TOTA running on Laptops and on Compaq IPAQs equipped with 802.11b and Personal Java. IPAQ connects locally in the MANET mode (i.e. without requiring access points) creating the skeleton of the TOTA network. Tuples are being propagated through multicast sockets to all the nodes in the one-hop neighbor. The use of multicast sockets has been chosen to improve the communication speed by avoiding 802.11b unicast handshake. By considering the way in which tuples are propagated, TOTA is very well suited for this kind of broadcast communication. We think that this is a very important feature, because it will allow in the future implementing TOTA also on really simple devices (e.g. micro sensors) that cannot be provided with sophisticate communication mechanisms. Other than this communication mechanism, at the core of the TOTA middleware there is a simple event-based engine, that monitors network reconfigurations and the income of new tuples and react either by triggering propagation of already stored tuples or by generating an event directed to the event interface. Actually we own only a dozen of IPAQs and laptops on which to run the system. Since the effective testing of TOTA would require a larger number of devices, we have implemented an emulator to analyze TOTA behavior in presence of hundreds of nodes. The emulator, developed in Java, enables examining TOTA behavior in a MANET scenario, in which nodes topology can be rearranged dynamically either by a drag and drop user interface or by autonomous nodes' movements. The strength of our emulator is that, by adopting well-defined interfaces between the emulator and the application layers, the *same* code "installed" on the emulated devices can be installed on Personal Java real devices (e.g. Compaq IPAQs) enabled with wireless connectivity. This allow to test application first in the emulator, then to transfer them directly in a network of real devices. In order to rend the emulated scenario as close as possible to the real scenario, devices' battery consumption and wireless network glitches have been emulated as well. A simplified applet version of the TOTA emulator can be accessed and used at our research group Web site (http://www.agentgroup.unimo.it).

3 Location and Space in TOTA

Before describing how to realize location-based and content-based access in TOTA, it is fundamental to explain how nodes in a P2P computer network can be made aware of their spatial location. This information, in fact, is fundamental in both kind of access methods as we will see in the next sections. By creating an overlaid, distributed data structure, TOTA tuples intrinsically provides a notion of space in the network. For instance, a tuple incrementing one of its fields as it gets far away from the source identifies a sort of "structure of space" defining the network distances from the source. Moreover, TOTA allows dealing with spatial concepts in a much more flexible way. Although at the primitive level the space is the network space, and distances are measured in terms of hops from peer to peer, it is also possible to exploit more physically-grounded concepts of space. These may be required by several pervasive computing scenarios in which application agents need to interact with and acquire awareness of the physical space. For instance, if some sort of localization mechanism, whether GSP or beacon-based triangulation [7], is available to peers, then tuples propagation rules can also be expressed exploiting the available spatial information. Specifically, one can bound the propagation of a tuple to a portion of physical space by having the propagation procedure - as the tuple propagates from node to node - check in the local tuple space the local spatial coordinates, so as to deciding whether to further propagate the tuple or not. In addition, one could think at mapping the peers of a TOTA network in any sort of virtual space. This space, that must be supported by an appropriate routing mechanism allowing distant peers to be neighbors in the virtual space (e.g., the normal IP protocol), can then be used to propagate tuple so as to realize content-based routing policies, as in CAN [18] and Pastry [21].

4 Location Based Information Access

When dealing with mobile and P2P computing, a key issue is how to effectively exploit location-based information (e.g., a specific location from which a service is accessed). This information can in fact provide a notable added value to mobility: for instance, location-dependent yellow-pages could provide users driving in a city with information on the closest gas station, or with the list of closest

Chinese restaurants, and adapt such information while the users change its position. These examples are rooted on the concept of location based information access: an agent uses location information to constrain the scope of requests to a specific physical location. To realize such kind of location based information access in TOTA we can envision the following solution: an agent looking for some information will create a tuple having as content the description of what it is looking for (e.g. gas station) and having a propagation rule that propagates the tuple within a specified locality scope. More in detail, the tuple can be programmed to flood the network following an epidemic communication schema, but stopping propagating once a specified critical distance (e.g. 1Km) from the source has been reached. Peers, through the use of the TOTA event interface, can subscribe to the income of query tuples they can handle (of course, a general agreement on the syntax and the semantics of queries must be established) and react to this query tuple accordingly. In particular it must be noted that the query tuple creates, during its propagation, a data structure that enables the query recipient to send information back to the enquiring agent. This can be simply achieved by injecting an answer tuple in the network that propagates following downhill the query tuple's val field (see figure 2). It is worth noting, that the presented approach is adaptive to peer movements, since the intended shape of the tuples is fully maintained by the middleware.

```
Query Tuple
C = (description,val)
P = (propagate flooding the
network, until the critical 1Km distance has been reached.
Increase val by the hop distance at every hop, and always store
the tuple  in intermediate nodes)
```

```
Answer Tuple
C = (description,location)
P = (propagate following
downhill the val of the associated QueryTuple, incrementing
distance value by one at every hop)
```

5   Content Based Information Access

From another point of view, the utility of an P2P computer network derives primarily from the data and information it holds (think at sensor networks). The identity of the individual node that store the data tends to be less relevant. Accordingly, suitable interaction models and communication abstractions should be content-based, in the sense they should provide access to information on a content-basis rather than on the identity or the location of the device in which information is stored. Here the main issue is how to provide such kind of access to information avoiding the trivial solution of flooding the network with requests (i.e. querying all the peers whether or not they have the desired information).

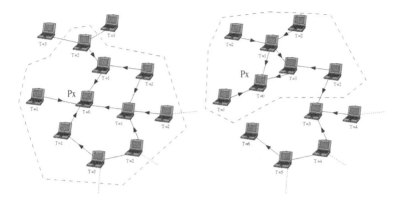

Fig. 2. (left) A TOTA tuple enabling the access to information within a three-hop locality scope. (right) when the tuple source moves, the locality scope change accordingly, thus providing an adaptive location-based access.

An effective solution to this problem has been proposed in [19]: in this approach the particular node that stores a given information is determined by the content of the information itself (indicated by a list of keywords). Hence all data with the same general content (i.e. indicated by the same keywords) will be routed to the same network node (not necessarily the node that originally gathered the data). This is achieved by having the list of keywords being hashed (via a predefined hash function) to a particular physical location and by routing the data to node closest to that physical location. To this purpose a MANET routing mechanism like GPSR [[9] can be conveniently used. Requests can follow a similar schema: a request for an information described by a specific list of keywords is sent to the node at the location indicated by the hashing of the list of keywords. In this way, information and requests meet in a rendez-vous node within the network without any kind of flooding being involved. This schema can be easily implemented within the TOTA middleware. Once nodes have been localized a node wanting to publish an information will inject in the network the following Info tuple. This tuple embeds in its propagation rule the GPSR routing algorithm described in [[9], that basically takes advantage of nodes location to forward packets following simple Euclidean consideration to bring the packet at every hop closer to the destination. The destination peer (rendez-vous) is determined applying a proper hash function (on which all the nodes agrees) to the content of the tuple. The query tuple to retrieve information follows a similar process, but, other than being routed to the rendez-vous node, it also creates a structure to route back information to the enquiring peer. Finally, on each node, there will be an agent subscribed to the income of query tuples it can handle and that will inject an answer tuple (see figure 3). It is worth noting that the approach is adaptive to peer mobility, since tuples are maintained despite changes in network topology, and it is also robust against peer failure since tuples will be routed to the alive peer closest to the target location.

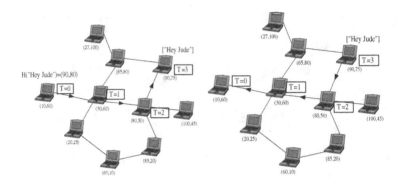

Fig. 3. (left) Px is looking for the mp3 file "Hey Jude". It evaluates H("Hey Jude") that results in (90,80). It then send a tuple to that location, that also create an overlaid structure to eventually route back information once found. (right) the peer closest to (90,80) receives the tuple and replies with a tuple that follows the trial left by the previous tuple to reach the enquiring peer.

```
Info Tuple
C = (data)
P = (propagate using GPSR routing algorithm
to the node closest to coordinates H(data))

Query Tuple
C = (data,val)
P = (propagate using GPSR routing
algorithm to the node closest to coordinates H(data). Increase val
by the hop distance at every hop, and always store the tuple  in
intermediate nodes)
```

6   Related Work

A number of recent proposals address the problem of defining effective interaction mechanisms in mobile and P2P computing scenarios. In particular, location-based access and content-based access have emerged as very useful interaction mechanisms and lots of proposals deal with them. Considering location-based access approaches, [[20] proposes a method to gather contextual information in a MANET scenario that is quite similar to the one we exploit in TOTA for the same purpose. There, each peer in the MANET dynamically builds via propagation a distributed data structure (i.e., a shortest path tree) to gather contextual, location-sensitive, information from other peers in the network. TOTA is much more flexible: the possibility of programming propagation rules makes it possible to express coordination patterns and to drive navigation, other than just gather contextual information. In addition, TOTA enables the definition of abstract overlay networks to be exploited for content-based routing. The DataSpace approach [[8] is centered on modeling the physical space as a collection of spatially addressable areas (called datacubes). All the computing devices spread in physical space inhabit these datacubes and are registered in a so called datacube registry accordingly to their physical location. Devices can be accessed on a spatial basis: Queries for printers within a specific building are firstly routed to the datacube associated to the building and then forwarded to those printing devices registered in the datacube registry. The main service provided in DataSpace is thus location-based access to information and resources. This approach is very different from TOTA: DataSpace is based on a look-up discovery and direct communication model. In TOTA, instead, all the interactions between agents are mediated by distributed tuples, thus promoting uncoupled and indirect communication model. Moreover TOTA is intended for a broader set of application rather then only location-based information access. Coming to content-based access, most of the proposals in the area introduces novel "overlay network" architectures, and define the specific algorithms for building such networks, re-organize them in response to dynamic network changes, and route data and requests across the overlay network. Some of these proposals focuses on the problem of Internet-scale peer-to-peer routing (e.g., CAN [[18], Pastry [21] and Chord [23]), other on more specific P2P scenarios(e.g., GHT [[19] and INS/Twine [[1]). However, to our knowledge, none of these proposals provide a configurable framework with which to define and customize the structure of the overlay network and the associated policy. TOTA can provide this feature via a simple and intuitive programming model, and can make it possible to define, say, libraries of tuples with which to implement any needed content-based policy for data and service access. As a final note, we emphasize that (i) recent approaches in the area modular robots [[22] exploit the idea of propagating "hormones" across the robot agents so as to achieve a globally coherent behavior in robot's reshaping activities; (ii) in the popular simulation game "The Sims" [[24], characters move and act accordingly to specific fields that are assumed to be spread in the simulated environment and sensed by characters depending on situations (e.g., they sense the food field when hungry); (iii) ant-based optimization systems [[2],[17] exploit a virtual environment in which ants can spread pheromones, diffusing and evaporating in the environment according to specific rules. (iv) amorphous computers [[3],[16] exploit propagation of fields to let particles self-organize their activities. Although serving different purposes, these approaches definitely share with TOTA the same physical inspiration.

7   Conclusion and Future Works

The TOTA middleware, by relying on distributed tuples to be propagated over a network as sorts of electromagnetic fields, provides an effective support to support distributed applications in dynamic network scenarios, as we have tried to shown via several application examples. Several issues are still to be solved for our first prototype implementation to definitely fulfill its promises. First, experiments and performance evaluations are needed to test the limits of usability and the scalability of TOTA, by quantifying the TOTA delays in updating the tuples' distributed structures in response to dynamic changes. Second, we must try to develop more and more applications upon the TOTA middleware to test the actual effectiveness of the abstractions proposed. Third, we must compulsory integrate proper access control model to rule accesses to distributed tuples and their updates.

Acknowledgements. Work supported by the Italian MIUR and CNR in the "Progetto Strategico IS-MANET, Infrastructures for Mobile ad-hoc Networks".

References

1. M. Balazinska, H. Balakrishnan, D. Karger, "INS/Twine: A Scalable Peer-to-Peer Architecture for Intentional Resource Discovery", Pervasive 2002 - International Conference on Pervasive Computing, Zurich, Switzerland, August 2002.
2. E. Bonabeau, M. Dorigo, G. Theraulaz, "Swarm Intelligence", Oxford University Press, 1999.
3. W. Butera, "Programming a Paintable Computer", PhD Thesis, MIT Media Lab, Feb. 2002.
4. G. Cabri, L. Leonardi, F. Zambonelli, "Engineering Mobile Agent Applications via Context-Dependent Coordination", IEEE Transactions on Software Engineering, 28(11), Nov. 2002.
5. G. Cugola, A. Fuggetta, E. De Nitto, "The JEDI Event-based Infrastructure and its Application to the Development of the OPSS WFMS", IEEE Transactions on Software Engineering, 27(9): 827-850, Sept. 2001.
6. Gnutella, http://gnutella.wego.com
7. J. Hightower, G. Borriello, "Location Systems for Ubiquitous Computing", IEEE Computer, 34(8): 57-66, Aug. 2001.
8. T. Imielinski, S. Goel, "Dataspace - querying and monitoring deeply networked collections in physical space", IEEE Personal Communications Magazine, October 2000, pp. 4-9.
9. B. Karp, H. Kung, "GPSR: Greedy Perimeter Stateless Routing for Wireless Networks", Mobicom 2000, Boston, MA, USA.
10. Kazaa, http://www.kazaa.com/en/index.php
11. M. Mamei, F. Zambonelli, L. Leonardi, "Tuples On The Air: a Middleware for Context-Aware Computing in Dynamic Networks", 1st International ICDCS Workshop on Mobile Computing Middleware (MCM03) Providence, Rhode Island. May 2003.
12. M. Mamei, F. Zambonelli, "Self-Maintained Distributed Data Structure Over Mobile Ad-Hoc Network", Technical Report No. DISMI-2003-23, University of Modena and Reggio Emilia, August 2003.
13. MOTION, IST Project, IST-1999-11400, http://www.motion.softeco.it
14. Morpheus, http://www.musiccity.com
15. International Workshop on Mobile Teamwork Support, http://www.infosys.tuwien.ac.at/motion/mts/
16. R. Nagpal, "Programmable Self-Assembly Using Biologically-Inspired Multiagent Control", 1st International Conference on Autonomous Agents and Multiagent Systems, Bologna (I), ACM Press, July 2002.

17. V. Parunak, S. Bruekner, J. Sauter, "ERIM's Approach to Fine-Grained Agents", NASA/JPL Workshop on Radical Agent Concepts, Greenbelt (MD), Jan. 2002.
18. S. Ratsanamy, P. Francis, M. Handley, R. Karp, "A Scalable Content-Addressable Network", ACM SIGCOMM Conference 2001, San Diego (CA), ACM Press, Aug. 2001.
19. S. Ratsanamy et al., "GHT: A Geographic Hash Table for Data-Centric Storage", 1st ACM Int. Workshop on Wireless Sensor Networks and Applications, Atlanta, Georgia, USA, September 2002.
20. G.C. Roman, C. Julien, Q. Huang, "Network Abstractions for Context-Aware Mobile Computing", 24th International Conference on Software Engineering, Orlando (FL), ACM Press, May 2002.
21. A. Rowstron, P. Druschel, "Pastry: Scalable, Decentralized Object Location and Routing for Large-Scale Peer-to-Peer Systems", 18th IFIP/ACM Conference on Distributed Systems Platforms, Heidelberg (D), Nov. 2001.
22. W. Shen, B. Salemi, P. Will, "Hormone-Inspired Adaptive Communication and Distributed Control for CONRO Self-Reconfigurable Robots", IEEE Transactions on Robotics and Automation, Oct. 2002.
23. I. Stoica, R. Morris, D. Karger, M. Kaashoek, H. Balakrishnan, "Chord: A Scalable Peer-to-peer Lookup Service for Internet Applications", ACM SIGCOMM 2001, San Deigo, CA, August 2001, pp. 149-160.
24. The Sims, http://www.thesims.com

K-Trek: A Peer-to-Peer Approach to Distribute Knowledge in Large Environments

Paolo Busetta[1], Paolo Bouquet[2,1], Giordano Adami[1], Matteo Bonifacio[2,1], and
Francesco Palmieri[3]

[1] ITC-irst – Povo, Trento, Italy
{busetta,gioadami}@itc.it
[2] University of Trento – Trento, Italy
{bouquet,bonifacio}@dit.unitn.it
[3] Palmieri Consulting – Roma, Italy
francesco.palmieri@tiscali.it

Abstract. In this paper, we explore an architecture, called *K-Trek*, that enables mobile users to *travel across knowledge* distributed over large geographical areas (ranging from large public buildings to national parks). Our aim is to provide, distribute, and enrich the environment with location-sensitive information for use by agents on board mobile and static devices. Local interactions among K-Trek devices and the distribution of data in the larger environment follow some typical peer-to-peer patterns and techniques. We introduce the architecture, discuss some of its potential knowledge management applications, and present a few experimental results obtained by means of simulation.

1 Introduction

In this paper, we explore an architecture, called *K-Trek*, that supports a form of *context-aware computing*. K-Trek enables mobile users to *travel across knowledge* distributed over a large geographical area (ranging from large public buildings to a national park). This is obtained by providing, distributing, and enriching the environment with location-sensitive information for use by agents on board of mobile and static devices.

Context-aware computing is an area of active research at the very heart of *pervasive computing* and *ambient intelligence* [1], even if a clear focus has yet to emerge (see for instance the recent [2]). Context-awareness is usually defined as sensitivity to the user's state, the environment where she currently is, and the current physical environment [3]. Distinguishing features of our approach with respect to the known literature are:

- our definition of *context*, derived by applying the formal framework described in [4] to knowledge management issues, is based on data accumulated and categorized by each user during an extended period of time. An explicit negotiation phase (which subsumes traditional feature-based selections based on user preferences or profiling as particular cases) is used to filter or annotate information given to and left by users during their movements;
- no long-range, permanent wireless networks or sensors of any kind are involved. Instead, we "augment" the environment, as well as mobile devices, with very low cost,

G. Moro, C. Sartori, and M.P. Singh (Eds.): AP2PC 2003, LNAI 2872, pp. 174–185, 2004.
© Springer-Verlag Berlin Heidelberg 2004

easily available hardware for wireless, short range communication. Bluetooth [5] is our reference technology, but the architecture can be easily adapted to future standards as they will emerge;
- agents on board of static as well as mobile devices can exploit the users they get in contact with for transporting information to agents they cannot directly reach.

K-Trek adopts some typical peer-to-peer patterns and techniques. Small peer-to-peer networks are formed on-the-fly and enable localized, context-aware interactions among agents. User movement is exploited to provide message transport in the larger environment, in a way similar to query propagation on some well-known peer-to-peer networks. This mechanism is effectively a particular form of *ad hoc* wide area networking that does not need any permanent long-distance communication infrastructure.

This paper is organized as follows. Next section introduces the concept of context as intended in the field of *distributed knowledge management*, and discusses how it can be applied to represent location-sensitive information. Sec. 3 describes the architecture of K-Trek. Context awareness in K-Trek is discussed in more detail in Sec. 4. We present, in Sec. 5, a few application scenarios. We conclude with some experimental results collected by simulating different scenarios (Sec. 6).

2 Context in Distributed Knowledge Management

In several recent papers, the idea of *Distributed Knowledge Management* (DKM) was proposed as a new and promising approach to the design and implementation of systems for managing knowledge within complex organizations and, in general, in scenarios in which there is a multiplicity of autonomous knowledge sources [6]. The main idea was that, over time, different people (or groups of people) produce heterogeneous and partial views (called *contexts*) on the information available within an organization, each from their own perspective (*principle of autonomy*), and that these views – far from being an obstacle to management and coordinated action – are a potential source of innovation and knowledge creation, if suitably managed (*principle of coordination*). As mentioned above, this definition of context is a direct derivation of the work on the contextual reasoning by Giunchiglia and his group [4,7].

Current work on DKM focuses on issues of semantic autonomy and coordination. An experimental testbed has been developed in a peer-to-peer system called KEx (*Knowledge Exchange*) [8]. KEx embodies the functionality for developing one or more local views (contexts) for each so-called K-Peer, and automatically discovering mappings among contexts using a complex algorithm for semantic matching [9]. In KEx, contexts are graphs of concepts that are used to index or annotate document bases, data bases, and in the future Web services. By means of context mappings, a K-Peer user can navigate through the knowledge available within different parts of an organization by adopting her own perspective, rather than the perspective of the knowledge's original owners, thus facilitating the discovery of documents or services classified according to unfamiliar terminology. During this process, the user may also discover new concepts, which in turn she can use to enrich her own contexts.

The work presented here explores a different direction of DKM, which is closely related to what is called *ambient intelligence*. We imagine a scenario in which knowledge is context-dependent not only because it embodies the (semantic) perspectives of different people (as for KEx), but also because (i) it says something about a specific location of a given environment, and (ii) is physically stored in that location. To understand the underlying intuition, we suggest an analogy with signs in the physical world, which provide the intended information only if they are placed in the location in which they were designed to stay. For example, a sign describing the history of an old building ("This palace was built in ... ") provides useful (and true) information only if it is physically attached to that building; and a sign indicating a distance of 50 km from Trento provides true information only if the sign is not moved to another location or to point in the wrong direction.

3   K-Trek: An Overview

K-Trek is based on three main types of device, called *K-Trek devices* (Fig. 1):

K-Beacon: a static device (such as an embedded system with integrated Bluetooth board) which stores contextual information about a specific location (i.e., the location where it is placed), and can interact in various forms with other K-Trek devices;

K-Voyager: any mobile device – such as a PDA or a last generation mobile phone – with one or more K-Trek applications on board;

K-Plug: any device with a standard network interface that acts as a gateway between K-Trek devices and back-end servers.

K-Trek devices communicate via two types of networks, described below:

– *K-Trek micro networks*, i.e. on-the-fly networks that connect a limited number of K-Trek devices in a very small geographical area, and

– *K-Trek Wide Area Network (K-wan)*, i.e. a wide-area, message-based, asynchronous network, where mobile K-Trek devices act as temporary bridges between disconnected devices.

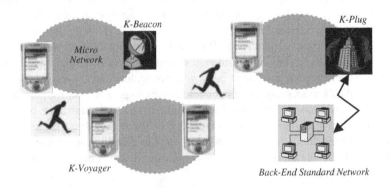

Fig. 1. K-Trek: main components

3.1   Micro Networking with Localized Resources

The main feature of K-Trek is the ability of setting up "micro networks" on-the-fly, i.e. networks that cover a very small geographical area (no more than a few tens of meters) with a limited number of devices and limited bandwidth, without the need for dedicated, static equipment (wires, routers, access points, or other paraphernalia)[1].

Special light-weight message handling agents are responsible for communication among K-Trek devices in a micro network. The agent tasks include the most basic peer-to-peer interaction, i.e. discovery. To this end, they periodically broadcast *announcements*. For instance, a K-Beacon announcement contains the K-Beacon's contact information and a set of short messages, sent by local application agents and directed to the agents on passing K-Voyagers. The processing of this announcement is discussed later, in Sec. 4.

This discovery-based approach, inspired by peer-to-peer systems[2], contrasts with location-aware systems based on geographical coordinates, commonly adopted with mobile phones and other wireless networks, for various reasons. First, no location sensor such as a Global Positioning System (GPS) is needed. Second, since there are no coordinates, there is no need for geo-referencing information to be delivered to users, as it is commonly required when central services are involved (typically with mobile phones), or when local applications need to retrieve data already on board of the user's mobile device or to access a centralized directory.

Note that, in general, communication happens while the user is moving, thus the time of contact between two devices can be short. This, and the limitations on bandwidth, impose strong constraints on the protocols, concerning in particular the frequency of announcements and the amount of data exchanged. However, these constraints may be loosened after a careful study of the characteristics of a specific scenario, which may reveal peculiar user patterns (possibly induced, e.g. by some human-computer interface mechanism such as a sound that invites the user to look at the screen and thus to slow down), or may impose a specific behavior (e.g., stopping whenever the K-Voyager signals that it is in contact with a K-Beacon).

3.2   K-Wan: A Wide-Area Asynchronous Network

The second type of network is what we call K-Trek Wide Area Network (K-wan), designed for certain types of knowledge management applications. A K-wan is a wide-area, message-based, asynchronous network, where messages may be delivered long after being posted, and only stochastic guarantees are given concerning their actual delivery, latency, and the geographical area of distribution. As discussed later, a K-wan exploits the users' movements for message transport, thus no special equipment is required other than what is required to set up micro-networks (that is, Bluetooth boards). A K-wan may

---

[1] As mentioned in the introduction, our reference technology is Bluetooth [5], because it is suitable to very low-cost, low-power, wireless devices, and it is commonly built into many last-generation mobile phones and PDAs. What we call a micro network is commonly referred to as a *pico network* in Bluetooth; we purposely differentiate our terminology, which refers to a high-level architecture. The definition of K-Trek device is independent from Bluetooth.

[2] The Sweden company Pocit Labs produced a Bluetooth-based peer-to-peer network called BlueTalk, similar to our micro-network. Unfortunately, they went out of business in June 2002.

remind one of a *partial mesh* network, where each node is connected to each other node either directly or by means of other intermediate nodes that act as routers. However, in a K-wan no routing is possible since user movements are not predictable, thus messages are broadcasted, adopting a very different propagation strategy than in mesh networks. This strategy may be improved in future, if some intelligence (including user profiling and machine learning techniques) is able to predict the future user movements, or in specific domains where user movements are well known (e.g., devices on board of public transport vehicles).

The message handling agents implement some micro networking mechanisms in order to support transport within a K-wan. One of these mechanisms is applied after a K-Voyager discovers a K-Beacon, as described in Sec. 3.1 above, and consists of two complementary actions. The first is the downloading of any message addressed to the K-Beacon that is contained in a dedicated K-wan buffer on board of the K-Voyager; in other words, a K-Voyager delivers, to the K-Beacons it gets in contact with, anything addressed to them that was picked up during its trip. Conversely, the second action is uploading messages onto the K-Voyager, sent from the K-Beacon and addressed to agents running remotely.

The second mechanism needed by K-Wan is applied between K-Voyagers. The announcement mechanism of Sec. 3.1 enables K-Voyagers to discover each other; this is followed by the exchange of the contents of their K-wan buffers, in a truly peer-to-peer fashion. At the end of this process, any message addressed to either of the two K-Voyagers is delivered to the appropriate agent and discarded from both buffers (since it reached its destination), while all others are duplicated.

This buffer content exchange happens whenever two users carrying K-Trek devices get close by, without any human involvement. This effectively implies that messages spread around the geographical area covered by moving K-Trek users as a sort of benign – but highly infectious – virus. Various mechanisms – such as setting expiration dates on messages, maintaining lists of those already delivered, managing buffer overflows – keeps things under control. However, a number of questions arise, e.g. what buffer size is required, what is the probability of reaching the destination, which geographical area is covered; the answers are affected by many factors, the most important being the pattern of movement of users. We return on this topic in Sec. 6.

The last major micro networking mechanism used by a K-wan involves the third type of K-Trek device, K-Plugs. A K-Plug can be any device (e.g., a personal computer or a Bluetooth *access point*) with a standard network interface that acts as a gateway between devices on a K-wan and back-end servers. To this end, all K-Plugs provide access to a single, centralized mailbox service. When a K-Voyager gets within the range of a K-Plug, a set of peer-to-peer protocols similar to those presented above are used to deposit messages for agents on back-end systems, and to pick up messages addressed to the K-Voyager (or its user) and for other K-Trek devices; the first are immediately delivered to their destination agents, while the others are deposited in the K-wan buffer.

We expect that more than one K-Plug are part of a K-wan. Ideally, they should be located in places where, sooner or later, most if not all users pass by.[3] In situations where

---

[3] For this reason, and to reduce the amount of circulating messages, a K-Trek administrator may configure K-Plugs so that K-Voyagers can pick up messages for themselves and for K-Beacons,

the paths followed by users can be predicted, messages for a K-Beacon K are distributed only by the K-Plugs along the paths that touch K. Since message duplications are likely while delivery cannot be guaranteed, care is taken in the mailbox administration, for instance by making sure that messages for K-Beacons are not removed until expired or requested by their senders (possibly after an application-level handshake).

Finally, a note on security. To the usual security problems of wireless environments, a K-wan adds something of its own because of its virus-like message transport mechanism. For instance, if no care is taken, a denial-of-service attack could be easily performed by somebody generating many apparently innocent messages with very long expiration dates. Thus, the K-wan buffer management is a particularly sensitive issue.

A K-wan is particularly suited to cases where low-power embedded systems distributed on a large territory need to perform occasional exchanges of non-critical data (e.g., collecting data from sensors detecting animal or tourist movements in a national park). These scenarios currently require either expensive links (such as microwaves or satellite), or people physically going to each device for uploading and downloading data via floppy disks or other media. As shown in the examples in the concluding section of this paper, a careful analysis can predict the performance of a K-wan with some precision. To this end, we have developed analysis tools that can be used to set up a K-wan so that any required level of performance (e.g., maximum time for delivery) is achieved, thus making a K-wan appealing for a large number of application scenarios.

4 Context-Sensitive Mobile Applications in K-Trek

Our first objective is to enable the exchange of contextually relevant information among the K-Trek devices temporarily connected in a micro-network. Context here is used in two distinct senses:

1. *Context as location*: This is the more traditional sense of context in context-aware applications. However, K-Trek supports a particular form of location-awareness, where the "location" is determined not by geographic coordinates but by the co-presence of other K-Trek devices (e.g., a meeting can happen anywhere as long as all the required participants are present);
2. *Context as perspective*: Context here is used in the same sense of DKM, and refers to the conceptual graphs mentioned for KEx. In the simplest case, a context is nothing more than a set of labels indicating features or user preferences, possibly enriched off-line with linguistic information from thesauruses or data bases such as WordNet [10]; the context mapping mentioned for KEx is reduced, for devices with limited capabilities, to plain label matching. Whenever a micro-network is established, K-Voyagers discover whatever resources are available on other K-Trek devices, attempt to perform mappings between the contexts they have on board and those on board the others, and act consequently (e.g., they may report on the findings to their users). Context-sensitivity is achieved by "augmenting" the environment with K-Beacons, with their own contexts on board, representing or annotating local

---

but not for other K-Voyagers. Other distribution-limiting parameters are also available to the administrator.

information such as data generated by local sources (typically on embedded systems) or information left by other mobile devices.

Application agents running on a K-Voyager are associated to one or more contexts. By operating on the K-Voyager's GUI, the user decides which applications, and which contexts, to keep active. This means that user gets *only information relevant to her at that particular time at that particular location* – which is to say, a K-Voyager is context-aware as commonly meant [3]. Since the interaction is two-way, also data flowing from K-Voyagers to K-Beacons can be annotated with contextual information, so agents on the static device can get additional information on mobile users and possibly select only that information that is of their interest.

User contexts can be edited by users; this is a typical off-line process, better performed on a more convenient platform than a mobile device, e.g. a PC. Similarly, contexts on board of K-Beacons are typically edited off-line and downloaded by a system configurator. In the future, it is foreseeable that contexts may be acquired semi-automatically by K-Trek devices themselves, e.g. in a mixed-initiative process where some of the information collected by a K-Voyager during a trip is suggested to the user for addition to her contexts.

In the following, we illustrate the interaction of a K-Voyager with a K-Beacon; the same pattern applies when interacting with K-Plugs or other K-Voyagers. When the message handling agent on board of the K-Voyager receives a K-Beacon announcement, it performs a discrimination of the content, then a first type of context-sensitive processing. Application messages addressed to a remote system or to a different K-Voyager are stored in the K-wan buffer; their processing has been discussed above. The others (i.e., those addressed to either anybody or specifically to this K-Voyager) are filtered against the user contexts. As mentioned above, currently this process is limited to little more than plain matching between the labels in the contexts and those on the messages; we expect, in a not-too-distant future, to be able to perform something more sophisticated, up to the full context mapping of KEx (Sec. 2).

Eventually, the messages left after filtering are delivered to their destination agents. Typically, these messages are further application-specific announcements or local information to be shown to the user. Apart from those described in Sec. 3.2, further interactions between K-Beacon and K-Voyager are driven by the application agents, for instance to retrieve or deposit data or obtain services from K-Beacon agents. Since a K-Voyager may fall within reach of multiple K-Beacons, application agents must be able to handle simultaneous interactions.

5   Distributed Knowledge Management Applications on K-Trek

Most things that one can imagine doing in the physical world by putting a sign, leaving a mark, depositing a form in a mailbox, attaching a "post-it" card, and so on, can be done electronically with K-Trek, with the exception of those actions that require knowledge of the exact location and direction of the user (e.g., direction-giving relative to the user position, such as "move for 20 meters on your left and you will see the Colosseum", cannot be supported without additional sensors).

Looking at K-trek from a broader knowledge management perspective, its architecture is suitable to situations in which:

- the physical environment is populated by objects whose value can be increased by either delivering to, or collecting information from, other objects or users;
- linking these "informative" objects by means of an information network based on long-distance wireless connections is unfeasible, because of costs or environmental constraints;
- mobile actors in the environment need to locally exchange information either with informative objects or with other actors;
- mobile actors move across the environment along paths that, statistically, connect all the informative objects;
- an environment administrator has an interest in enhancing the environment through the provision of infrastructural services;
- there may be external actors that have an interest in "owning" the informative processes related to one or more objects.

A first example of potential K-Trek enabled environment is natural parks and, in general, geographically dispersed entertainment environments such as archaeological sites. Parks are populated by objects such as natural attractions, routes or historical sites whose value can be enhanced if they are able to exchange information with users, other objects, the administrator, or the "owner" of the site (an entity that has an interest in updating and collecting the information that belong to the site). For example, a historical site may receive information: from a school of architecture in order to update its description; from a visitor that wants to leave a message to those that will visit the site in future ("virtual post-it"); and, from a member of the maintenance staff that has periodically to asses its status. Conversely, the site can provide: architectural information to a visitor whose context shows an interest in architecture; maintenance information to inspectors, previously deposited by members of the maintenance staff; and, information about number of visits, type of users and the kind of information they deposit on the site to the park administrator. Visitors and maintainers unintentionally provide the "lazy" communication channel needed to ensure information delivery, update, and collection by K-wan.

Another scenario involves field management activities of geographically distributed industrial settings. Relevant objects are industrial sites or components (power stations, junction boxes, and so on) that generate information about their status and collect information about those maintenance activities that must be performed and assessed in site. Here, since the certainty of information delivery and collection is more critical, maintenance visits are intentionally scheduled not just as a function of each maintenance task, but also for enabling the circulation of information across the overall system. For example, maintainer A that has to visit and asses the status of site 1, has a route that passes in front of site 2 whose maintenance is under the responsibility of the maintainer B. In such case, A deposits his visit report on site 1 and automatically collects the visit report of B done on site 2. The latter will be delivered to the environment administrator whose task is to monitor the overall system.

The scenario above provides an example on how K-wan can handle certain levels of information criticality when the administrator is able to exploit the value of predictable "visit paths" in terms of connections that will happen with a known frequency and with a known level of reliability. Another good example is represented, in a urban environment, by mailmen that, in addition to their usual task of mail delivery, might deliver to and collects updates from those K-Beacons that are positioned on their typical routes.

In summary, the peculiarities of K-wan make it useful for specific – but not at all uncommon – classes of applications, the most important being the non-real time ("lazy") monitoring and control of large territories. For instance, the application domains mentioned above would benefit from the collection of statistics (e.g., on tourists' preferences, on the state of natural resources), of summaries of notes or forms left locally by passing users (e.g., tourist satisfaction forms), of data coming from embedded processors (e.g., usage statistics of industrial equipment). K-wan supports this kind of data collection at a much lower cost than networks requiring direct connection between data source and destination, including WiFi (IEEE standard 802.11b) and GSM/GPRS (used by cell phones), both in terms of infrastructure and power consumption. The same is true for the lazy distribution of data or configuration parameters (even software) from a centralized place to users or K-Beacons.

It is worth to stress again that the annotation of messages with information taken from the originating agent's contexts helps in performing typical knowledge management tasks, varying from the ability to support communities of mobile users to classical data mining processes such as understanding tourists' interests, identifying patterns of visit per user category, and so on.

6 Quantitative Studies on K-Wan

Before deploying a knowledge management solution, even before developing any software for K-Trek, we deemed it necessary to assess the characteristics of a K-wan and to define a set of criteria for network design. This is a very complex task, because a large number of factors influence the network behavior: for instance, the number of mobile users, their patterns of movements, the number and location of K-Beacons and K-Plugs, the size of the K-wan buffers, the lifetime of messages. The general question to be answered can be formulated as follows: given a certain configuration, what is the probability that a message reaches its destination within a given timeframe? or, equivalently, which factors should a network designer focus on, so that messages are delivered on time with a given probability (possibly 100%)?

The most effective way to answer this question seems to be simulation. For our initial studies, we adopted a multi-agent simulation tool, called NetLogo [11] – easy to use, ideally suited to classroom experiments but not adequate to complex scenarios analysis; that notwithstanding, it revealed to be enough for our objectives. Ultimately, our aim is to build a library of models that cover a reasonable large number of situations, and use it as a design tool for a K-wan. In the following, we discuss two simple models and present some of the collected results.

Objective of our first model was to understand if we could identify any correlations among a selected set of parameters on a relatively small scale scenario. The model has not been thought with reference to any specific domain. A grid of roads, whose overall size and density was controlled via parameters, was randomly generated and a set of travelers with K-Voyagers scattered over them. Travelers followed random walks at a

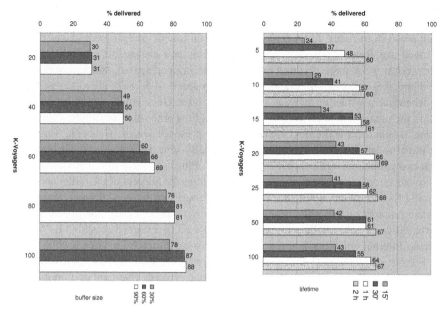

Fig. 2. Experimental Results - left: generic model; right: tourism in town

fixed speed, and bounced back when reaching the border of the grid. A set of K-Beacons and K-Plugs were randomly scattered over the grid. A constant number of messages (5) were generated by K-Beacons with random destinations, which could be either specific K-Voyagers or generic back-end applications (that is, any K-Plug). We ran a large batch of simulations, varying road density, number of K-Voyagers, K-Beacons, and K-Plugs, lifetime of messages, and size of the K-wan buffers.

The graph on the left of Fig. 2 contains an extract from one of the many statistics we elaborated, the most interesting in our opinion. The horizontal bars tell the average percentage of messages that reached their destination as a function of the number of K-Voyagers involved (shown on the left) and the size of the K-Wan buffer. The latter was set as a percentage of the total number of circulating messages; the three bars in each cluster show the results with different values (30, 60, e 90% respectively). All other simulation parameters had a negligeable influence on the outcome. In summary, what the graph shows is that the buffer size had a relatively limited influence, while the most important factor is the density of K-Voyagers. This is not surprising – as any doctor would tell, the highest the density of the population, the highest the chance for a virus to spread. No matter how good this result looks like, we refrain from jumping to definitive conclusions, since there is too a large number of arbitrary configuration choices (e.g., the way we distributed roads), policies (e.g., concerning buffer overflow management), and behaviors (e.g., paths followed by travelers) to consider this model of general applicability.

Differently from the previous one, the second model was built by analyzing a realistic scenario, which is also a potential target domain: tourism in a historical town. We recreated a partial and slightly simplified map of the town center of Trento, Italy, roughly corresponding to a square whose side is 600 mt long. This historical center features a thick network of roads, fairly typical of medieval towns, open to pedestrians only. We assumed that Bluetooth devices can communicate at a distance of up to 30 mt, which experiments show to be a conservative estimate in open spaces. Mobile users crossed the mapped area following a random walk at a speed of 5 km/h; also, they could stop anywhere for a while, or leave and come back later. On average, a mobile user stayed within the area for an hour. We put 4 K-Plugs at the corner of busy streets. Twenty food outlets (restaurants and cafes) advertised their presence with K-Beacons. Similarly to the previous model, these K-Beacons periodically sent messages to K-Voyagers or to back-end applications (thus, delivered to any K-Plug).

In our reference application, a message contains the address of the outlet owning the sending K-Beacon and a note left by a passing tourist with a K-Voyagers; a note could contain remarks on the outlet, a suggested meeting location, a satisfaction form for the tourist office. A note can be sent either to another K-Trek user (that is, to a K-Voyager), or to an Internet email account (by means of an e-mail server, i.e. via a K-Plug).

For our simple model, we assumed that every K-Beacon had always two messages to deliver. A new message was generated when one expired. The number of mobile users was constant over time. Message destinations were chosen randomly in a set formed by the K-Voyagers plus 4 e-mail addresses; for instance, given 96 users, there was a 4% probability that a message had to be delivered to the e-mail server via a K-Plug. We set the K-wan buffer size to 50% of the number of circulating messages, i.e. 20. Our goal was to determine the probability that a message reached its destination, as a function of its lifetime and the number of mobile users.

The graph on the right of Fig. 2 summarizes the results we obtained after simulating a 12 hours period by discrete cycles corresponding to a simulated period of 10 seconds each. It can easily be seen that the message lifetime, which varied between 15 minutes and two hours, not surprisingly had an important impact. After analysis, we found out that undelivered messages were for K-Voyager users that left the area too soon to be reached, while e-mails were always delivered (apart from unrealistic cases of very short lifetime, not shown in the table). The number of mobile users has an important influence, too, in a slightly surprising way. Indeed, with high density, messages lifetime decreases its importance, indicating that messages spread around more quickly than with lower densities; still, the best case has been achieved with a relatively low number of K-Voyagers. The reason seems to be the buffer size - indeed, the quicker messages spread around, the higher the chance of buffer overflows (our management policy is FIFO). For our reference application, we consider these results satisfactory.

7   Conclusions

We have introduced an architecture, called K-Trek, that provides context-sensitive information to mobile devices and "lazy" distribution of data over a wide area network. K-Trek adopts some typical peer-to-peer communication patterns. No location sensor is required; commonly available short-distance communication hardware (Bluetooth today, and emerging standards in future) is exploited. Data exchange, both local and long-distance, is much cheaper than in wireless networks such as WiFi and GSM/GPRS, both in terms of required hardware and power consumption. K-Trek is suitable to situations where the deployment of a large scale infrastructure faces serious constraints in terms of cost, environmental impact, or geographical coverage; we have presented a few application domains showing these characteristics. Simulations have focused on the reliability of long-distance communication, and have shown the effectiveness and limitations of K-Trek for this purpose. Future work will be directed at practical experimentation in real world cases.

References

1. Ducatel, K., Bogdanowicz, M., Scapolo, F., Leijten, J., Burgelman, J.C.: Scenarios for ambient intelligence in 2010. Technical report, Information Society Technologies Programme of the European Union Commission (IST) (2001) http://www.cordis.lu/ist/.
2. Abowd, G.D., Ebling, M., Hunt, G., Lei, H., Gellersen, H.: Context-aware computing. IEEE Pervasive Computing **1** (2002)
3. Schilit, B., Adams, N., Want, R.: Context-aware computing applications. In: IEEE Workshop on Mobile Computing Systems and Applications, Santa Cruz, CA, US (1994)
4. Ghidini, C., Giunchiglia, F.: Local Models Semantics, or Contextual Reasoning = Locality + Compatibility. Artificial Intelligence **127** (2001) 221–259
5. Bluetooth SIG, I.: The Official Bluetooth Wireless Info Site (2002) http://www.bluetooth.com/.
6. Bonifacio, M., Bouquet, P., Traverso, P.: Enabling Distributed Knowledge Management. Managerial and Technological Implications. Novatica and Informatik/Informatique **III** (2002)
7. Benerecetti, M., Bouquet, P., Ghidini, C.: Contextual Reasoning Distilled. Journal of Theoretical and Experimental Artificial Intelligence **12** (2000) 279–305
8. Bonifacio, M., Bouquet, P., Mameli, G., Nori, M.: KEx: a peer-to-peer solution for Distributed Knowledge Management. In Karagiannis, D., Reimer, U., eds.: Fourth International Conference on Practical Aspects of Knowledge Management (PAKM-2002), Vienna (Austria) (2002)
9. Bouquet, P., Serafini, L., Zanobini, S.: Semantic coordination: a new approach and an application. In Sycara, K., ed.: Second International Semantic Web Conference (ISWC-03). Lecture Notes in Computer Science (LNCS), Sanibel Island (Florida, USA) (2003)
10. Fellbaum, C., ed.: WordNet: An Electronic Lexical Database. The MIT Press, Cambridge, US (1998)
11. Wilensky, U.: NetLogo (1999) http://ccl.northwestern.edu/netlogo/.

Improving Peer-to-Peer Resource Discovery Using Mobile Agent Based Referrals

Prithviraj(Raj) Dasgupta

Department of Computer Science
University of Nebraska, Omaha, NE 68182.
pdasgupta@mail.unomaha.edu
Phone: (402) 554 4966, Fax: (402) 554 3284

Abstract. A peer-to-peer(P2P) system consists of a decentralized, distributed network of nodes that is capable of sharing resources and services without centralized supervision. A major functionality in P2P networks is locating resources or services present on remote nodes. Traditional techniques for resource discovery include blind searches among the nodes using query flooding, or, positioning resources strategically to enable rapid lookup using distributed hash tables. In this paper, we propose a mobile agent based referral service that directs resources queries intelligently towards the nodes possessing the resource. The mobile agents adaptively learn paths called trails within the P2P network to enable rapid location of resources. Preliminary results of our algorithm demonstrate that the agent based technique performs favorably with existing P2P resource discovery protocols.

Keywords: Peer-to-peer systems, mobile agents, intelligent resource discovery, multi-agent learning, rumor-mongering.

1 Introduction

The rapid growth of the Internet over the past decade has enabled several technologies for online human interaction. Users of the World Wide Web can exchange information in different formats including text and multimedia using different devices ranging from wireless mobile devices to desktop computers. User interaction across a variety of applications and devices requires that the software processes enabling the communication should be able to interact and exchange resources and information with each other as peers. Peer-to-peer(P2P) systems are becoming an attractive computing paradigm to share resources in a heterogenous environment of connected users.

P2P systems comprise an overlay network where the nodes can interact and share resources with one another. Since every node is a peer and there is no central controlling authority, the system is decentralized and distributed. This makes P2P networks attractive for connecting thousands of users without worrying about scalability and centralized control issues. However, the distributed nature of the network also makes it difficult to locate resources. The most common

G. Moro, C. Sartori, and M.P. Singh (Eds.): AP2PC 2003, LNAI 2872, pp. 186–197, 2004.
© Springer-Verlag Berlin Heidelberg 2004

resource discovery protocols in P2P networks are query flooding and distributed hash tables(DHT). However, flooding generates excessive network traffic while DHT-s require additional overhead for distribued updates. The traditional P2P resource discovery protocol can be improved if a node initiating a query has an idea of where to look for resources without maintaining a distributed hash. In this paper, we propose an intelligent agent based mechanism where a query is encapsulated in a mobile agent that gets forwarded in the direction of the resource aided by referrals given by the nodes it visits, until the resource is located. Both referrals given by nodes and trails followed by mobile agents within the P2P network are adaptively learnt to enable rapid discovery of resources. Simulation results of our agent based resource discovery algorithm shows that it compares favorably with traditional P2P resource discovery techniques.

2   Peer-to-Peer Network Protocols

A P2P system is a decentralized and distributed network of nodes that is capable of sharing and distributing resources between themselves. The primary objective of a node in a P2P network is to search and acquire resources and services available on other nodes in the network and, simultaneously allow other nodes to access resources present on the node itself. For this every node uses a node discovery protocol to determine other nodes in the network and a resource discovery protocol to determine resources on other peer nodes. The node discovery protocol consists of two messages. A newly joined node sends out a *ping* message to probe and discover other nodes in the network. Existing nodes that receive the ping message and willing to have the new node as a neighbor respond with a *pong* message. After a node becomes aware of its peer nodes it uses the resource discovery protocol to discover resources that are possibly present on those peers. The resource discovery protocol comprises the *query* message that is forwarded to successive peers until the resource is discovered or the lifetime of the message expires. If the resource is found on a peer node a *queryHit* message is sent back from the node containing the resource to the node that originated the query. The requesting node and the providing node then decide on the download protocol for the resource.

2.1   Informed Search in a P2P Network

The traditional resource discovery P2P protocol performs an uninformed search for a resource within the network. A significant performance improvement can be obtained if the resource discovery protcol can be provided with a heuristic-based informed search. Software agents provide a suitable paradigm for implementing an informed search mechanism in a P2P network. An agent is a piece of software code that can continue to execute the actions programmed into it without continuous supervision by a central authority. In the next section, we describe a multi agent based framework for implementing the protocols in a P2P system.

3   Agent Framework for a P2P System

An agent enabled P2P system must implement the basic P2P protocols described in Section 2. In addition, the agents can be used to perform computations that improve the efficiency of the basic P2P protocols. Our first step in this research was to design and implement a multi-agent based system to support the traditional P2P node and resource discovery protocols. A peer node is implemented as an agent server running on a particular port within a computer. The agent server is capable of hosting agents and sending and receiving mobile agents from other nodes. Each agent server contains a stationary *Controller Agent* and a stationary *Information Agent*. The controller agent creates and manages other agents for the node and also interacts with the user through a GUI while the information agent provides an interface to the information contained within the node to other agents visiting the node.

The node discovery protocol is implemented using the mobile *Reconnaissance Agent*. The traditional node discovery protocol uses a flooding technique to discover other nodes. In [4] we have described a gossip based controlled flooding algorithm where the reconnaissance agent uses an incentive driven model to selectively discover addresses during the node discovery protocol.

The resource discovery protocol is implemented in our system using the mobile *Search Agent*. The traditional resource discovery protocol uses a blind search where the query, encapsulated by the search agent, gets flooded across the network until the resource is located or the search boundary is reached. We envisage that the resource discovery protocol can be significantly improved if the search agent performs a heuristic based informed search among the nodes of the P2P network. However, informed search in a P2P network is complicated because the topology of the network and availability of resources can change dynamically as nodes join and leave the network. In the next section we describe an adaptive learning algorithm used by search agents for improving the traditional resource discovery protocol in a multi-agent P2P system.

4   Intelligent Resource Discovery Using Mobile Agents

Our intelligent resource discovery protocol is inspired by the foraging activity used by social insects such as ants [2] to locate food sources. In several ant species, ants searching for food leave behind a pheromone trail along the path from their nest to the food source. Ants searching for the food source later on use the trail as positive reinforcement to lead themselves to the food source. Ants also show a high affinity to an established trail and are reluctant to deviate to trail-less but more efficient paths towards the food source even if one exists.

In our intelligent resource discovery algorithm mobile search agents mimic the actions of ants. When a P2P network is initially established there is no trail information. A search agent dispatched along a trail-less path is called a *foraging* search agent. The foraging search agent performs a blind search for a resource and establishes a trail. Later search agents called *follower* search agents can utilize the trail to discover resources. However, resource discovery in P2P networks is different from the foraging in an ant society in the following ways:

- **Heterogenous Resources.** Ants always discover the same resource; viz., food. However, in a P2P network the characteristics of the resource being searched for, such as the resource name and resource type, are specified by the user's query. Therefore, trails can only be used to direct a search agent towards nodes where resources have been previously located. However, the same trail should not be followed repeatedly because it is unlikely that all resources will be present at the same node.
- **Occasional Foraging.** Although positive feedback from the pheromone along a trail reinforces the affinity of ants towards the trail, it prevents them from discovering more efficient routes. Occasional explorations or forages along trail-less paths can sometimes lead to the discovery of more efficient routes.
- **Reliability of Trail Information.** A P2P network is a decentralized environment where it is difficult to authenticate every node. Malicious nodes can try to divert search agents along incorrect trails to sabotage the network. Therefore, before deploying a search agent along a trail, the trail information should be associated with parameters such as reputation or reliability of the node that originates the trail information.
- **Variable Resource Location.** In ant algorithms, the location of the food source is fixed. However, in P2P networks the location of resources can change with time as existing nodes leave the network and new nodes with new resources join the network. Therefore, the foraging and trail-following behavior should be combined into the route taken by a search agent.

The characteristics of the resource discovery protocol in P2P networks mentioned above imply that a trail laid by a foraging search agent should not be followed blindly by follower search agents. A search agent therefore decides probabilistically whether to forage along a new path or to follow along an existing trail at each node that it visits. This allows search agents to selectively explore trail-less paths in the P2P network. We have also assumed, perhaps a bit naively, that the probablistic decision to follow a trail also reflects the search agent's reliability about the trail information.

The path explored by a foraging search agent is determined from referrals to neighboring node addresses obtained from every node that the search agent visits. The node referral algorithm uses an adaptive node ranking mechanism to accommodate dynamic joining and leaving of nodes in a P2P network. The next section specifies the algorithm for intelligent resource discovery used by the search agents in our system.

4.1   Algorithm for Intelligent Resource Discovery

The steps of the intelligent resource discovery algorithm are as follows:

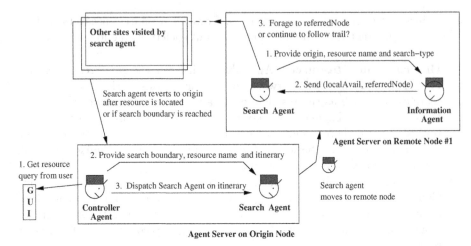

Fig. 1. Schematic for the intelligent the resource discovery protocol showing different agents and their interactions.

1. The controller agent on the origin node obtains the query containing the resource name and other attributes from the user through a GUI.
2. The controller agent creates a mobile search agent and provides it with a search boundary. The search boundary specifies the maximum number of nodes the search agent should visit before abandoning the search in case the resource is not located.
3. The search agent probabilistically decides whether to follow an existing trail or to forage along a trail-less path. The probability value is drawn from a uniform distribution $U[min, max]$ where min and max are determined experimentally from the minimum and maximum probabilities of foraging that optimize the number of hops made by a search agent to locate a resource. If the origin node has no trail information obtained by a previously created foraging search agent, the decision is to forage.
4. The itinerary of a follower search agent comprises the node addresses contained in the trail it is following. The itinerary of a foraging search agent contains the addresses of nodes returned during the node discovery phase.
5. The search agent visits each site on its itinerary. At each node the search agent interacts with the information agent present on the node. The search agent reveals the address of its origin, the name of the resource it is looking for, and its search type (forage or follow) to the information agent.
6. The information agent reponds with a pair of values (*localAvailabity, referredNode*). The former value has boolean type and denotes whether the resource is available locally on the node being currently visited. If the resource is not locally available, the latter value denotes the address of a node which lies along a path to resourceful nodes. The address of *referredNode* is determined using the node referral algorithm described in Section 4.2.

7. If *(localAvailability == true)* the search agent reverts to its origin with the address of the current node on which the resource was located. The trail consisting of the addresses of nodes visited by the search agent is stored within the origin node for use by follower agents for later resource queries originated from the same node.

8. If *(localAvailability == false)* and the search agent is a follower, the search agent decides probabilistically whether to remain a trail-follower or to begin foraging. Foraging search agents are forwarded to *referredNode* while follower search agents continue along their trail. The probability value is drawn from the uniform distribution $U[min, max]$ where min and max are determined experimentally as before. If a follower search agent chooses to become a foraging search agent it continues to behave as a foraging search agent on subsequent sites it visits. The transition of a follower agent into a foraging agent also enables efficient resource location. As more and more queries are initiated by nodes within the network, the number of trails leading to resourceful nodes goes on increasing. If a new resourceful node joins the network at this time there would be no trails leading to it because no foraging agents have visited it before. If follower agents always followed their trail without ever foraging, they would never be able to locate possibly useful resources on the newly joined node. Occasional foraging enables the search agent to investigate trail-less paths that can possibly lead to newly joined resourceful nodes.

9. If the search agent reaches its search boundary before the resource is located it reverts to its origin and reports unavailability of the resource within the P2P network.

The ratio between followers and foraging agents varies dynamically depending on the progress of the search. At every hop along its trail a follower agent decides whether begin foraging instead of following its trail with a probability p. After i hops the ratio between the foragers and followers is given by:

$$r = \frac{1}{(1-p)^i} - 1.$$

A high value of p (close to 1) creates many foraging agents which leads to an inefficient blind search. On the other hand, a low value of p(close to 0) leads to excessive trail following and is inefficient in discovering resources along trail-less path or on newly joined nodes. The ratio between foraging and follower agents given above implies that there are many follower agents when nodes close to the origin of the search query are being searched (i is small). As the search proceeds (i increases) and follower agents visit successive remote locations unsuccessfully, more and more followers transition to foraging to explore trail-less paths for the resource. In the worst case, when the resource is not located after a large number of hops (i is large) and the search boundary is not yet reached, every follower agent becomes a foraging agent.

The information agent on a node maintains three hashtables to enable node referrals. The *resource Table* contains information about resources locally present within the node. The *visitedAgentTable* maintains information about search agents from other nodes that have visited the current node. The key of this hashtable is the *origin* of the visited search agent. The other attributes of the table are *resourceName* and *forwardedNode* which denote the name of the resource that the last search agent from *origin* was searching for and the node to which that search agent was forwarded respectively. The entries of the *forwardingTable* contain the addresses of neighbor nodes of the current node and a corresponding rank for each neighbor node used to determine referrals. The neighbor addresses are discovered during the node discovery phase. The rank of a node is dynamically updated depending on the availability of resources along paths containing the node. While giving a referral to a search agent, a node with a higher rank is given more preference; ties between nodes with the same rank are broken at random.

4.2   Node Referral Algorithm

Our node referral algorithm is based on the premise that a route or trail that leads to the discovery of one resource is likely to be a successful trail for discovering future resources as well. We believe that this is a reasonable assumption because studies of P2P networks [7,14] show that nodes are either altruistic and share many resources or are ungenerous and share few or no resources. Our node referral algorithm gives preference to referrals for nodes that are altrustic or those that lie along a path to altruistic nodes. The flow diagram for the node referral algorithm is shown in Figure 2. Initially all neighbor nodes in the *forwardingTable* have the same rank (zero). When a search agent arrives on a node it provides its origin, resource name and search type (forage or follow) to the information agent on that node. The algorithm for determining the values *(localAvailablity, referredNode)* returned to the search agent by the information agent are illustrated in Figure 2. Key features of the algortihm are described as follows:

1. If the resource is not available locally the *visitedAgentTable* is checked to determine whether a search agent from the same origin had visited the node earlier.
2. Since only one search agent is created for a particular resource query, if a search agent from the same origin has already visited the current node searching for the same resource, the current path of the search agent contains a cycle. Cycles within trails are eliminated by setting *referredNode* to highest ranked node in the *forwardingTable* excluding the node to which the previous search agent from the same origin looking for the same resource was forwarded.
3. If the search agent is a foraging agent set *referredNode* as the node with the current highest rank inside *forwardingTable* and update the forwarded node entry inside the *visitedAgentTable* for the the search agent's origin with *referredNode*.

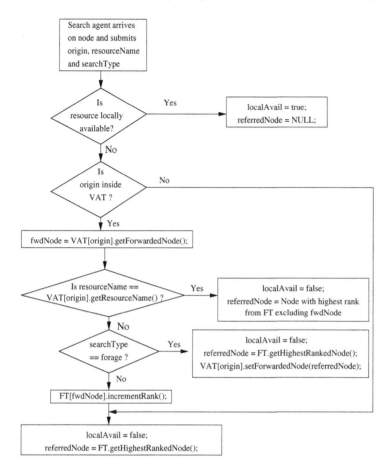

Fig. 2. Flow diagram for node referral algorithm used by the information agent on a node. VAT and FT are abbreviations for *visitedAgentTable* and *forwardingTable* respectively.

4. If the search agent is a follower agent it means that the current node lies along a trail that has been foraged earlier by a foraging search agent from the same origin. The follower search agent arrived on the node because the earlier foraging had led to a successful resource discovery, and, therefore, a trail including the current node had been constructed. This implies that the node that was referred to the earlier foraging agent(*fwdNode* in Figure 2) is a node along a path to a resourceful node. Therefore, the rank of node *fwdNode* in the *forwardingTable* is incremented by one. *referredNode* is once again set to the node with the current highest rank in the *forwardingTable*.

When a node leaves the network, its neighbor node entry is removed from the *forwardingTable* on all nodes which had the leaving node as a neighbor so that its address can no longer be given as a valid *referredNode*. When a node joins the network its address is added to the *forwardingTable* on its neighbor nodes determined by the node discovery protocol. The rank of the neighbor nodes of the newly joined node is set to zero within its *forwardingTable* is set to zero. The rank of the newly joined node in other nodes' *forwardingTable* is set to a random value distributed uniformly between the current highest and lowest ranks within each *forwardingTable*. The random selection of a rank value ensures that the newly joined node also gets a fair chance to be given as a *referredNode* to some search agent.

5   Experimental Results

We have used the Java based IBM Aglets SDK [9] to implement as our mobile agent platform. The P2P network used for our simulation contained $N = 10$ nodes. The message boundary for a resource query was selected random between $N/2$ and $2N/3$ hops. Based on a study of resource sharing by nodes in P2P networks[14] $N/3$ of the nodes were resourceful (more than 20 resources per node) while the rest were scarce in resources (5 or less resources per node). Since our objective is to analyze our resource discovery algorithm, we assumed that the P2P network has already been set up by the node discovery protocol and the *forwardingTable* at each node was already initialized. All resource queries were initiated from the same node and a resourceful node was at least 3 hops away from the origin. All results were averaged over 4 simulation runs.

Figure 3(a) shows the effect of varying the probability p with which a search agent decides to forage at each node that it visits. $p = 0$ means that the search agent is always a follower. However, to set up the first trail in the network at least one foraging agent needs to be created. Therefore, we started our simulations with a small value of $p = 0.05$ and gradually increased p towards 1.0. The results of our experiments illustrate that resources were located with the least number of hops when the search agent combines following and foraging with a slight preference towards foraging($p = 0.55$ to 0.65). The average number of hops to locate a resource with these values of p is $0.45 * N$. With query flooding, the number of messages in the worst case is $(N - 1)$. Therefore, the traffic generated by the agent enabled resource discovery algorithm is less thanquery flooding. We believe the reason for the preference to foraging is due to the fact that resources are present of different nodes and trail following tends to lead to the node that had been previously resourceful for a different resource. Therefore, follower search agents alone are inadequate to accommodate variable location of the resource in subsequent queries.

Our next simulation shows the result of nodes joining and leaving the P2P network on our resource discovery algorithm in Figure 3(b). For this set of simulations we have set $p = 0.6$ as the foraging probability based on the results from our previous experiment. We start with $N = 10$ and selectively remove and add nodes. First we successively removed nodes with scarce resources(t_1 in Figure 3(b)) until the network contains more then $N/2$ resourceful nodes. This allows resources to be located more easily in the network and the number of hops

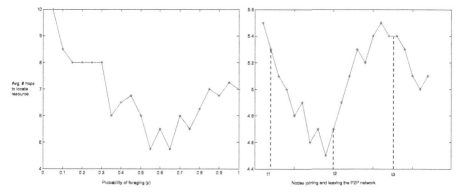

Fig. 3. Average number of hops to locate a resource with (a) different values of the probability of foraging used by search agents and (b) nodes joining and leaving the P2P network dynamically.

to locate a resoure reduces. Next we restored the nodes with scarce resources and successively removed the resourceful nodes(t_2). Consequently, the number of hops to locate a resource increased as the network got more and more popluated with nodes that are scarce in resources. Finally, we introduced two resourceful nodes in the network(t_3) and the number of hops required to locate resources slightly diminished.

In the previous experiment we had assumed that a resource does not get shared with other nodes after it is downloaded to concentrate on the performance of our resource discovery algorithm in response to dynamic addition and removal nodes in the network. When resources are shared after downloading, the nodes that are initially scarce in resources become resourceful and resources get located more rapidly. In such a scenario, follower search agents are more successful in locating resources (the optimum value of p shown in Figure 3(a) reduces to around 0.4) as resources become more available. Therefore, in a P2P network in which most nodes are resourceful, following is a preferred strategy over foraging.

6   Related Work

P2P systems have become an area of active research and development since the popularity of online resource sharing services such as Freenet [5], Gnutella [6], Napster[10] and SETI@home[15]. The most common techniques for P2P resource discovery include query flooding [6,10] and distributed hash tables(DHT). Query flooding produces considerable network traffic by blindly forwarding the query across the network. Some researchers have also proposed controlled query flooding using rumor mongering protocols[11]. Improvements to query flooding include strategic placement of resources on nodes within distributed hash tables(DHT) to improve resource availability and enable rapid lookup[16,13,20]. However, DHT-s require additional overhead in the form of updates to local hash tables within a node when nodes and resources join or leave the network, and, forwarding the updates to neighbor nodes. Enhancements to DHT based techniques include clever routing algorithms and strategic selection of the update set among the neighbor nodes[12,17], super-peer networks[19], and text based content ranking[3]. However, query flooding and DHT based techniques focus more on resource management and do not incorporate the information obtained from previous resource queries for future searches. Our mobile agent based resource discovery algorithm uses trails to direct future searches towards previously located resourceful nodes.

The Anthill framework[1] employs intelligent agents for node and resource discovery. Mobile agents called ants move across the nodes in a P2P network to discover resources. In anthill, *InsertAnts* are used to disseminate information about resources from one node to another while *SearchAnts* move across nodes to discover resources. Ants backtrack along the path they travelled and update routing tables at each node to enable future ants to locate resources more efficiently. In contrast our algorithm avoids table updates at each node along the path of every ant and uses the trail traced by a search agent as a referral for directing future search agents in the possible direction of the resource.

7   Conclusion and Future Work

In this paper, we have described an algorithm for intelligent resource discovery in a P2P system using mobile intelligent agents. The simulation results obtained from our system indicates that an informed search technique for resource discovery based on trails established from previous searches improves the resource discovery protocol a P2P network.

This work is the first step in our research on agent enabled P2P systems. We envisage that a significant improvement can be obtained in the resource discovery protocol if a node originating a resource query sends multiple search agents to search for the resource. We are currently developing a controlled flooding algorithm that dispatches search agents for an optimal cover of the P2P network. Another enhancement to the algorithm described in this paper allows search agents from different nodes can exchange trail information with each other. Appropriate techniques need to be developed to ensure the security and reliability of shared trail information. Finally, we are working on reliable and secure P2P interactions and studying the overhead of secure communication between agents in a P2P system.

The P2P system described in this paper is a simulation of P2P network using agent servers to model peer nodes. In the future, we plan to overlay our agent framework over a P2P community such as JXTA[8] to compare the performance of agent enabled intelligent P2P systems with traditional P2P networks. From our preliminary results described in this paper, we envisage that agent enabled P2P systems are likely to compare favorably with network based P2P systems.

References

1. O. Babaoglu, H. Meling and A. Montresor, "Anthill: A framework for the development of agent-based peer-to-peer systems," Proceedings of the 22nd International Conference on Distributed Computing Systems, Vienna, Austria, 2002, pp. 15-22.
2. E. Bonabeau, M. Dorigo, G. Theraulaz, "Swarm Intelligence: From Natural to Artificial Systems," Oxford University Press, 1999.
3. F. Cuenca-Acuna, C. Peery, R. Martin, and T. Nguyen, "Planetp: Using gossiping to build content addressable peer-to-peer information sharing communities," Technical Report, DCS-TR-487, Department of Computer Science, Rutgers University,2002.
4. P. Dasgupta, "Incentive Driven Node Discovery in a P2P Network Using Mobile Intelligent Agents," (to appear) Proceedings of the Seventh International Conference on Artificial Intelligence, Las Vegas, NV, June 2003.
5. Freenet, URL http://www.freeproject.org
6. Gnutella, URL http://www.gnutella.com
7. P. Golle, K. Leyton-Brown I. Mironov and M. Lillibridge, "Incentives for sharing in peer-to-peer networks," Proceedings of the 2nd International Workshop on Electronic Commerce, (Lecture Notes in Computer Science, vol. 2232, Springer Verlag), Heidelberg, Germany, 2001, pp. 75-87.
8. JXTA URL http://www.jxta.org
9. D. Lange and M. Oshima, "Programming and deploying java mobile agents with aglets," Addison Wesley, 1998.
10. Napster, URL http://www.napster.com
11. M. Portmann and A. Seneviratne, "Cost-effective broadcast for fully decentralized peer-to-peer networks," Computer Communication, Special Issue on Ubiquitous Computing, Elsevier Science, Autumn 2002.
12. S. Ratnasamy, P. Francis, M. Handley, R. Karp, and S. Shenker, "A scalable content-addressable network," Proceedings of ACM SIGCOMM, San Diego, CA, USA, 2001, pp. 161-172.
13. A. Rowstron and P. Druschel, "Pastry: Scalable, distributed object location and routing for large-scale peer-to-peer systems", Proceedings of the IFIP/ACM International Conference on Distributed Systems Platforms (Middleware), Heidelberg, Germany, 2001, pp. 329-350.
14. S. Saroiu, K. Gummadi, and S. Gribble, "A measurement study of peer-to-peer file sharing systems, In MMCN, Jan. 2002.
15. SETI URL http:// setiathome.ssl.berkeley.edu
16. I. Stoica, R. Morris, D. Karger, F. Kaashoek, and H. Balakrishnan, "Chord: A peer-to-peer lookup service for internet applications," Proceedings of the ACM SIGCOMM Conference, San Diego, CA, USA, 2001.
17. C. Tang, Z. Xu and M. Mahalingam, "PeerSearch: Efficient Information retrieval in P2P Networks," Hewlett-Packard Labs, Technical Report HPL-2002-198, 2002.
18. B. Yang and H. Garcia-Molina, "Improving search in peer-to-peer networks," Proceedings of the 22nd International Conference on Distributed Computing Systems (ICDCS'02), Vienna, Austria, July 2002, pp. 5-14.
19. B. Yang and H. Garcia-Molina, "Designing a super-peer network," Proceedings of the 19th International Conference on Data Engineering, Bangalore, India, March 2003.
20. B. Y. Zhao, J. D. Kubiatowicz, and A. D. Joseph, "Tapestry: An infrastructure for fault resilient wide-area location and routing," Technical Report UCB CSD-01-1141, University of California, Berkeley, 2001.

Mobile Agents for Locating Documents in Ad Hoc Networks

Khaled Nagi[1], Iman Elghandour[1], and Birgitta König-Ries[2]

[1] Computer Science Department, Faculty of Engineering, Alexandria University,
Egypt.
nagi@ipd.uni-karlsruhe.de, ielghand@alexeng.edu.eg
[2] Institute for Program Structures and Data Organization, Universität Karlsruhe,
Germany.
koenig@ipd.uni-karlsruhe.de

Abstract. The wide availability of mobile devices equipped with wireless communication capabilities results in highly dynamic communities of mobile users. An interesting application in such an environment is decentralized peer-to-peer file sharing. Locating files in a highly dynamic network while minimizing the consumption of scarce resources is challenging. Since the availability of files changes significantly over time, an asynchronous approach to searching is promising. In this paper, we show why existing file sharing systems cannot be used here and introduce our approach based on mobile agents.

1 Introduction

The growing number of mobile devices with wireless communication capabilities has sparked interest in a new form of wireless networks: ad-hoc networks [1], [2], [3]. These are collections of autonomous nodes that communicate by forming a multi-hop wireless network maintaining connectivity without using underlying infrastructure. From a user's point of view, file sharing as in peer-to-peer systems like Gnutella [4] seems to be an attractive application for these networks. However, existing P2P file exchange systems are not usable in ad-hoc networks for the following reasons.

- *The highly dynamic topology* caused by the mobility of the nodes and frequent (dis-)connections makes it hard to maintain overlay structures.
- *The limited resources of the nodes* in terms of power and memory capacity severely restrict the amount of messages that can be send and the amount of information that can be replicated across nodes.
- *The limited bandwidth* requires that traffic be kept minimal.

In this paper, we present a mobile agents based approach to asynchronous file sharing [5] in ad-hoc networks, which complements the synchronous service discovery, which we develop in the DIANE project [6].

G. Moro, C. Sartori, and M.P. Singh (Eds.): AP2PC 2003, LNAI 2872, pp. 198–204, 2004.

2   Application Scenario

Helped by subsidized programs, nowadays, more and more students (e.g., in our campus at the University of Karlsruhe) are equipped with notebooks, tabletpcs, or PDAs. Students use the devices to take notes in classes. Now, in order to exchange notes (something that is routinely done), it is no longer necessary to physically exchange and copy them, rather, an electronic exchange becomes feasible. It is obvious that such information cannot be posted on a centralized server and a sort of Gnutella on the ad-hoc network is needed. Consider, e.g., Anna, a computer science student. In two weeks, she has to pass a database exam. Anna finds out that she needs (either electronically or as a hard copy) additional information for her preparation such as lecture notes, solutions of exercises or a collection of likely exam questions put together by older students. Anna is not in a hurry, she just wants those documents before the exam. In return, she is willing to offer her collection of documents to other students. Using the DIANE system, she can search the nodes currently available in the network. However, it is quite likely that at any given point in time not everybody who owns some information will be part of the existing ad-hoc network. An alternative producing a more complete result set is to propagate her request *asynchronously*.

Anna composes her request using a piece of software on her PDA: "Find notes about SQL lectures and exercises. *Format*: PDF. *Deadline*: 05/28/03. *Contact information*: I am daily at the library from 2 to 4 p.m., or you can mail to anna@student.myUni.edu. *Priority*: low, increases after a week from now."

As Anna meets Marc and Michael, her request is transferred to their PDAs. However, neither of them possesses the document she needs. After a couple of days Marc meets Susan and the request is passed on to her. She has some of the documents Anna is interested in. Susan can send Anna an email with the matching documents if electronically available or can request a physical meeting for the handout.

Requests at the PDAs should not be immediately purged. They will reside there and wait for further physical encounters in case they meet others with relevant documents. Additionally, if a document, say *Exercise5.doc*, is found; the search software will be intelligent enough to guess that there must be *Exercise1.doc* to *Exercise4.doc* somewhere in the net. In this case, a search subtask is started. This customized search intelligence will be programmed by Anna and the code must be propagated together with the request. Once the deadline is reached the requests are dropped. There are several technical challenges to be considered in this scenario:

- *Searching for documents must be done on a wider basis.* That is why asynchronous service discovery is considered in our work.
- *Each node has its own semantics concerning the representation of meta-information about the documents.* This semantics must be understood by the nodes issuing and receiving requests. There are a number of approaches to this problem, e.g., the one used in the DIANE project [6].
- *The number of nodes to which a request is propagated must be affected by the approaching deadline.* Clearly, we need a priority mechanism.

- *Adaptation of the search plan.* As search plan may be modified during the course of the search, the plan should be, at least virtually, consolidated and the partial results must be merged to fit the original search request.

In the following sections, we introduce our asynchronous mobile agents based approach to searching documents in an ad-hoc network meeting these challenges.

3   System Architecture

A search operation consists of data about the request and code implementing the search. For the search to be carried out, the data *must* be propagated through the network, whereas propagating the code is dependent on the nature of the application. Migrating both data and code is the basic definition of *mobile agents* as we use them. Choosing the right degree of *agency* in the system depends on the following factors: *the non-monolithic nature of the system, the need for dynamic code adaptation, definition of search plan,* and *security* issues. An analysis of the impact of each factor on our decision for using mobile agents can be found in [5].

We use the following system architecture to support search requests: The life of an agent starts at the node initiating the request (*root node*). The agent continually clones itself, dispatches the clones to neighboring nodes upon detecting their presence, and hence propagates the request through the network. If a document is found at a node, the agent informs the root node that issued the request. The current framework supports three contact methods: *directly* if the root node is within radio-range, through *physical meeting* using the information in the request or through *email*.

Figure 1 illustrates the components of mobile agent and hosting platform. Both are implemented using J2ME. The *service discoverer* implements the search intelligence. Based on the description of the *search request*, it communicates with the hosting environment for service discovery through the *interaction manager*. Upon discovery of a document, the contact information is sent to the hosting environment to establish the peer-to-peer communication and the information interchange. The *persistence manager* governs the life-cycle of the agent (see Section 4). The *migration manager* establishes the negotiation before code cloning and transfer. The hosting platform maintains a *directory* of information services that the owner of the device is willing to share and a *domain ontology* used for matching. The *query processor* answers the search requests. The *communication manager* interacts with the outside world.

4   Agent Operation

The following problem arises when an agent is cloned and the child agent migrates: During agent cloning, information is transferred from parent to child. Shortly after migration, while the node on which the parent resides and the one the child migrated to are still within radio range, information can be communicated from the child to the parent. Later on, as nodes move or leave the

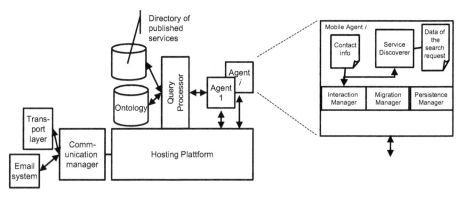

Fig. 1. Architecture of the mobile agent and the hosting platform.

network, this is no longer true. Thus, nodes cannot communicate control parameters to their ancestor nor to older siblings. In the following, we try to make the best possible *estimation* of these parameters. They are related to the documents found, the agent's age in the network, its priority, and the clustering behavior of the nodes in the network. Before explaining the agent life cycle in detail, we investigate these parameters and their interrelations and present our approach to estimating their values taking into account the lack of communication between arbitrary agents in the hierarchy.

In the following, we denote an agent a's parameter as p $(p(a))$ whenever we are looking at it from within (outside) the agent. Also, we use $a.parent$ to denote a's parent, $a.root$ to denote the initial agent issuing the request, and $a.known\_rel$ to denote the set of agents known to the agent (including agents along the path from the root agent to this agent, older siblings along this path, and current direct children).

Document relevance. Denoted $R(i)$, where i is a document at a node, is an index of the relevance degree $[0..1]$ of a document in accordance to the requested document description. In DIANE, methods to estimate $R(i)$ are being developed.

Hit ratio. The *Hit Ratio* (HR) is the ratio of documents discovered until now to the whole set requested by the root node. This can be formulated as:

$$HR = N_f/N_t \tag{1}$$

where N_f is the total number of relevant documents found at this node, N_t is the number of topmost documents the user is interested in. However, due to the lack of continuous information flow between all agents of the same origin, maintaining a global HR is not possible. Each agent has only an estimate based on its known relatives, denoted $HR(a.known\_rel)$: children of a node send feedback with the number of matching documents found locally (right after migration, i.e., while radio connection still exists). The parent node determines the total number of documents found by its children to provide future children with a better estimate of the hit ratio. The *fruitfulness* of the search along a path is thus indicated by a combination of $HR(a.known\_rel)$ and its rate of change along the path from $a.root$ to a, denoted $HR'(a.known\_rel)$.

Hop count. In contrast to typical file sharing and exchange systems, the *Hop Count* (HC) is made variable to provide an early pruning of a path in the network that is not promising and to allow to longer pursue paths in *fruitful* areas of the network.

$$HC(a) = \begin{cases} HC(a.parent) + f(HR(a.known\_rel), HR'(a.known\_rel)) & ; HR'(a.known\_rel) \geq T \\ HC(a.parent) - 1 & ; HR'(a.known\_rel) < T \end{cases}$$
(2)

where T is the threshold and f is a suitable function.

Clustering ratio. The *Clustering Ratio* (CR) represents the rate of change in the list of physical recent neighbors (rn) of a node within a time window t. This is a list maintained by each agent, which contains all the nodes that the agent has sensed in its physical proximity. CR is the ratio between the new nodes added to the whole size of the list;

$$CR = ND_{ch}/ND_{sz}$$
(3)

where ND_{ch} is the number of new nodes added to the recent neighbor list and ND_{sz} is the total size of the recent neighbor list. If the CR is above a certain threshold the node is entering a new community and the agent should intensify its efforts to propagate. A lower CR indicates that the community is currently stable and, hence, the agent should decrease its priority of populating the network.

Priority. In our system, we define two values for the *priority* (P) of an agent.

$$P = \begin{cases} High & ; PV \geq T\_Priority \\ Low & ; PV < T\_Priority \end{cases}$$
(4)

$$PV = f(deadline, CR, HR)$$
(5)

The *deadline* is given the highest weight in this function. Additionally, we include the effect of the clustering ratio and the hit ratio in our calculation.

Depending on the control parameters governing its execution and the search plan embedded in the agent, the life cycle of a non-root agent[1] will vary. A typical life cycle is shown in Figure 2-left. The agent can be in one of the following states.

– *Initial processing at the node upon its arrival (st1):* The agent checks for the availability of enough system resources depending on the initial priority for the agent. Eventually, it may decide to kill the agent (ev0) (see Figure 2-right for details).
– *In a waiting state (st2):* The agent remains waiting for events to occur or a killing decision is taken by either itself or the hosting platform.

---

[1] The life cycle of the root node differs slightly since it is the request initiator and it receives the matching documents/invitations for meetings.

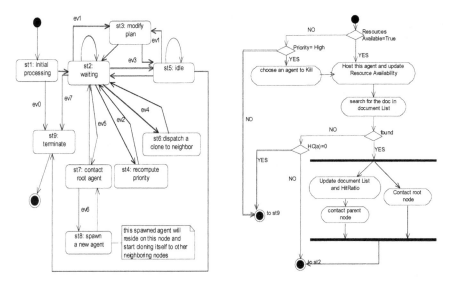

Fig. 2. Agent life cycle at a non-root node.

- *Modifying the agent plan (st3):* The local plan at this node must be merged and modified. This modification takes place if an arriving agent happens to be a clone with a newer plan (ev1).
- *Re-computing priority (st4):* Occurs when one of the parameters affecting the priority changes (ev2).
- *In an idle state (st5):* Entered if the *CR* is below a certain level (ev3).
- *Dispatching a clone to a neighboring node (st6):* Occurs if a neighbor is sensed (ev4). If the agent, with its current status of plans and intermediate results, is not in the physical recent neighbors list, the cloning and dispatching take place.
- *Contacting the root agent (st7):* Takes place if matching documents are found (ev5), it may lead to *spawning a new agent (st8)* if a subplan is created (ev6).
- *Terminating state (st9):* The agent kills itself (if the deadline of the request is reached, its *HC* reaches zero, or a newer copy with an updated plan arrives), or is killed by a decision of the hosting platform due to lack of resources (ev7).

5   Future Work

Currently, we are working on an extensive simulation model to analyze the behavior of the system; in parallel we are developing a functional prototype to be used as a test bed at our campus. In our analysis, we concentrate on performance metrics, such as the degree of propagation of agents within the network as compared to the purely synchronous approach. We also investigate the impact of each of the control parameters on the performance of the mobile agents and the resource consumption in the network in terms of superfluous migrations.

Here, we target some good settings of the control parameters before the actual deployment.

References

1. Corson, S., Macker, J.: Mobile ad-hoc networking (manet): Routing protocol performance issues and evaluation considerations. RFC 2501 (1999)
2. Koodli, R., Perkins, C.: Service discovery in on-demand ad-hoc networks. Manet working group internet draft (2002)
3. Wu, J., Zitterbart, M.: Service awareness and its challenges in mobile ad-hoc networks. In: Proc. of the GI Jahrestagung. LNI (2001)
4. Gnutella File Sharing, http://gnutella.wego.com
5. Nagi, K., König-Ries, B.: Asynchronous service discovery in mobile ad-hoc networks. In: Proc. of the Workshop "Persistence, Scalability, Transactions - Database Mechanisms for Mobile Applications". LNI (2003)
6. DIANE: Dienste in Ad-hoc-Netzen. (Services in Ad-hoc Networks), http://www.ipd.uni-karlsruhe.de/Diane

Author Index